Bloom's Modern Critical Views

Modern Critical Views

GEORGE ELIOT

Modern Critical Views

GEORGE ELIOT

Edited with an introduction by

Harold Bloom

Sterling Professor of the Humanities
Yale University

1986
CHELSEA HOUSE PUBLISHERS
New York
New Haven   Philadelphia

PROJECT EDITORS: Emily Bestler, James Uebbing
ASSOCIATE EDITOR: Maria Behan
EDITORIAL COORDINATOR: Karyn Gullen Browne
EDITORIAL STAFF: Laura Ludwig, Linda Grossman, Perry King
DESIGN: Susan Lusk

Cover illustration by Richard Martin

Printed and bound in the United States of America

Library of Congress Cataloging in Publication Data

George Eliot.
     (Modern critical views)
     Bibliography: p.
     Includes index.
     1. Eliot, George, 1819–1880—Criticism and
interpretation—Addresses, essays, lectures.   I. Bloom,
Harold.   II. Series.
PR4688.G37   1986   823'.8   85-17508
ISBN 0–87754–660–6

Chelsea House Publishers
Harold Steinberg, Chairman and Publisher
Susan Lusk, Vice President
A Division of Chelsea House Educational Communications, Inc.
133 Christopher Street, New York, NY 10014

Contents

Editor's Note

This volume gathers together what is, in its editor's judgment, a representative selection of the best criticism available on the novels of George Eliot. The essays and excerpts range in time from 1948 to the present, and are arranged here in the chronological order of their publication.

The editor's "Introduction" divides itself between a discussion of Eliot's moral stance, as revealed in her letters, and some of the aesthetic perplexities generated by that stance in *Daniel Deronda*. F. R. Leavis fittingly begins the chronological sequence of the criticism with his analysis of Eliot's early phase, the *Scenes from Clerical Life* and *Adam Bede*. Dorothy Van Ghent's reading of *Adam Bede* follows, leading into John Holloway's meditation upon Eliot as Victorian sage, primarily in *Silas Marner*, but also in the vision of "the system of nature" elsewhere in her fiction. With Barbara Hardy's astute account of what she calls "the moment of disenchantment," Eliot's characteristic negation or negative epiphany, something of the darker wisdom of the sage is further revealed. The commentary upon *The Mill on the Floss* by Walter Allen addresses itself to Eliot's somber greatness, and brings to a close a broad movement in Eliot criticism that began with Leavis.

A new movement can be felt with the criticism of the seventies, commencing here with Richard Ellmann's witty biographical critique of Dorothea's husbands in *Middlemarch*, and with the moving reflection upon traditions of English country workers by their descendant Raymond Williams, in his view of "knowable communities" in several of the novels. A very different critical mode, Deconstruction, is introduced by J. Hillis Miller in his lively reading of *Middlemarch*, and yet another, feminist analysis, in Elizabeth Weed's grimly funny "The Liquidation of Maggie Tulliver," an exegesis of *The Mill on the Floss* very different from Walter Allen's. Robert Caserio's structurally informed contrast of *Felix Holt* and *Bleak House*, and Neil Hertz's deconstruction of *Middlemarch* conclude the critical selections here from the seventies.

A good introduction to the critical pluralism of the eighties is provided by the three contending readings of Chapter 85 of *Middlemarch* by Barbara Hardy, J. Hillis Miller and Richard Poirier. *Middlemarch* is again the text analyzed by George Levine, but with a very different emphasis upon what he calls the novel's "scientific texture." A sharp contrast is then introduced by the defense of *Daniel Deronda* as Biblical romance and parable by Barry V. Qualls. The final essay, Martin Price's meditation upon "the nature of decision" in *Daniel Deronda*, *Middlemarch* and elsewhere in Eliot, takes us full circle back to the concern with Eliot's moral stance expressed in my introductory remarks, where some exception is taken to Price's nobly resigned conclusions.

Introduction

*Even taken in its derivative meaning of outline, what is form but the
limit of that difference by which we discriminate one object from
another?—a limit determined partly by the intrinsic relations or
composition of the object, & partly by the extrinsic action of other bodies
upon it. This is true whether the object is a rock or a man . . .*
—GEORGE ELIOT, "Notes on Forms in Art"

It was Freud, in our time, who taught us again what the pre-
Socratics taught: *ethos* is the *daimon*, character is fate. A generation before
Freud, George Eliot taught the same unhappy truth to her contemporaries.
If character is fate, then in a harsh sense there can be no accidents.
Character presumably is less volatile than personality, and we tend to
disdain anyone who would say: personality is fate. Personalities suffer
accidents; characters endure fate. If we seek major personalities among
the great novelists, we find many competitors: Balzac, Tolstoi, Dickens,
Henry James, even the enigmatic Conrad. By general agreement, the
grand instance of a moral character would be George Eliot. She has a
nearly unique spiritual authority, best characterized by the English critic
Walter Allen about twenty years ago:

> George Eliot is the first novelist in the world in some things, and they
> are the things that come within the scope of her moral interpretation
> of life. Circumscribed though it was, it was certainly not narrow; nor
> did she ever forget the difficulty attendant upon the moral life and
> the complexity that goes to its making.

Her peculiar gift, almost unique despite her place in a tradition
of displaced Protestantism that includes Samuel Richardson's *Clarissa*
and Wordsworth's poetry, is to dramatize her interpretations in such a way
as to abolish the demarcations between aesthetic pleasure and moral
renunciation. Richardson's heroine, Clarissa Harlowe, and Wordsworth
in his best poems share in a compensatory formula: experiential loss can
be transformed into imaginative gain. Eliot's imagination, despite its

Wordsworthian antecedents, and despite the ways in which Clarissa Harlowe is the authentic precursor of Dorothea Brooke in *Middlemarch*, is too severe to accept the formula of compensation. The beauty of renunciation in Eliot's fiction does not result from a transformation of loss, but rather from a strength that is in no way dependent upon exchange or gain. Eliot presents us with the puzzle of what might be called the Moral Sublime. To her contemporaries, this was no puzzle. F. W. H. Myers, remembered now as a "psychic researcher" (a marvelous metaphor that we oddly use as a title for those who quest after spooks) and as the father of L. H. Myers, author of the novel *The Near and the Far*, wrote a famous description of Eliot's 1873 visit to Cambridge:

> I remember how at Cambridge I walked with her once in the Fellows' Garden of Trinity, on an evening of rainy May; and she, stirred somewhat beyond her wont, and taking as her text the three words which had been used so often as the inspiring trumpet-call of men—the words God, Immortality, Duty—pronounced with terrible earnestness how inconceivable was the first, how unbelievable was the second, and yet how peremptory and absolute the third. Never, perhaps, have sterner accents confirmed the sovereignty of impersonal and unrecompensing Law. I listened, and night fell; her grave, majestic countenance turned towards me like a sybil's in the gloom; it was as though she withdrew from my grasp, one by one, the two scrolls of promise and left me the third scroll only, awful with inevitable fates. And when we stood at length and parted, amid that columnar circuit of forest trees, beneath the last twilight of starless skies, I seemed to be gazing, like Titus at Jerusalem, on vacant seats and empty halls—on a sanctuary with no Presence to hallow it, and heaven left empty of God.

However this may sound now, Myers intended no ironies. As the sybil of "unrecompensing Law," Eliot joined the austere company of nineteenth-century prose prophets: Carlyle, Ruskin, Newman and Arnold in England; Emerson in America; Schopenhauer, Nietzsche, Kierkegaard and finally Freud on the Continent. But this ninefold, though story-tellers of a sort, wrote no novels. Eliot's deepest affinities were scarcely with Dickens, Thackeray, and Trollope, and yet her formal achievement requires us to read her as we read them. This causes difficulties, since Eliot was not a great stylist, and was far more immersed in philosophical than in narrative tradition. Yet her frequent clumsiness in authorial asides and her hesitations in storytelling matter not at all. We do not even regret her absolute lack of any sense of the comic, which never dares take revenge upon her anyway. Wordsworth at his strongest, as in "Resolution and Independence," still can be unintentionally funny (which inspired the splendid parodies of the poem's leech-gatherer and its solipsistic bard in Lewis Carroll's "White Knight's Ballad," and Edward Lear's "Incidents in the Life of my uncle Arly"). But I have seen no effective parodies of George Eliot, and doubt their possibility. It is usually unwise to be witty concerning our desperate need, not only to decide upon right action, but also to will such action, against pleasure and against what we take to be self-interest. Like Freud, Eliot ultimately is an inescapable moralist, precisely delineating our discomfort with culture, and remorselessly weighing the economics of the psyche's civil wars.

II

George Eliot is not one of the great letter writers. Her letters matter because they are hers, and in some sense do tell part of her own story, but they do not yield to a continuous reading. On a scale of nineteenth-century letter-writing by important literary figures, in which Keats would rank first, and Walter Pater last (the Paterian prose style is never present in his letters), Eliot would find a place about dead center. She is always herself in her letters, too much herself perhaps, but that self is rugged, honest, and formidably inspiring. Our contemporary feminist critics seem to me a touch uncomfortable with Eliot. Here she is on extending the franchise to women, in a letter to John Morley (May 14, 1867):

> Thanks for your kind practical remembrance. Your attitude in relation to Female Enfranchisement seems to be very nearly mine. If I were called on to act in the matter, I would certainly not oppose any plan which held out a reasonable promise of tending to establish as far as possible an equivalence of advantages for the two sexes, as to education and the possibilities of free development. I fear you may have misunderstood something I said the other evening about nature. I never meant to urge the "intention of Nature" argument, which is to me a pitiable fallacy. I mean that as a fact of mere zoological evolution, woman seems to me to have the worst share in existence. But for that very reason I would the more contend that in the moral evolution we have "an art which does mend nature"—an art which "itself is nature." It is the function of love in the largest sense, to mitigate the harshness of all fatalities. And in the thorough recognition of that worse share, I think there is a basis for a sublimer resignation in woman and a more regenerating tenderness in man.
>
> However, I repeat that I do not trust very confidently to my own impressions on this subject. The peculiarities of my own lot may have caused me to have idiosyncrasies rather than an average judgment. The one conviction on the matter which I hold with some tenacity is, that

through all transitions the goal towards which we are proceeding is a more clearly discerned distinctness of function (allowing always for exceptional cases of individual organization) with as near an approach to equivalence of good for woman and for man as can be secured by the effort of growing moral force to lighten the pressure of hard non-moral outward conditions. It is rather superfluous, perhaps injudicious, to plunge into such deeps as these in a hasty note, but it is difficult to resist the desire to botch imperfect talk with a little imperfect writing.

This is a strong insistence upon form in life as in art, upon the limit of that difference by which we discriminate one object from another. I have heard feminist critics decry it as defeatism, though Eliot speaks of "mere zoological evolution" as bringing about every woman's "worse share in existence." "A sublimer resignation in woman" is not exactly a popular goal these days, but Eliot never speaks of the sublime without profundity and an awareness of human loss. When she praises Ruskin as a teacher "with the inspiration of a Hebrew prophet," she also judges him to be "strongly akin to the sublimest part of Wordsworth," a judgment clearly based upon the Wordsworthian source of Ruskin's tropes for the sense of loss that dominates the sublime experience. The harshness of being a woman, however mitigated by societal reform, will remain, Eliot reminds us, since we cannot mend nature and its unfairness. Her allusion to the Shakespearean "art which does mend nature," and which "itself is nature" (*Winter's Tale*, IV.iv.88–96) subtly emends Shakespeare in the deliberately wistful hope for a moral evolution of love between the sexes. What dominates this letter to Morley is a harsh plangency, yet it is anything but defeatism. Perhaps Eliot should have spoken of a "resigned sublimity" rather than a "sublime resignation," but her art, and life, give the lie to any contemporary feminist demeaning of the author of *Middlemarch*, who shares with Jane Austen and Emily Dickinson the eminence of being the strongest women writers in the English language.

III

All seven novels by Eliot were immensely popular in her own lifetime. Today there is common consent that *The Mill on the Floss* (1860) and *Middlemarch* (1871–72) are as vital as they were more than a century ago. *Adam Bede* (1859) is respected but not widely read or studied, while *Romola* (1862–63) is rightly forgotten. *Felix Holt, the Radical* (1866) retains some current interest, but less perhaps than *Adam Bede*. *Silas Marner* (1861) remains an extraordinary reading experience, and probably is undervalued by most critics. Rereading it after decades away from it, I find astonishing mythological power throughout its apparently serene pastoralism. The problematic novel by Eliot is of course *Daniel Deronda* (1876), which has divided its readers and will go on confusing them. Dr. Leavis and others proposed the radical solution of quarrying a new novel, *Gwendolyn Harleth*, out of the book, thus creating an achievement for Eliot not unlike the *Emma* or *Persuasion* of Jane Austen. In this drastic operation, the hero, Daniel Deronda himself, was to be all but discarded, primarily on the grounds that his endless nobility was wearisome. Deronda is an incipient Zionist leader who is nine-tenths a prig and only one-tenth a passionate idealist. He simply is not a male Dorothea Brooke, as his scenes with Gwendolyn Harleth invariably show. She vaults off the page; he lacks personality, or else possesses so much character that he sinks with it, into a veritable bathos in a few places.

And yet, as many critics keep remarking, Deronda is not quite so easily discarded, because the remarkable Gwendolyn is convincingly in love with him and also because the even more remarkable George Eliot is in love with him also. Her portrait of George Henry Lewes, her common-law husband, as Will Ladislaw in *Middlemarch* does not persuade us that he is a wholly fit partner, whether for George Eliot or for Dorothea Brooke. Deronda sometimes makes me think him a Jewish Caspar Goodwood, just as Gwendolyn seems half-way between Elizabeth Bennet and Isabel Archer. Henry James, in his equivocal *"Daniel Deronda: A Conversation,"* neatly gives his "Theodora" a positive judgment of Deronda, "Pulcheria" a rather more pungent negative one, and the judicious "Constantius" an ambiguous balance between the two:

> *Theodora.* And the advice he gives Gwendolyn, the things he says to her, they are the very essence of wisdom, of warm human wisdom, knowing life and feeling it. "Keep you fear as a safeguard, it may make consequences passionately present to you." What can be better than that?

> *Pulcheria.* Nothing, perhaps. But what can be drearier than a novel in which the function of the hero—young, handsome, and brilliant—is to give didactic advice, in a proverbial form, to the young, beautiful, and brilliant heroine?

> *Constantius.* That is not putting it quite fairly. The function of Deronda is to have Gwendolyn fall in love with him . . .

Constantius adds, rather mordantly: "Poor Gwendolyn's falling in love with Deronda is part of her own luckless history, not of his." The implied view of Deronda here is not too far from that of Robert Louis

Stevenson, for whom the visionary Zionist was "the Prince of Prigs."
Against all this must be set the reaction of George Eliot herself,
dismissing "the laudation of readers who cut the book into scraps and
talk of nothing in it but Gwendolyn. I meant everything in the book
to be related to everything else there." We can test this relatedness
in one of the novel's great moments, when Gwendolyn is compelled to
recognize a rejection that she legitimately cannot be expected to understand:

> That was the sort of crisis which was at this moment beginning in
> Gwendolyn's small life: she was for the first time feeling the pressure
> of a vast mysterious movement, for the first time being dislodged from
> her supremacy in her own world, and getting a sense that her horizon
> was but a dipping onward of an existence with which her own was
> revolving. All the troubles of her wifehood and widowhood had still left
> her with the implicit impression which had accompanied her from
> childhood, that whatever surrounded her was somehow specially for
> her, and it was because of this that no personal jealousy had been roused
> in her in relation to Deronda: she could not spontaneously think of
> him as rightfully belonging to others more than to her. But here
> had come a shock which went deeper than personal jealousy—something
> spiritual and vaguely tremendous that thrust her away, and yet quelled
> all anger into self-humiliation.

Perhaps this is Eliot's greatest power: to represent the falling away
of a solipsism, not ignoble as an involuntary movement, into the terror
of a sublime solitude. Gwendolyn after all is losing not only her potential
lover, but her virtual superego, though a superego very different from
the Freudian model. The Freudian superego demands that the hapless
ego surrender its aggressivities, and then continues to torment the ego
for being too aggressive still. But Deronda is the gravest and most
gentlemanly of consciences, perhaps because he mysteriously associates
his own shrouded origins with Gwendolyn's undeveloped self. This is the
subtle surmise of Martin Price in his *Forms of Life*, a study of "Character
and Moral Imagination in the Novel." Price reads Gwendolyn as a
character terrorized by her own empty strength of will, oppressed by the
potential solitude to which her own will may convey her. Ironically,
that fear of the sublime attracts its own doom in the sadistic Grandcourt,
who marries Gwendolyn in certainly the most dreadful of all mismatches,
even in Eliot. Her strength blocked, her will thwarted, Gwendolyn
seems condemned to perpetual death-in-life, until George Eliot rescues
her heroine by one of her characteristic drownings, thus relieving
Gwendolyn of her error but depriving the reader of a splendidly hateful
object in Grandcourt, who is one of Eliot's negative triumphs.

Eliot is masterly in never quiet explaining precisely what draws Deronda to Gwendolyn. Absurd high-mindedness aside, it does seem that Deronda needs the lady's well-developed sense of self, as Price suggests. Himself a kind of changeling, Deronda needs to enact rescue-fantasies, with Gwendolyn taking the place of the absent mother. If that seems too close to Freud's essay "Family Romances," and too far from Eliot's fiction, then we ought to recall the yearnings of Dorothea Brooke and of Lydgate in *Middlemarch*, and Eliot's own lifelong yearnings to "rescue" distinguished male intellectuals. Instilling a moral conscience in the charming Gwendolyn may seem a curious training for a future Zionist uplifter, but in Eliot's universe it is perhaps an inevitable induction for someone determined to be a prophet of his people's moral regeneration.

Price sums up Gwendolyn by associating her with Estella in *Great Expectations* and with Marianne Dashwood in *Sense and Sensibility*. Like them, the even more charming and forceful Gwendolyn must be reduced in scope and intensity in order to become a better person, or perhaps only an imperfect solipsist. Price is very much in Eliot's mode when he counts and accepts the cost of assigning sublimity to *moral* energy: "There is a loss of scale as one dwindles to a moral being; yet it is also the emergence of a self from the welter of assertion and impulse that has often provided an impressive substitute." Something in the reader, something not necessarily daemonic, wants to protest, wants to ask Eliot: "Must there always be a loss in scope? Must one *dwindle* to a moral being?"

IV

Eliot herself, in her letters, gives one answer theoretically (and it is consistent with the burden of *Daniel Deronda*, and a very different one pragmatically), since she palpably gains scale even as she gorgeously augments her self as a moral being. Whatever her letters may lack as narrative, or in Ruskinian madness, they continuously teach us the necessity of confronting our own moral evasions and self-disenchantments. Here she is in full strength, writing to Mrs. Harriet Beecher Stowe on October 29, 1876:

> As to the Jewish element in "Deronda," I expected from first to last in writing it, that it would create much stronger resistance and even repulsion than it has actually met with. But precisely because I felt that the usual attitude of Christians towards Jews is—I hardly know whether to say more impious or more stupid when viewed in the light of their professed principles, I therefore felt urged to treat Jews with such sympathy and understanding as my nature and knowledge could attain

to. Moreover, not only towards the Jews, but towards all oriental peoples with whom we English come in contact, a spirit of arrogance and contemptuous dictatorialness is observable which has become a national disgrace to us. There is nothing I should care more to do, if it were possible, than to rouse the imagination of men and women to a vision of human claims in those races of their fellow-men who most differ from them in customs and beliefs. But towards the Hebrews we western people who have been reared in Christianity, have a peculiar debt and, whether we acknowledge it or not, a peculiar thoroughness of fellowship in religious and moral sentiment. Can anything be more disgusting than to hear people called "educated" making small jokes about eating ham, and showing themselves empty of any real knowledge as to the relation of their own social and religious life to the history of the people they think themselves witty in insulting? They hardly know that Christ was a Jew. And I find men educated at Rugby supposing that Christ spoke Greek. To my feeling, this deadness to the history which has prepared half our world for us, this inability to find interest in any form of life that is not clad in the same coat-tails and flounces as our own lies very close to the worst kind of irreligion. The best that can be said of it is, that it is a sign of the intellectual narrowness—in plain English, the stupidity, which is still the average mark of our culture.

Yes, I expected more aversion than I have found . . . I sum up with the writer of the Book of Maccabees—"if I have done well, and as befits the subject, it is what I desired, but if I have done ill, it is what I could attain unto" . . .

Confronted by that power of moral earnestness, the critic is properly disarmed. It hardly suffices to murmur that Deronda is the Prince of Prigs, or to lament that Gwendolyn's imaginative force and human charm deserved something better than a dwindling down into moral coherence. Eliot is too modest in summing up with the barely inspired writer of the Book of the Maccabees. She sums up with the author of Job, and with Tolstoi. *Daniel Deronda* may be a more vexed creation than *The Mill on the Floss* or *Middlemarch*, but it carries their moral authority, Biblical and Tolstoyan. No one after Eliot has achieved her peculiar and invaluable synthesis between the moral and aesthetic, and perhaps it never will be achieved again.

F. R. LEAVIS

The Early Phase

There is general agreement that an appraisal of George Eliot must be a good deal preoccupied with major discriminations—that the body of her work exhibits within itself striking differences not merely of kind, but between the more and the less satisfactory, and exhibits them in such a way that the history of her art has to be seen as something less happy in its main lines than just an unfolding of her genius, a prosperous development of her distinctive powers, with growing maturity. It is generally assumed that this aspect of her performance is significantly related to the fact of her having displayed impressive intellectual gifts outside her art, so that she was a distinguished figure in the world of Herbert Spencer and the *Westminster Review* before she became a novelist. And there is something like a unanimity to the effect that it is distinctive of her, among great novelists, to be peculiarly addicted to moral preoccupations.

The force of this last—what it amounts to or intends, and the significance it has for criticism—is elusive; and it seems well to start with a preliminary glance at what, from his hours with the critics, the reader is likely to recall as a large established blur across the field of vision. Henry James seems to me to have shown finer intelligence than anyone else in writing about George Eliot, and, he, in his review of the Cross *Life* of her, tells us that, for her, the novel 'was not primarily a picture of life, capable of deriving a high value from its form, but a moralized fable, the last word of a philosophy endeavouring to teach by example.' The blur is seen here in that misleading antithesis, which, illusory as it is, James's commentary insists on. What, we ask, is the 'form' from which a 'picture of life' derives its value? As we should expect, the term 'aesthetic,' with its trail of confusion, turns up in the neighbourhood (it is a term the literary critic would do well to abjure). James notes, as characterizing 'that side of George Eliot's nature which was weakest,' the 'absence of free aesthetic life,' and he says that her 'figures and situations' are 'not *seen* in the irresponsible plastic way.' But, we ask, in what great, in what interesting, novel *are* the figures and situations seen in an 'irresponsible plastic way' (a useful determination of one of the intentions of 'aesthetic')? Is there any great novelist whose preoccupation with 'form' is not a matter of his responsibility towards a rich human interest, or complexity of interests, profoundly realized?—a responsibility involving, of its very nature, imaginative sympathy, moral discrimination and judgment of relative human value?

The art distinguished by the corresponding irresponsibility might be supposed to be represented by the dreary brilliance of *Salammbô* and *La Tentation.* But we know that this is so far from James's intention that he finds even *Madame Bovary*, much as he admires it, an instance of preoccupation with 'form' that is insufficiently a preoccupation with human value and moral interest. In fact, his verdict on *Madame Bovary* may fairly be taken to be of no very different order from that implied when George Eliot finds *Le Père Goriot* 'a hateful book'—the phrase that, curiously enough, provides the occasion for James's remarks about her lack of 'free aesthetic life.'

That the antithesis I quote from Henry James is unsatisfactory and doesn't promote clear thinking is no doubt obvious enough. And the reader may note that James's essay dates sixty years back. Yet his handling of the matter seems to me representative: I don't know of anything written about George Eliot that, touching on this matter of her distinctive moral preoccupation, does anything essentially more helpful towards defining the distinctive quality of her art. James, then, is a critic one reads with close attention, and, coming on so challenging a formulation in so intelligent a context, one is provoked to comment that, while, among the great novelists, George Eliot must certainly have her difference, it can hardly be of the kind such an antithetical way of putting things suggests. Though such formulations may have their colourable grounds, there must, one reflects, be something more important to say about the moral seriousness of George Eliot's novels; otherwise she would hardly be the great novelist one knows her to be. There are certain conditions of art from which she cannot be exempt while remaining an artist.

A tentative comparison or two may help to define the direction in which the appraising critic should turn his inquiries. Consider her against, not Flaubert, but two novelists concerning whose greatness one has no uneasy sense of a need to hedge. In her own language she ranks with Jane Austen and Conrad, both of whom, in their different ways, present sharp contrasts with her. To take Conrad first: there is no novelist of whom it can more fitly be said that his figures and situations are *seen*, and James would have testified to his intense and triumphant preoccupation with 'form.' He went to school to the French masters, and is in the tradition of Flaubert. But he is a greater novelist than Flaubert because of the greater range and depth of his interest in humanity and the greater intensity of his moral preoccupation: he is not open to the kind of criticism that James brings against *Madame Bovary*. *Nostromo* is a masterpiece of 'form' in senses of the term congenial to the discussion of Flaubert's art, but to appreciate Conrad's 'form' is to take stock of a process of relative valuation conducted by him in the face of life: what do men live by? what *can* men live by?—these are the questions that animate his theme. His organization is devoted to exhibiting in the concrete a representative set of radical attitudes, so ordered as to bring out the significance of each in relation to a total sense of human life. The dramatic imagination at work is an intensely moral imagination, the vividness of which is inalienably a judging and a valuing. With such economy has each 'figure' and 'situation' its significance in a taut inclusive scheme that *Nostromo* might more reasonably than any of George Eliot's fictions except *Silas Marner* (which has something of the fairy-tale about it, and is in any case a minor work) be called a 'moralized fable.'

What, then, in this matter of the relation between their moral interests and their art, is the difference between Conrad and George Eliot? (Their sensibilities, of course, differ, but that is not the question.) I had better here give the whole of the sentence of James's, of which above I quoted a part:

> Still, what even a jotting may *not* have said after a first perusal of *Le Père Goriot* is eloquent; it illuminates the author's general attitude with regard to the novel, which, for her, was not primarily a picture of life, capable of deriving a high value from its form, but a moralized fable, the last word of a philosophy endeavouring to teach by example.

—To find the difference in didactism doesn't take us very far; not much to the point is said about a work of art in calling it didactic—unless one is meaning to judge it adversely. In that case one is judging that the intention to communicate an attitude hasn't become sufficiently more than an intention; hasn't, that is, justified itself as art in the realized concreteness that speaks for itself and *enacts* its moral significance. But whatever criticism the weaker parts of George Eliot may lie open to no one is going to characterize her by an inclusive judgment of that kind. And it is her greatness we are concerned with.

James speaks of a 'philosophy endeavouring to teach by example': perhaps, it may be suggested, the clue we want is to be found in the 'philosophy'? And the context shows that James does, in attempting to define her peculiar quality, intend to stress George Eliot's robust powers of intellectual labour and her stamina in the realm of abstract thought—he speaks elsewhere of her 'exemption from cerebral lassitude.' But actually it is not easy to see how, in so far as her intellectual distinction appears in the strength of her art, it constitutes an essential difference between her and Conrad. She has no more of a philosophy than he has, and he, on the other hand, is, in his work, clearly a man of great intelligence and confirmed intellectual habit, whose 'picture of life' embodies much reflective analysis and sustained thought about fundamentals.

What can, nevertheless, be said, with obvious truth, is that Conrad is more completely an artist. It is not that he had no intellectual career outside his art—that he did nothing comparable to translating Strauss, Spinoza and Feuerbach, and editing *The Westminster Review.* It is that he transmutes more completely into the created work the interests he brings in. No doubt the two facts are related: the fact that he was novelist and seaman and not novelist and high-level intellectual middleman has a bearing on the fact that he achieved a wholeness in art (it will be observed that the change of phrase involves a certain change of force, but the shift is legitimate, I think) not characteristic of George Eliot. But it must not be concluded that the point about her is that her novels contain unabsorbed intellectual elements—patches, say, of tough or drily abstract thinking undigested by her art. The relevant characteristic, rather, is apt to strike the reader as something quite other than toughness or dryness; we note it as an emotional quality, something that strikes us as the direct (and sometimes embarrassing) presence of the author's own personal need. Conrad, we know, had been in his time hard-pressed; the evidence is everywhere in his work, but, in any one of the great novels, it comes to us out of the complex impersonalized whole. There can, of course, be no question of saying simply that the opposite is true of George Eliot: she is a great novelist, and has achieved her triumphs of creative art. Nor is it quite simply a matter of distinguishing between what is strong in her work and what is weak. At her best she has the impersonality of genius, but there is characteristic work of hers that is rightly admired where the quality of the sensibility can often be felt to have intimate relations with her weakness.

That is, the critic appraising her is faced with a task of discrimination. I began by reporting general agreement to this effect. The point of my comparison is to suggest that the discriminating actually needing to be done will be on different lines from those generally assumed.

And that is equally the conclusion prompted by a comparative glance at Jane Austen. Though the fashionable cult tends to suggest otherwise, she doesn't differ from George Eliot by not being earnestly moral. The vitality of her art is a matter of a preoccupation with moral problems that is subtle and intense because of the pressure of personal need. As for the essential difference (leaving aside the differences in the nature of the need and in range of interests), is it something that can be related to the fact that Jane Austen, while unmistakably very intelligent, can lay no claim to a massive intellect like George Eliot's, capable of maintaining a specialized intellectual life? Perhaps; but what again strikes us in the intellectual writer is an emotional quality, one to which there is no equivalent in Jane Austen. And it is not merely a matter of a difference of theme and interest—of George Eliot's dealing with (say) the agonized conscience and with religious need as Jane Austen doesn't. There could be this difference without what is as a matter of fact associated with it in George Eliot's work: a tendency towards that kind of direct presence of the author which has to be stigmatized as weakness.

But this is to anticipate.

The large discrimination generally made in respect of George Eliot is a simple one. Henry James's account is subtler than any other I know, but isn't worked out to consistency. He says (though the generalization is implicitly criticized by the context, being inadequate to his perception):

> We feel in her, always, that she proceeds from the abstract to the concrete; that her figures and situations are evolved, as the phrase is, from her moral consciousness, and are only indirectly the products of observation.

What this gives us is, according to the accepted view, one half of her—the unsatisfactory half. The great George Eliot, according to this view, is the novelist of reminiscence; the George Eliot who writes out of her memories of childhood and youth, renders the poignancy and charm of personal experience, and gives us, in a mellow light, the England of her young days, and of the days then still alive in family tradition. Her classics are *Scenes of Clerical Life, Adam Bede, The Mill on the Floss,* and *Silas Marner.* With these books she exhausted her material, and in order to continue a novelist had to bring the other half of herself into play—to hand over, in fact, to the intellectual. *Romola* is the product of an exhausting and misguided labour of excogitation and historical reconstruction (a judgment no one is likely to dispute). *Felix Holt* and *Daniel Deronda* also represent the distinguished intellectual rather than the great novelist; in them she 'proceeds from the abstract to the concrete,' 'her figures and situations are evolved from her moral consciousness,' they 'are deeply studied and massively supported, but . . .'—Henry James's phrases fairly convey the accepted view.

It should be said at once that he is not to be identified with it (he discriminates firmly, for instance, in respect of *Daniel Deronda*). Still, he expresses for us admirably what has for long been the current idea of her development, and he does in such passages as this endorse the view that, in the later novels, the intellectual gets the upper hand:

> The truth is, perception and reflection at the outset divided George Eliot's great talent between them; but as time went on circumstances led the latter to develop itself at the expense of the former—one of these circumstances being apparently the influence of George Henry Lewes.

And we don't feel that he is inclined to dissociate himself to any significant extent when, in the *Conversation* about *Daniel Deronda*, he makes Constantius say:

> She strikes me as a person who certainly has naturally a taste for general considerations, but who has fallen upon an age and a circle which have compelled her to give them an exaggerated attention. She does not strike me as naturally a critic, less still as naturally a sceptic; her spontaneous part is to observe life and to feel it—to feel it with admirable depth. Contemplation, sympathy and faith—something like that, I should say, would have been her natural scale.

At any rate, that gives what appears to be still the established notion of George Eliot.

It will have been noted above that I left out *Middlemarch*. And it will have been commented that *Middlemarch*, which, with *Felix Holt* between, comes in order of production after *Romola* and doesn't at all represent a reversion to the phase of 'spontaneity,' has for at least two decades been pretty generally acclaimed as one of the great masterpieces of English fiction. That is true. Virginia Woolf, a good index of cultivated acceptance in that period, writes (in *The Common Reader*, first series):

> It is not that her power diminishes, for, to our thinking, it is at its highest in the mature *Middlemarch*, the magnificent book which, with all its imperfections, is one of the few English novels written for grown-up people.

This judgment, in a characteristic and not very satisfactory essay on George Eliot, must be set to Mrs. Woolf's credit as a critic; there is no doubt that it has had a good deal to do with the established recognition of *Middlemarch*.

But Mrs. Woolf makes no serious attempt at the work of general revision such a judgment implies, and the appreciation of George Eliot's *œuvre* has not been put on a critical basis and reduced to consistency. For if you think so highly of *Middlemarch*, then, to be consistent, you must be more qualified in your praise of the early things than persisting convention recognizes. Isn't there, in fact, a certain devaluing to be done? The key word in that sentence quoted from Mrs. Woolf is 'mature.' Her distinguished father (whose book on George Eliot in *The English Men of Letters* has his characteristic virtues) supplies, where their popularity is concerned, the key word for the earlier works when he speaks of a 'loss of charm' involved in her development after *The Mill on the Floss*. At the risk of appearing priggish one may suggest that there is a tendency to overrate charm. Certainly charm is overrated when it is preferred to maturity.

Going back in one's mind over the earlier works, what can one note as their attractions and their claims? There is *Scenes of Clerical Life*, which is to-day, perhaps, not much read. And indeed only with an effort can one appreciate why these stories should have made such an impact when they came out. One of them, *Mr. Gilfil's Love-Story*, is charming in a rather slight way. Without the charm the pathos would hardly be very memorable, and the charm is characteristic of the earlier George Eliot: it is the atmospheric richness of the past seen through home tradition and the associations of childhood. Of the other two, *The Sad Fortunes of the Rev. Amos Barton* and *Janet's Repentance*, one feels that they might have appeared in any Victorian family magazine. This is unfair, no doubt; the imaginative and morally earnest sympathy that finds a moving theme in the ordinariness of undistinguished lives—there we have the essential George Eliot; the magazine writer would not have had that touch in pathos and humour, and there is some justice in Leslie Stephen's finding an 'indication of a profoundly reflective intellect' in 'the constant, though not obtrusive, suggestion of the depths below the surface of trivial life.' But *Scenes of Clerical Life* would not have been remembered if nothing had followed.

George Eliot did no more prentice-work (the greater part of the *Scenes* may fairly be called that): *Adam Bede* is unmistakably qualified to be a popular classic—which, in so far as there are such to-day, it still is. There is no need here to offer an appreciation of its attractions; they are as plain as they are genuine, and they have had full critical justice done them. Criticism, it seems to me, is faced with the ungrateful office of asking whether, much as *Adam Bede* deserves its currency as a classic (and of the classical English novels it has been among the most widely read), the implicit valuation it enjoys in general acceptance doesn't represent something more than justice. The point can perhaps be made by suggesting that the book is too much the sum of its specifiable attractions to be among the great novels—that it is too resolvable into the separate interests that we can see the author to have started with. Of these, a main one, clearly, is given in Mrs. Poyser and that mellow presentation of rustic life (as George Eliot recalled it from her childhood) for which Mrs. Poyser's kitchen is the centre. This deserves all the admiration it has received. And this is the moment to say that juxtaposition with George Eliot is a test that disposes finally of the 'Shakespearean' Hardy: if the adjective is to be used at all, it applies much more fitly to the rich creativeness of the art that seems truly to draw its sap from life and is free from all suspicion of Shakespeareanizing. George Eliot's rustic life is convincingly real even when most charming (and she doesn't always mellow her presentation of it with charm).

We have another of the main interests with which George Eliot started in Dinah, that idealized recollection of the Methodist aunt. Dinah, a delicate undertaking, is sufficiently successful, but one has, in appraising her in relation to the total significance of the book, to observe, with a stress on the limiting of implication the word, that the success is conditioned by the 'charm' that invests her as it does the world she moves in and belongs to. She is idealized as Adam is idealized; they are in keeping. Adam, we know, is a tribute to her father; but he is also the Ideal Craftsman, embodying the Dignity of Labour. He too is *réussi*, but compare him with George Eliot's other tribute to her father, Caleb Garth of *Middlemarch*, who is in keeping with *his* context, and the suggestion that the idealizing element in the book named after Adam involves limiting judgments for the critic gets, I think, an obvious force.

Mrs. Poyser, Dinah and Adam—these three represent interests that George Eliot wanted to use in a novel. To make a novel out of them she had to provide something else. The Dinah theme entails the scene in prison, and so there had to be a love-story and a seduction. George Eliot works them into her given material with convincing skill; the entanglement of Arthur Donnithorne with Hetty Sorrel—the first casual self-indulgence, the progressive yielding to temptation, the inexorable Nemesis—involves a favourite moral-psychological theme of hers, and she handles it in a personal way. And yet—does one want ever to read that large part of the book again? does it gain by re-reading? doesn't this only confirm one's feeling that, while as Victorian fiction—a means of passing the time—the love-story must be granted its distinction, yet, judged by the expectations with which one approaches a great novelist, it offers nothing proportionate to the time it takes (even if we cut the large amount of general reflection)? Satisfactory at its own level as the unity is that the author has induced in her materials, there is not at work in the whole any pressure from her profounder experience to compel an inevitable development; so that we don't feel moved to discuss with any warmth whether or not she was right to take Lewes's suggestion, and whether or not Dinah *would* really have become Mrs. Adam Bede. We are not engaged in such a way as to give any force to the question whether the marriage is convincing or otherwise; there is no sense of inevitability to outrage. These comments of Henry James's seem to me just:

> In *Silas Marner*, in *Adam Bede*, the quality seems gilded by a sort of autumn haze, an afternoon light, of meditation, which mitigates the sharpness of the portraiture. I doubt very much whether the author herself had a clear vision, for instance, of the marriage of Dinah Morris to Adam, or of the rescue of Hetty from the scaffold at the eleventh hour. The reason of this may be, indeed, that her perception was a perception of nature much more than of art, and that these particular incidents do not belong to nature (to my sense at least); by which I do not mean that they belong to a very happy art. I cite them, on the contrary, as an evidence of artistic weakness; they are a very good example of the view in which a story must have marriages and rescues in the nick of time, as a matter of course.

James indicates here the relation between the charm and what he calls the 'art.' They are not identical, of course; but what I have called 'charm' and described as an idealizing element means an abeyance of the profounder responsibility, so that, without being shocked, we can have together in the same book the 'art' to which James refers—the vaguely realized that draws its confidence from convention—and such genuinely moving things as the story of Hetty Sorrel's wanderings. And here I will anticipate and make the point that it is because the notorious scandal of Stephen Guest in *The Mill on the Floss* has nothing to do with 'art,' but is a different kind of thing altogether, that it is interesting and significant.

It is a related point that if 'charm' prevails in *Adam Bede* (and, as Henry James indicates, in *Silas Marner*), there should be another word for what we find in *The Mill on the Floss*. The fresh directness of a child's vision that we have there, in the autobiographical part, is something very different from the 'afternoon light' of reminiscence. This recaptured early vision, in its combination of clarity with rich 'significance,' is for us, no doubt, enchanting; but it doesn't idealize, or soften with a haze of sentiment (and it can't consort with 'art'). Instead of Mrs. Poyser and her setting we have the uncles and aunts. The bearing of the change is plain if we ask whether there could have been a Dinah in this company. Could there have been an Adam? They both belong to a different world.

In fact, the Gleggs and the Pullets and the Dodson clan associate, not with the frequenters of Mrs. Poyser's kitchen, but with the tribe that forgathers at Stone Court waiting for Peter Featherstone to die. The intensity of Maggie's naïve vision is rendered with the convincing truth of genius; but the rendering brings in the intelligence that goes with the genius and is *of* it, and the force of the whole effect is the product of understanding. This is an obvious enough point. I make it because I want to observe that, although the supremely mature mind of *Middlemarch* is not yet manifested in *The Mill on the Floss*, the creative powers at work here owe their successes as much to a very fine intelligence as to powers of feeling and remembering—a fact that, even if it is an obvious one, the customary stress nevertheless leaves unattended to, though it is one that must get its full value if George Eliot's development is to be understood. I will underline it by saying that the presentment of the Dodson clan is of marked sociological interest—not accidentally, but because of the intellectual qualifications of the novelist.

But of course the most striking quality of *The Mill on the Floss* is that which goes with the strong autobiographical element. It strikes us as an emotional tone. We feel an urgency, a resonance, a personal vibration, adverting us of the poignantly immediate presence of the author. Since the vividness, the penetration and the irresistible truth of the best of the book are clearly bound up with this quality, to suggest that it also entails limitations that the critic cannot ignore, since they in turn are inseparable from disastrous weaknesses in George Eliot's handling of her themes, is perhaps a delicate business. But the çase is so: the emotional quality represents something, a need or hunger in George Eliot, that shows itself to be insidious company for her intelligence—apt to supplant it and take command. The acknowledged weaknesses and faults of *The Mill on the Floss*, in fact, are of a more interesting kind than the accepted view recognizes.

That Maggie Tulliver is essentially identical with the young Mary Ann Evans we all know. She has the intellectual potentiality for which the environment into which she is born doesn't provide much encouragement; she has the desperate need for affection and intimate personal relations; and above all she has the need for an emotional exaltation, a religious enthusiasm, that shall transfigure the ordinariness of daily life and sweep her up in an inspired devotion of self to some ideal purpose.

There is, however, a difference between Maggie Tulliver and Mary Ann Evans: Maggie is beautiful. She is triumphantly beautiful, after having been the ugly duckling. The experience of a sensitive child in this latter rôle among insensitive adults is evoked with great poignancy: George Eliot had only to remember. The glow that comes with imagining the duckling turned swan hardly needs analysing; it can be felt in every relevant page, and it is innocent enough. But it is intimately related to things in the book that common consent finds deplorable, and it is necessary to realize this in order to realize their nature and significance and see what the weaknesses of *The Mill on the Floss* really are.

There is Stephen Guest, who is universally recognized to be a sad lapse on George Eliot's part. He is a more significant lapse, I think, than criticism commonly allows. Here is Leslie Stephen:

> George Eliot did not herself understand what a mere hairdresser's block she was describing in Mr. Stephen Guest. He is another instance of her incapacity for portraying the opposite sex. No man could have intro- duced such a character without perceiving what an impression must be made upon his readers. We cannot help regreting Maggie's fate; she is touching and attractive to the last; but I, at least, cannot help wishing that the third volume could have been suppressed. I am inclined to sympa- thize with the readers of *Clarissa Harlowe* when they entreated Richardson to save Lovelace's soul. Do, I mentally exclaim, save this charming Maggie from damning herself by this irrelevant and discordant degradation.

That the presentment of Stephen Guest is unmistakably feminine no one will be disposed to deny, but not only is the assumption of a general incapacity refuted by a whole gallery of triumphs, Stephen himself is sufficiently 'there' to give the drama a convincing force. Animus against him for his success with Maggie and exasperation with George Eliot for allowing it shouldn't lead us to dispute that plain fact—they don't really amount to a judgment of his unreality. To call him a 'mere hairdresser's block' is to express a valuation—a valuation extremely different from George Eliot's. And if we ourselves differ from her in the same way (who doesn't?), we must be careful about the implication of the adjective when we agree that her valuation is surprising. For Leslie Stephen Maggie's entanglement with Stephen Guest is an 'irrelevant and discordant degradation.'—Irrelevant to what and discordant with what?—

> The whole theme of the book is surely the contrast between the 'beauti- ful soul' and the commonplace surroundings. It is the awakening of the spiritual and imaginative nature and the need of finding some room for the play of the higher faculties, whether in the direction of religious mysticism or of human affection.

—It is bad enough that the girl who is distinguished not only by beauty but by intelligence should be made to fall for a provincial dandy; the scandal or incredibility (runs the argument) becomes even worse when we add that she is addicted to Thomas à Kempis and has an exalted spiritual nature. Renunciation is a main theme in her history and in her daily meditations; but—when temptation takes the form of Mr. Stephen Guest! It is incredible, or insufferable in so far as we have to accept it, for temptation at this level can have nothing to do with the theme of renunciation as we have become familiar with it in Maggie's spiritual life—it is 'irrelevant and discordant.' This is the position.

Actually, the soulful side of Maggie, her hunger for ideal exalta-tions, as it is given us in the earlier part of the book, is just what should make us say, on reflection, that her weakness for Stephen Guest is not so surprising after all. It is commonly accepted, this soulful side of Maggie, with what seems to me a remarkable absence of criticism. It is offered by George Eliot herself—and this of course is the main point—with a remark-able absence of criticism. There is, somewhere, a discordance, a discrep-ancy, a failure to reduce things to a due relevance: it is a characteristic and significant failure in George Eliot. It is a discordance, not between her ability to present Maggie's yearnings and her ability to present Ste-phen Guest as an irresistible temptation, but between her presentment of those yearnings on the one hand and her own distinction of intelligence on the other.

That part of Maggie's make-up is done convincingly enough; it is done from the inside. One's criticism is that it is done too purely from the inside. Maggie's emotional and spiritual stresses, her exaltations and renunciations, exhibit, naturally, all the marks of immaturity; they involve confusions and immature valuations; they belong to a stage of develop-ment at which the capacity to make some essential distinctions has not yet been arrived at—at which the poised impersonality that is one of the conditions of being able to make them can't be achieved. There is nothing against George Eliot's presenting this immaturity with tender sympathy; but we ask, and ought to ask, of a great novelist something more. 'Sympathy and understanding' is the common formula of praise, but understanding, in any strict sense, is just what she doesn't show. To understand immaturity would be to 'place' it, with however subtle an implication, by relating it to mature experience. But when George Eliot touches on these given intensities of Maggie's inner life the vibration comes directly and simply from the novelist, precluding the presence of a maturer intelligence than Maggie's own. It is in these places that we are most likely to make with conscious critical intent the comment that in

George Eliot's presentment of Maggie there is an element of self-idealization. The criticism sharpens itself when we say that with the self-idealization there goes an element of self-pity. George Eliot's attitude to her own immaturity as represented by Maggie is the reverse of a mature one.

Maggie Tulliver, in fact, represents an immaturity that George Eliot never leaves safely behind her. We have it wherever we have this note, and where it prevails her intelligence and mature judgment are out of action:

> Maggie in her brown frock, with her eyes reddened and her heavy hair pushed back, looking from the bed where her father lay, to the dull walls of this sad chamber which was the centre of her world, was a creature full of eager, passionate longings for all that was beautiful and glad; thirsty for all knowledge; with an ear straining after dreamy music that died away and would not come nearer to her; with a blind, unconscious yearning for something that would link together the wonderful impressions of this mysterious life, and give her soul a sense of home in it.

This 'blind, unconscious yearning' never, for all the intellectual contacts it makes as Maggie grows up and from which it acquires a sense of consciousness, learns to understand itself: Maggie remains quite naïve about its nature. She is quite incapable of analysing it into the varied potentialities it associates. In the earlier part of the book, from which the passage just quoted comes, the religious and idealistic aspect of the yearning is not complicated by any disconcerting insurgence from out of the depths beneath its vagueness. But with that passage compare this:

> In poor Maggie's highly-strung, hungry nature—just come away from a third-rate schoolroom, with all its jarring sounds and petty round of tasks—these apparently trivial causes had the effect of rousing and exalting her imagination in a way that was mysterious to herself. It was not that she thought distinctly of Mr. Stephen Guest, or dwelt on the indications that he looked at her with admiration; it was rather that she felt the half-remote presence of a world of love and beauty and delight, made up of vague, mingled images from all the poetry she had ever read, or had ever woven in her dreamy reveries.

The juxtaposition of the two passages makes us revert to a sentence quoted above from Leslie Stephen, and see in it a hint that he, pretty plainly, missed:

> It is the awakening of the spiritual and imaginative nature and the need of finding some room for the play of the higher faculties, whether in the direction of religious mysticism or of human affection.

—For the second alternative we need to couple with 'religious mysticism' a phrase more suggestive of emotional intensity than Leslie Stephen's. And we then can't help asking whether the 'play of the higher faculties' that is as intimately associated with a passion for Stephen Guest as the two last-quoted paragraphs together bring out can be as purely concerned with the 'higher' as Maggie and George Eliot believe (unchallenged, it seems, by Leslie Stephen).

Obviously there is a large lack of self-knowledge in Maggie—a very natural one, but shared, more remarkably, by George Eliot. Maggie, it is true, has the most painful throes of conscience and they ultimately prevail. But she has no sense that Stephen Guest (apart, of course, from the insufficient strength of moral fibre betrayed under the strain of temptation—and it is to Maggie he succumbs) is not worthy of her spiritual and idealistic nature. There is no hint that, if Fate had allowed them to come together innocently, she wouldn't have found him a pretty satisfactory soul-mate; there, for George Eliot, lies the tragedy—it is conscience opposes. Yet the ordinary nature of the fascination is made quite plain:

> And then, to have the footstool placed carefully by a too self-confident personage—not any self-confident personage, but one in particular, who suddenly looks humble and anxious, and lingers, bending still, to ask if there is not some draught in that position between the window and the fireplace, and if he may not be allowed to move the work-table for her—these things will summon a little of the too-ready, traitorous tenderness into a woman's eyes, compelled as she is in her girlish time to learn her life-lessons in very trivial language.

And it is quite plain that George Eliot shares to the full the sense of Stephen's irresistibleness—the vibration establishes it beyond a doubt:

> For hours Maggie felt as if her struggle had been in vain. For hours every other thought that she strove to summon was thrust aside by the image of Stephen waiting for the single word that would bring him to her. She did not *read* the letter: she heard him uttering it, and the voice shook her with its old strange power. . . . And yet that promise of joy in the place of sadness did not make the dire force of the temptation to Maggie. It was Stephen's tone of misery, it was the doubt in the justice of her own resolve, that made the balance tremble, and made her once start from her seat to reach the pen and paper, and write 'Come.'

There is no suggestion of any antipathy between this fascination and Maggie's 'higher faculties,' apart from the moral veto that imposes renunciation. The positive counterpart of renunciation in the 'higher' realm to which this last is supposed to belong is the exaltation, transcending all conflicts and quotidian stalenesses, that goes with an irresistibly ideal self-devotion. It is significant that the passages describing such an exaltation, whether as longed for or as attained—and there are many in George Eliot's works—have a close affinity in tone and feeling with this (from the chapter significantly headed, *Borne along by the tide*):

> And they went. Maggie felt that she was being led down the garden among the roses, being helped with firm tender care into the boat, having the cushion and cloak arranged for her feet, and her parasol opened for her (which she had forgotten)—all this by the stronger presence that seemed to bear her along without any act of her own will, like the added self which comes with the sudden exalting influence of a strong tonic—and she felt nothing else.

—The satisfaction got by George Eliot from imaginative participation in exalted enthusiasms and self-devotions would, if she could suddenly have gained the power of analysis that in these regions she lacked, have surprised her by the association of elements it represented.

The passage just quoted gives the start of the expedition with Stephen in which chance, the stream and the tide are allowed, temporarily, to decide Maggie's inner conflict. It has been remarked that George Eliot has a fondness for using boats, water and chance in this way. But there are distinctions to be made. The way in which Maggie, exhausted by the struggle, surrenders to the chance that leaves her to embark alone with Stephen, and then, with inert will, lets the boat carry her downstream until it is too late, so that the choice seems taken from her and the decision compelled—all this is admirable. *This* is insight and understanding, and comes from the psychologist who is to analyse for us Gwendolen Harleth's acceptance of Grandcourt. But the end of *The Mill on the Floss* belongs to another kind of art. Some might place it under the 'art' referred to by Henry James. And it is certainly a 'dramatic' close of a kind congenial to the Victorian novel-reader. But it has for the critic more significance than this suggests: George Eliot is, emotionally, fully engaged in it. The qualifying 'emotionally' is necessary because of the criticism that has to be urged: something so like a kind of daydream indulgence we are all familiar with could not have imposed itself on the novelist as the right ending if her mature intelligence had been fully engaged, giving her full self-knowledge. The flooded river has no symbolic or metaphorical value. It is only the dreamed-of perfect accident that gives us the opportunity for the dreamed-of heroic act—the act that shall vindicate us against a harshly misjudging world, bring emotional fulfilment and (in others) changes of heart, and provide a gloriously tragic curtain. Not that the sentimental in it is embarrassingly gross, but the finality is not that of great art, and the significance is what I have suggested—a revealed immaturity.

The success of *Silas Marner*, that charming minor masterpiece, is conditioned by the absence of personal immediacy; it is a success of reminiscent and enchanted recreation: *Silas Marner* has in it, in its solid way, something of the fairy tale. That 'solid' presents itself because of the way in which the moral fable is realized in terms of a substantial real world. But this, though re-seen through adult experience, is the world of childhood and youth—the world as directly known then, and what is hardly distinguishable from that, the world as known through family reminiscence, conveyed in anecdote and fireside history. The mood of enchanted adult reminiscence blends with the re-captured traditional aura to give the world of *Silas Marner* its atmosphere. And it is this atmosphere that conditions the success of the moral intention. We take this intention quite seriously, or, rather, we are duly affected by a realized moral significance; the whole history has been conceived in a profoundly and essentially moral imagination. But the atmosphere precludes too direct a reference to our working standards of probability—that is, to our everyday sense of how things happen; so that there is an answer to Leslie Stephen when he comments on *Silas Marner* in its quality of moral fable:

> The supposed event—the moral recovery of a nature reduced by injustice and isolation to the borders of sanity—strikes one perhaps as more pretty than probable. At least, if one had to dispose of a deserted child, the experiment of dropping it by the cottage of a solitary in the hope that he would bring it up to its advantage and to his own regeneration would hardly be tried by a judicious philanthropist.

Leslie Stephen, of course, is really concerned to make a limiting judgment, that which is made in effect when he says:

> But in truth the whole story is conceived in a way which makes a pleasant conclusion natural and harmonious.

There is nothing that strikes us as false about the story; its charm depends upon our being convinced of its moral truth. But in our description of the satisfaction got from it, 'charm' remains the significant word.

The force of the limiting implication may be brought out by a comparative reference to another masterpiece of fiction that it is natural to bring under the head of 'moral fable': Dickens's *Hard Times*. The heightened reality of that great book (which combines a perfection of 'art' in the Flaubertian sense with an un-Flaubertian moral strength and human richness) has in it nothing of the fairy tale, and is such as to preclude pleasantness altogether; the satisfaction given depends on a moral significance that can have no relations with charm. But the comparison is, of course, unfair: *Hard Times* has a large and complex theme, involving its author's profoundest response to contemporary civilization, while *Silas Marner* is modestly conscious of its minor quality.

The unfairness may be compensated by taking up Leslie Stephen's suggestion that '*Silas Marner* is . . . scarcely equalled in English literature, unless by Mr. Hardy's rustics, in *Far from the Madding Crowd* and other early works.' Actually, the comparison is to George Eliot's advantage (enormously so), and to Hardy's detriment, in ways already suggested. The praises that have been given to George Eliot for the talk at the Rainbow are deserved. It is indeed remarkable that a woman should have been able to present so convincingly an exclusively masculine *milieu*. It is the more remarkable when we recall the deplorable Bob Jakin of *The Mill on the Floss*, who is so obviously and embarrassingly a feminine product.

Silas Marner closes the first phase of George Eliot's creative life. She finds that, if she is to go on being a novelist, it must be one of a very different kind. And *Romola*, her first attempt to achieve the necessary inventiveness, might well have justified the conviction that her creative life was over.

DOROTHY VAN GHENT

"*Adam Bede*"

In Chapter 17 of *Adam Bede*, "the story pauses a little" and George Eliot sets forth her aim as a novelist, an aim which she describes as "the faithful representing of commonplace things," of things *as they are*, not "as they never have been and never will be"; and we are reminded of a similar aim as expressed by Defoe's Moll Flanders, who said, "I am giving an account of what was, not of what ought or ought not to be." It is the vocation of the "realistic" novelist to represent life in this way; . . . but, as Defoe brought us to a consideration of the shaping changes which the "real" undergoes as it is submitted to art, even to the most "realistic" art, so George Eliot brings us back to the same consideration of the transforming effect of composition upon things-as-they-are. Her strongest effort, she says, is to avoid an "arbitrary picture," and

> to give a faithful account of men and things as they have mirrored themselves in my mind. The mirror is doubtless defective; the outlines will sometimes be disturbed, the reflection faint or confused; but I feel as much bound to tell you as precisely as I can what that reflection is, as if I were in the witness-box, narrating my experience on oath.

We cannot avoid observing that the "mirror" is at times defective, but since it is for the most part clear and well lighted we are not primarily concerned with the defects; more interesting is the analogy of the mirror itself—the novelist's mind as a mirror from whose "reflections" of "men and things" he draws his account. Men and things, then, do not leap to his page directly out of the "real" but, before they get there, take a

From *The English Novel: Form and Function*. Copyright © 1953 by Dorothy Van Ghent. Harper and Brothers.

journey through the "mirror." But the mirror which the mind offers is not at all like other mirrors; even—leaving out of consideration defective glasses—very clear minds are not like very clear mirrors. Dangerous as analogies are, a spoon would be a better one, where, in the concave, as we tip it toward us, we see our head compressed and a half-moon scooped out of it on top as if it were a dime-store flowerpot for our viney hair, our body tapered to vanishing at the hips, and the whole upside down; or, in the convex, our eyelids are as large as foreheads, our forehead is as small as an eyelid, our cheeks hang down from our face like shoulders, and our shoulders hide under them like little ears. The "mirror" of the mind shapes what it sees. It does not passively "reflect" things-as-they-are, but creates thing-as-they-are. Though we can clearly discriminate the quality of intention shown by a realistic art—and it usually reduces finally to a choice of materials from the field of the quotidian, the commonplace, the mediocre—yet its aim of veraciousness is necessarily one of veraciousness to what the artist sees in the shape-giving, significance-endowing medium of his own mind, and in this sense the mythopoeic art of *Wuthering Heights* is as veracious as the realistic art of *Adam Bede*.

The singularity of the world of *Wuthering Heights* is its innocence of "good" and "evil" in any civilized ethical meaning of these terms; it is a world shaped by kinetic rather than by ethical forces, and its innocence is that of the laws of dynamics (Catherine's fatal choice, for instance, is essentially a choice of stasis and a denial of motion; it is as if an electron or a star should "choose" to stand still). *Adam Bede* offers the radical contrast of a world shaped through and through by moral judgment and moral evaluation. We are prone, perhaps, to think of a perfectly amoral vision, such as Emily Brontë's, as a vision not of things-as-they-are but as a subjective creation of things-as-they-never-were-but-might-be, and, on the other hand, to think of an ethical vision, such as George Eliot's, as closer to things-as-they-are, more "objective," because of our own familiar addiction to moral judgments (however inapropos or cliché) and our difficulty in turning ethics out of doors. But, on a thought, it should be clear that a through and through ethically shaped world is as "created" a world as the other. The question is not one of *whether* things are really this way or that way, for either vision touches responsive similitudes within us, and God knows what things really are. The question is one of different organizations and different illuminations of the infinite possible qualities of things-as-they-are.

Technique is that which selects among the multitude of possible qualities, organizes them in the finite world of the novel, and holds them in a shape that can catch the light of our own awareness, which, without shapes to fall upon, is ignorant. Technique is like the concave or convex surface of the spoon, and the different turnings and inclinations to which it is liable; technique elongates or foreshortens, and while the rudimentary relationships of common experience remain still recognizable, it reveals astonishing bulges of significance, magnifies certain parts of the anatomy of life, of whose potentialities we had perhaps not been aware, humbles others. The massively slow movement of *Adam Bede* is one such shape-making technique. It is true that we are generally persuaded of the *actual* slow movement of rural life, and it is rural life—the life of villagers, tenant farmers, and peasantry—that George Eliot describes; but Dickens, in the first part of *Great Expectations*, is also dealing with people in a rural community, and yet the tempo or "pace" which he sets for these lives is one of shockingly abrupt accelerations.

> "Hold your noise!" cried a terrible voice, as a man started up from among the graves at the side of the church porch. "Keep still, you little devil, or I'll cut your throat!"

Emily Brontë deals with even more rurally isolated lives, but here the movement is one of furious assault: beasts attack, the tempest whirls and suffocates, emotions express themselves in howls, biting, kicking, trampling, bloodletting, homicidal and suicidal violence. In the context of this comparison let us set almost any random paragraph from *Adam Bede*. The movement is one of a massive leisureliness that gathers up as it goes a dense body of physical and moral detail, adding particle to particle and building layer upon layer with sea-depth patience.

> In the large wicker-bottomed arm-chair in the left-hand chimney-nook sat old Martin Poyser, a hale but shrunken and bleached image of his portly black-haired son—his head hanging forward a little, and his elbows pushed backwards so as to allow the whole of his fore-arm to rest on the arm of the chair. His blue handkerchief was spread over his knees, as was usual indoors, when it was not hanging over his head; and he sat watching what went forward with the quiet *outward* glance of healthy old age, which, disengaged from any interest in an inward drama, spies out pins upon the floor, follows one's minutest motions with an unexpectant purposeless tenacity, watches the flickering of the flame or the sun-gleams on the wall, counts the quarries on the floor, watches even the hand of the clock, and pleases itself with detecting a rhythm in the tick.

And here are the Poysers going to church:

> There were acquaintances at other gates who had to move aside and let them pass: at the gate of the Home Close there was half the dairy of cows

standing one behind the other, extremely slow to understand that their large bodies might be in the way; at the far gate there was the mare holding her head over the bars, and beside her the liver-coloured foal with its head towards its mother's flank, apparently still much embarrassed by its own straddling existence. The way lay entirely through Mr. Poyser's own fields till they reached the main road leading to the village, and he turned a keen eye on the stock and the crops as they went along, while Mrs. Poyser was ready to supply a running commentary on them all . . .

The damp hay that must be scattered and turned afresh tomorrow was not a cheering sight to Mr. Poyser, who during hay and corn harvest had often some mental struggles as to the benefits of a day of rest; but no temptation would have induced him to carry on any field-work, however early in the morning, on a Sunday; for had not Michael Holdsworth had a pair of oxen "sweltered" while he was ploughing on Good Friday? That was a demonstration that work on sacred days was a wicked thing; and with wickedness of any sort Martin Poyser was quite clear that he would have nothing to do, since money got by such means would never prosper.

"It a'most makes your fingers itch to be at the hay now the sun shines so," he observed, as they passed through the "Big Meadow." "But it's poor foolishness to think o' saving by going against your conscience. There's that Jim Wakefield, as they used to call 'Gentleman Wakefield,' used to do the same of a Sunday as o' week-days, and took no heed to right or wrong, as if there was nayther God nor devil. An' what's he come to? Why, I saw him myself last market-day a-carrying a basket wi' oranges in't."

"Ah, to be sure," said Mrs. Poyser, emphatically, "you make but a poor trap to catch luck if you go and bait it wi' wickedness. The money as is got so's like to burn holes i' your pocket. I'd niver wish us to leave our lads a sixpence but what was got i' the rightful way. And as for the weather, there's One above makes it, and we must put up wi't: it's nothing of a plague to what the wenches are."

Notwithstanding the interruption in their walk, the excellent habit which Mrs. Poyser's clock had of taking time by the forelock, had secured their arrival at the village while it was still a quarter to two, though almost every one who meant to go to church was already within the churchyard gates.

It would be difficult to quote at less length for these illustrations, for a leisurely pace can be illustrated only by its own leisureliness.

But what does "pace" *mean*? Of what is it the expressive signature? We have examined [previously], in the study of *Great Expectations*, what the tempo of that book means—how its abrupt shocks of timing, its ballet-like leaps, express the mysterious movements of a non-naturalistic world in which guilt has an objective being as palpable as that "fearful man, all in coarse grey, with a great iron on his leg" who starts up from among the graves; a world in which the secret inner life of the spirit does not wait on the slow processes of analysis and of naturalistic cause and effect, but suddenly appears before one on the staircase with hands stretched out, saying, "My boy! my dear boy!"; in short, an absurd world, quite contradicting commonsense, and one, therefore, in which things and people do not walk by the clock but dance pantomimic dances in the outrageous tempo of the absurd. In *Wuthering Heights*, the pace of assault is so deeply at the core of the book's feeling that comment seems superfluous: we cannot imagine this novel as moving otherwise than by violent attack—than by verbs of "snatching," "grinding," "crashing," "smashing," "thundering," "choking," "burning," "torturing," "murdering": for such excess is of the nature of that nonhuman Otherworld which, in Emily Brontë's vision, erupts grotesquely into the limited, the civilized, the moral, the static. And now, before attempting to define the expressive value of a very different kind of pace, let us consider somewhat more closely the types of material that, in *Adam Bede*, present themselves with the patient rhythms of day and night, of the seasons, of planting and harvest, of the generations of men, and of the thoughts of simple people who are bound by deep tradition to soil and to community.

We enter the description of Hall Farm in Chapter 6 at "the drowsiest time of the year, just before hay-harvest," and at "the drowsiest time of the day, too, for it is close upon three by the sun, and it is half-past three by Mrs. Poyser's handsome eight-day clock." If the reader will turn back to the passage quoted above, describing old Martin Poyser, he will find the clock again: old Martin watches its hands, not through engagement with time but through disengagement from it; he pleases himself with "detecting a rhythm in the tick" as he does with watching the sun-gleams on the wall and counting the quarries on the floor. And again, in the passage describing the Poysers on their way to church, we are told of "the excellent habit which Mrs. Poyser's clock had of taking time by the forelock," so that, despite interruptions in their walk, they arrive at the village "while it was still a quarter to two." The mechanism of the eight-day clock works in sympathy with the week, with the rhythm of workdays and Sabbath, and we are reminded in the same passage of that other scheduling of man's time which holds him to Sabbath observance no matter if the hay wants turning, for, as Mrs. Poyser says, "as for the weather, there's One above makes it, and we must put up wi't." We shall return to the clock, but we wish to note now the *kind* of life that this great mass of slow time carries with it. It is a kind of life that is signified by that wonderful kitchen at Hall Farm, with its polished surfaces of oak table and, of course, the oak clockcase—not "any of your varnished rubbish," but polished with "genuine 'elbow polish' "—the great round pewter dishes ranged on the shelves above the long deal dinner table, the jasper-shining hobs of the grate, mellow oak and bright brass; and it is signified by the Hall Farm dairy:

> such coolness, such purity, such fresh fragrance of new-pressed cheese, of firm butter, of wooden vessels perpetually bathed in pure water; such soft coloring of red earthenware and creamy surfaces, brown wood and polished tin, grey limestone and rich orange-red rust on the iron weights and hooks and hinges.

It is a kind of life that is signified, too, by the funeral of Thias Bede, that deeply reverend magical rite at which

> none of the old people held books—why should they? not one of them could read. But they knew a few "good words" by heart, and their withered lips now and then moved silently, following the service without any very clear comprehension indeed, but with a simple faith in its efficacy to ward off harm and bring blessing . . .

while old Lisbeth is comforted in her grief by "a vague belief that the psalm was doing her husband good," for

> it was part of that decent burial which she would have thought it a greater wrong to withhold from him than to have caused him many unhappy days while he was living. The more there was said about her husband, the more there was done for him, surely the safer he would be.

It is a kind of life that is signified by the chapter describing the schoolmaster, Bartle Massy, and his pupils—the stone sawyer, the brickmaker, the dyer—

> three big men, with the marks of their hard labour about them, anxiously bending over the worn books, and painfully making out, "The grass is green," "The sticks are dry," "The corn is ripe" . . . It was almost as if three rough animals were making humble efforts to learn how they might become human.

Bartle Massy himself has no critical place in the plot, but, like the schoolmaster in Goldsmith's "The Deserted Village," he is one more significant member of a community; and his kindness, his depth of feeling, his long habits of sacrifice and self-discipline, even his eccentricity, are of the richest texture of the community life. For it is the community that is the protagonist of this novel, the community as the repository of certain shared and knowledgeable values that have been developed out of ages of work and care and common kindness. The kitchen at Hall Farm shines in the sun, the dairy is clean and fragrant, Lisbeth's grief is alleviated by the funeral, and Bartle Massy's pupils make their toilsome efforts "to learn how they might become human," because of a moral development that has been made possible only by slow and difficult centuries of accreted recognitions, limitations, modulations, techniques.

Therefore the eight-day clock, with its minute rhythms for an old man's ear, with its rhythm for the daily work that starts at half past four, when the mowers' bottles have to be filled and the baking started, and with its weekly rhythm for the Sabbath. The clock is a monument not to time merely as time, but to the assured and saving values stored up through ages of experience. In one of her books George Eliot says, "There is no private life which has not been determined by a wider public life." In *Adam Bede*, this is the mute recognition by which the community lives: as imaginatively realized here, it is a recognition that personal good has communal determinations, that it is contingent upon the preservation of common values. But the statement bears also its converse, which might be phrased thus: "There is no public life which has not been determined by the narrower private life"; for the story of *Adam Bede* is a story of the irreparable damage wrought on the community by a private moment's frivolity.

Mrs. Poyser's clock at Hall Farm, the clock which has sublimated all time into good, is set for daylight saving (it has the "excellent habit" of "taking time by the forelock"). Not so the clocks of the gentlefolk at the Chase. Throughout that Thursday when Arthur twice meets Hetty in the wood, the clock is watched irritably. It is "about ten o'clock" when Arthur, time irritable and bored on his hands, goes to the stables; the "twelve o'clock sun" sees him galloping toward Norburne to see a friend; but Hetty is on his mind, and "the hand of the dial in the courtyard had scarcely cleared the last stroke of three" when he is again home; so that "it was scarcely four o'clock" when he is waiting at the gate of the wood. Hetty comes daily to learn lace mending of Mrs. Pomfret, the maid at the Chase, at four o'clock, and she tells Arthur that she always sets out for the farm "by eight o'clock." They exchange a look: "What a space of time those three moments were, while their eyes met and his arms touched her!" Arthur meditates irresolutely "more than an hour" on the false impression he feels he has created in the girl; but "the time must be filled up," and he dresses for dinner, "for his grandfather's dinner-hour was six"; meanwhile Hetty too is watching the clock, and at last "the minute-hand of the old-fashioned brazen-faced timepiece was on the last quarter of eight." In the shadows of the wood he kisses her. Then he pulls out his watch: "I wonder how late it is . . . twenty minutes past eight—but my watch is too fast." Back at the farm, Mrs. Poyser exclaims,

"What a time o'night this is to come home, Hetty . . . Look at the clock, do; why, it's going on for half-past nine, and I've sent the gells to bed this half-hour, and late enough too . . ."

"I did set out before eight, aunt," said Hetty, in a pettish tone, with a slight toss of her head. "But this clock's so much before the clock at the Chase, there's no telling what time it'll be when I get here."

"What! you'd be wanting the clock set by gentle-folks's time, would you? an' sit up burnin' candle, an' lie a-bed wi' the sun a-bakin' you like a cowcumber i' the frame? The clock hasn't been put forrard for the first time to-day, I reckon."

The pace of *Adam Bede* is set to Mrs. Poyser's clock, to all that slow toil and patient discipline that have made daylight—and living—valuable. Slower, organically, invisibly slow, are the months of Hetty's pregnancy; the Poysers' clock, the clock at the Chase, do not keep this time, with their eights and nines and half past nines. This other, deep, hidden, animal time drags the whole pace down to that of poor Hetty's "journey in despair," a blind automatism of animal night where the ticking of the human clock cannot be heard.

Hetty's very fragility is her claim to the saving disciplines of a traditional way of life. It is by her mediocrity that their value is tested, for without them she is abandoned to chaos. There is probably no other work that explores human suffering at the organic level with such deep authority as the chapter describing Hetty's journey from Oxford to Stonyshire. It is a suffering that has no issue in "illumination," no spiritual value for the sufferer, for Hetty is not the kind of character that sustains "illumination" through suffering. If she were, we should not have had the particular insight that *Adam Bede* affords into the moral meaning of time and tradition in the lives of simple people. Hetty is lost because she is more fragile than the others and therefore more dependent on the community disciplines (far more fragile, because of her class, than "Chad's Bess" of the village, for instance, who, with her looseness and silliness and—like Hetty—with false garnets in her ears, has a secure and accustomed place in the village life); lost from the only values that can support her mediocrity, she sinks into the chaos of animal fear, which, in the human being, is insanity. Other novelists have explored other kinds of suffering; one might draw up a chart or a dissertation, of no mean interest, that would show the hierarchies of human suffering as represented in literature and their psychological, ethical, and spiritual significance; surely Hetty's would be at the bottom of the scale (even lower, one would think, than that of some of the least human characters in Faulkner's novels, for Faulkner is interested in the "illumination" of which even idiots are capable). But its lowness and blindness in the scale of human suffering is its moving power. For Hetty is very human, very real, and if knowledge of suffering did not include hers, it would not include the broadest and commonest layer of human existence.

It is improbable that any but an English novelist would have interested himself in Hetty as a figure of tragic pathos. Flaubert would have despised her: the luxury fantasies of Emma Bovary (a French Hetty) have a richness and complexity of cultural experience, and a play of sensibility, that make Hetty's dreams of standing beside Arthur Donnithorne as a bride look thin indeed; and the fatality of Hetty's pregnancy would not have occurred to the author of *Madame Bovary*, nor all the mess of child murder, for these are quite English habits of interest (as we have been able to witness those habits in *The Heart of Mid-Lothian*—to whose plot *Adam Bede* is confessedly indebted—and shall again in Hardy's *Tess*); though Emma Bovary's adulterous experiences give her a far wider range of opportunity than Hetty's few moments with Arthur Donnithorne allow, Emma's child is a child by marriage and its existence has ironic rather than tragic significance; and the interest of Emma's adulteries is an interest in the adulterous psychology rather than an interest in spermatic and ovarian operations. Dostoevski could not have used Hetty, for she has less of God in her, a more meager spiritual capacity, than his imbeciles and whores; she is not capable even of that kind of "recognition" which leads the abused child in *The Possessed* and the carpenter in *Crime and Punishment* to hang themselves.

But the massy line of the book is deflected toward the end. ("The mirror," George Eliot says, "is doubtless defective; the outlines will sometimes be disturbed, the reflection faint or confused.") By Mrs. Poyser's clock, Hetty's last-minute reprieve cannot really be timed with a time integral to the rest of the novel, nor can Adam's marriage with Dinah. Henry James says of these events that he doubts very much "whether the author herself had a clear vision" of them, and suggests that the reason may be that George Eliot's perception

> was a perception of nature much more than of art, and that these particular incidents do not belong to nature (to my sense at least); by which I do not mean that they belong to a very happy art . . . they are a very good example of the view in which a story must have marriages and rescues in the nick of time, as a matter of course.

We should add Arthur Donnithorne's return in his interesting and picturesque ill-health. Hetty's reprieve, the marriage of Dinah and Adam,

Arthur's reconstruction through such suffering as Arthur is able to suffer—these are no compensation for and no real "illumination" of the tragedy of Hetty. They are the artificial illumination which so many Victorian novels indulged in, in the effort to justify to man God's ways or society's ways or nature's ways. But still there is left the ticking of the oak-cased clock, rubbed by human "elbow-polish," that paces the book through its greater part: the realization of value, clean as the clock-tick, radiant as the kitchen of Hall Farm, fragrant as the dairy; and the tragic realization of the loss of however simple human values, in Hetty's abandoned footsteps as she seeks the dark pool and caresses her own arms in the desire for life.

JOHN HOLLOWAY

"Silas Marner" and the System of Nature

George Eliot is quite plainly a novel-
ist who is also a sage. She speaks in her letters of 'The high responsibilities
of literature that undertakes to represent life'; she writes 'it is my way . . .
to urge the human sanctities . . . through pity and terror, as well as
admiration and delight', or 'My books have for their main bearing a
conclusion . . . without which I could not have dared to write any
representation of human life—namely, that . . . fellowship between man
and man . . . is not dependent on conceptions of what is not man: and
that the idea of God, so far as it has been a high spiritual influence, is the
ideal of a goodness entirely human'. But there is really no need to turn to
the letters. The didactic intention is perfectly clear from the novels alone.

In *Adam Bede*, for example—and it is George Eliot's first full-
length work—she says that so far from inventing ideal characters, her
'strongest effort is . . . to give a faithful account of men and things as they
have mirrored themselves in my mind'. Realistic pictures of obscure
mediocrity serve a didactic purpose: 'these fellow-mortals, every one, must
be accepted as they are . . . these people . . . it is needful you should
tolerate, pity and love: it is these more or less ugly, stupid, inconsistent
people whose movements of goodness you should be able to admire'.
Finally, she gives the lesson an autobiographical import: 'The way in
which I have come to the conclusion that human nature is lovable— . . .
its deep pathos, its sublime mysteries—has been by living a great deal
among people more or less commonplace and vulgar'.

From *The Victorian Sage: Studies in Argument.* Copyright © 1953 by Macmillan & Co.

But George Eliot is not interested only in people and in their good and bad qualities; she wishes, beyond this, to impart a vision of the world that reveals its whole design and value. Her teaching may be partly ethical, but it is ethics presented as a system and grounded on a wider metaphysical doctrine. Her early novels emphasize how an integrated scheme of values is a help to man—'No man can begin to mould himself on a faith or an idea without rising to a higher order of experience'—and she vividly indicates the forces in her own time that impelled men to seek such a scheme. For one class to be cultured and sophisticated another must be 'in unfragrant deafening factories, cramping itself in mines, sweating at furnaces . . . or else, spread over sheepwalks, and scattered in lonely houses and huts . . . where the rainy days look dreary. This wide national life is based entirely on . . . the emphasis of want. . . . Under such circumstances there are many . . . *who have absolutely needed an emphatic belief*: life in this unpleasurable shape demanding some *solution* even to unspeculative minds . . . something that good society calls "enthusiasm", something that will present motives in an entire absence of high prizes . . . that includes resignation for ourselves and active love for what is not ourselves'. This is an interesting passage for the social historian, and for the critic of nineteenth-century capitalism too; but its present importance lies in showing what was of concern to George Eliot as she wrote, and how we are justified in searching her novels for philosophy as well as ethics.

Moreover, she clearly saw that these principles did not lend themselves to abstract presentation; to be convincing they needed the methods of the imaginative writer. A striking passage in *Janet's Repentance* asserts that the influence which really promotes us to a higher order of experience is 'not calculable by algebra, not deducible by logic, but mysterious . . . ideas are often poor ghosts . . . they pass athwart us in thin vapour, and cannot make themselves felt. But sometimes they are made flesh; they . . . speak to us in appealing tones; they are *clothed in a living human soul, with all its conflicts, its faith*. . . . Then their presence is a power . . . and we are drawn after them with gentle compulsion'. We cannot but recognize, even in passing, how Dinah Morris, Maggie, Dorothea and others of George Eliot's characters are just such incarnations. And when, in *The Mill on The Floss*, she writes of the influence of Thomas à Kempis, this appeal of a nonlogical kind is related directly to how books are written. The *Imitation* still 'works miracles' because 'written down by a hand that waited for the heart's prompting'; expensive sermons and treatises that lack this essential carry no 'message', no 'key' to 'happiness' in the form of a key to understanding; their abstractions consequently cannot persuade.

Thus it is clear that George Eliot wished to convey the kind of message, and knew that she must use the distinctive methods, with which this enquiry is concerned. But in examining how her novels are moulded to conform to these requirements, there is something which is here of first importance as it was not with Disraeli. For George Eliot was a profoundly, perhaps excessively serious writer, and her novels are coloured through and through by her view of the world, and devoted in their whole dimensions to giving it a sustained expression, whereas most of Disraeli's novels are of lighter weight, and give expression to his more serious views more or less fitfully. It would, with George Eliot, be therefore a mistake to begin by noticing incidents, metaphors, snatches of conversation, or similar details. What must be given primary stress is the broad outline, the whole movement of her novels as examples of life that claim to be typical. 'How unspeakably superior', wrote Matthew Arnold, 'is the effect of the one moral impression left by a great action treated as a whole, to the effect produced by the most striking single thought or by the happiest image'. This is as true of the work of the sage-novelist as it is of classical drama or the epic poem. To ignore it is to miss the wood for the trees.

Silas Marner, perhaps because it is simple and short, shows this most plainly. It is worth examining in some detail. Silas the weaver, expelled from his little nonconformist community through a trick of blind chance, settles as a lonely bachelor in the obscure Midland village of Raveloe; one son of the local landlord steals his savings but is unsuspected, and Eppie, the daughter of another by a secret marriage, appears as a foundling at his cottage and he adopts her. Many years after, when she is a young woman about to marry, and her father Godfrey is middle-aged and has married again, the truth about her birth and about the robbery comes at last to light. Various things lend the tale its distinctive quality. First, the characters and their doings seem to belong to the same order of things as the non-human world that surrounds them. The little village, off the beaten track in its wooded hollow, is half submerged in the world of nature. The villagers are 'pressed close by primitive wants.' The passage of time and the rotation of the seasons affect humans and animals and plants all alike. Individuals are dominated by their environment. 'Marner's face and figure shrank and bent themselves into a constant mechanical relation to the objects of his life, so that he produced the same sort of impression as a handle or a crooked tube, which has no meaning standing apart'. It follows from this that all the people in the book are humble and obscure; they may be attractive or virtuous, but they are all nobodies. Silas is a poor weaver who finds hard words in the prayer-book, Godfrey Cass is a squireen's son and a barmaid's husband,

Eppie marries a gardener—even Nancy Lammeter, Godfrey's second wife, is only a trim farmer's daughter who does the baking and says ' 'oss'. Such, the tale implies, is the staple of men and women.

The pattern of events in which these people are involved is one of 'poetic justice': vice suffers, virtue is rewarded. Silas, though unfortunate at first, is a good man, and at last is made happy. Godfrey Cass, who refused to acknowledge his daughter, has no children by his second marriage. Dunstan Cass the rake, stealing Silas's money at night, falls into the pond and is drowned. But this justice is rough and partial. It is not vindictively stern, so much as impersonal and aloof and half-known; it takes a slow chance course, and meets human imperfections not with definite vengeance but with a drab pervasive sense of partial failure or limited success. For the peasantry of such places as Raveloe 'pain and mishap present a far wider range of possibilities than gladness and enjoyment'. For Silas in his time of misfortune the world is a strange and hopeless riddle. His money is taken, Eppie arrives, through the operation of forces that he venerates without comprehending. Done injustice by a sudden twist of fate, he comes to trust in the world again over a long period of years, as the imperceptible influence of Eppie gradually revives long-dead memories and emotions; over the same period his estrangement from the other villagers is slowly replaced by intimacy. His life is governed by habit, and so is theirs. We never learn whether his innocence ever became clear to the congregation that expelled him as a thief.

Though the book is so short, its unit of measurement is the generation: Silas young and old, Eppie the child and the bride, Godfrey the gay youth and the saddened, childless husband. The affairs of one generation are not finally settled except in the next, when Silas's happiness is completed by Eppie's marriage, and Godfrey's early transgressions punished by her refusal to become Miss Cass. Dunstan Cass's misdeeds are not even discovered until, twenty years after the robbery, his skeleton is found clutching the money-bags when the pond is drained; and this is brought to light through, of all things, Godfrey's activities as a virtuous, improving landlord. Well may the parish-clerk say 'there's windings i' things as they may carry you to the fur end o' the prayer-book afore you get back to 'em'. All in all, the world of the novel is one which, in its author's own words, 'never *can* be thoroughly joyous'. The unhappiness in it comes when natural generous feelings are atrophied by selfishness: Dunstan steals, Godfrey denies his daughter. And the consequences of sin are never quite obliterated; Godfrey must resign himself to childlessness, though resignation is itself a kind of content. Real happiness comes when numb unfeeling hardness, the state of mind for example of the grief-stricken and disillusioned Silas, slowly thaws to warmer emotions of kindliness and love.

This novel contains, therefore, though in little, a comprehensive vision of human life and the human situation. It does so through its deep and sustained sense of the influence of environment and of continuity between man and the rest of nature, through its selection as characters of ordinary people living drab and unremarkable lives, and through the whole course of its action, working out by imperceptible shifts or unpredictable swings of chance to a solution where virtue is tardily and modestly rewarded, and vice obscurely punished by some dull privation. The details of George Eliot's treatment operate within this broader framework.

GENERAL FEATURES OF THE NOVELS

Most of George Eliot's other books express the same vision of life, some of them amplifying it through their greater length or complexity. All except *Romola* and *Daniel Deronda* are set in the same historical period—that of the immediate past. This choice is significant. It is a time sufficiently near the present for manners to be familiar, dull and unremarkable, and for nothing to have the excitement or glamour of the remote past; and yet sufficiently remote for the rhythm of life to be slower, and for man to be more fully subservient to nature. *Felix Holt* (1866) has the 1830s for its period. 'The glory had not yet departed from the old coach-roads'. But besides their glories, the coaches evoke other memories; they take us back to the shepherd 'with a slow and slouching walk, timed by the walk of grazing beasts . . . his glance accustomed to rest on things very near the earth . . . his solar system . . . the parish', back to the great straggling hedgerows that hid the cottages, to the hamlet that 'turned its back on the road, and seemed to lie away from everything but its own patch of earth and sky', and the villagers, free alike from popish superstition, and from 'handlooms and mines to be the pioneers of Dissent'. The third chapter of this book is devoted entirely to a survey of historical trends at the time of the story, with the comment, 'These social changes in Treby parish are comparatively public matters . . . but there is no private life which has not been determined by a wider public life . . . that mutual influence of dissimilar destinies which we shall see gradually unfolding itself'. *Adam Bede* (1859) opens in the year 1799, when the village carpenter sings hymns as he works in his shop, and travellers go a-horseback, and 'there was yet a lingering after-glow' from the time of Wesley. The actions of *Middlemarch* (1871–2) and *The Mill on the Floss* (1860) seem also to be set in the 1830s; while *Silas Marner* (1861) is a story of the early nineteenth century 'when the spinning wheels hummed busily in the farmhouses' and pallid weavers, 'like the remnants of a disinherited race', were to be seen 'far away among the lanes, or deep in the bosom of the hills' and 'to the peasants of old times, the world outside their own direct experience was region of vagueness and mystery'.

The total impact of the novels also owes much to the sense they create of historical change; and of how, slowly, indirectly, in unexpected ways, it touches the lives of the characters. Inconspicuous as it is, this does much to suggest an integrated social continuity, of which personal relations between characters are only one part. *Janet's Repentance* portrays the gradual permeation of rural life by Evangelicalism; it records one instance of a general social change. The background of *The Mill on the Floss* is the expanding prosperity and material progress of the whole nation; and when the fortunes of the Tulliver family are at their lowest, Tom is carried up again by the rising prosperity of the firm he works for, with its many interrelated and developing commercial activities. At one point the story hangs upon whether or not to install steam plant in the Tullivers' old watermill. When Silas Marner goes back at last to the chapel in Lantern Yard where he worshipped as a young man, he finds everything swept away to make room for a modern factory with its crowds of workpeople. In *Felix Holt*, personal experience is determined by the Reform Bill's gradually taking effect, and still more by the slow shift of population from agriculture to industry.

But in this respect there is a more massive contribution. Real historical change is quite important in these novels, but it is less important than the complex interaction of town and countryside, of the pleasures or amusements of life with its work and business, of the various classes of society, and of social institutions like the church, the village inn, the bank, the chapel, the manor, the school and the workshop. It is an interesting contrast with Dickens. Varied though his social panorama may be, he is really interested in the occupations of only one social class—his business men are rarely seen in their offices, and if they are, it is usually not to work—and an occupation interests him not for its distinctive niche in the scheme of things, but for what it has of odd or picturesque or *macabre*. His characters sell curiosities or optical instruments or skeletons; they drive coaches or keep inns; they are ham actors, dancing-masters, fishermen; or if simply clerks or schoolmasters, they tend to be oddities or rogues in themselves. But for George Eliot every character has his distinctive occupational niche, and it is this which determines his nature and gives him what leverage he has upon the course of the action. Lawyer Dempster in *Janet's Repentance*, Mr. Tulliver in *The Mill on the Floss*, Lawyer Jermyn in *Felix Holt*, Bulstrode and Mr. Vincy and Caleb Garth and Lydgate in *Middlemarch*, Tito in *Romola* even—all of them have their livelihoods to earn, and their actions are largely governed by the need to do so in a world that is complex and slow to change.

Often these complexities are not treated fully in the novel, but they lend it a depth and variety of social colour. Adam Bede's getting a wife and following a career are not two processes, but one; and as the story proceeds, the relation between him and Arthur Donnithorne is a product of how they stand as rival lovers, and how they stand as landlord and bailiff. In *Middlemarch*, the love-affair of Lydgate and Rosamond is largely a projection of their social and economic standing. Similarly in a minor work like *Brother Jacob*: the story centres upon how a new shopping habit gradually spreads through a country town. 'In short', writes George Eliot, 'the business of manufacturing the more fanciful viands was fast passing out of the hands of maids and matrons in private families, and was becoming the work of a special commercial organ'. Mr. Freely, who is responsible for this 'corruption of Grimworth manners', 'made his way gradually into Grimworth homes, as his commodities did'. His engagement to a prosperous farmer's pretty daughter is an aspect of economic success.

Seeing the characters thus enmeshed in a wider context develops in George Eliot's readers the sense of a tortuous, half-unpredictable, slowly changing world of a thousand humdrum matters. 'Anyone watching keenly the stealthy convergence of human lots, sees a slow preparation of effects from one life on another . . . old provincial society had its share of this subtle movement; had not only its striking downfalls . . . but also those less marked vicissitudes which are constantly shifting the boundaries of social intercourse, and begetting new consciousness of interdependence . . . municipal town and rural parish gradually made fresh threads of connection—gradually, as the old stocking gave way to the savings-bank, and the worship of the solar guinea became extinct . . . settlers, too, came from distant counties, some with an alarming novelty of skill, others with an offensive advantage in cunning'. Lydgate exemplifies the first of these types, Bulstrode the second. The author, illustrating the general order of life by particular cases, is at pains to ensure that we see the wider drift.

George Eliot also uses the temporal scale of her novels for didactic ends. The slow movement of the natural world is stressed by the great span of time with which every novel deals—a span not packed with events in their variety, but necessary if we are to watch the full working out of even one event. *Silas Marner*, *The Mill on the Floss* and *Amos Barton* (if we take count of its epilogue) actually narrate events over a full generation. All of the other novels or *Scenes*, except *Adam Bede*, plunge back a full generation to depict the circumstances that originally created the situation of the novel. In *Felix Holt*, for example, the fortunes of all the chief characters except Felix are settled by the liaison, thirty-five years ago, between the local landowner's wife and her lawyer, and by the elderly minister's marriage as a young man to a Frenchwoman whose infant daughter is now a grown woman. *Daniel Deronda* tells how Daniel recovered the Judaic heritage of which he was deprived at birth. It is the same with the others.

The sense of a deterministic world where everything happens of necessity is increased in these novels by their stress on kinship. George Eliot is never tired of emphasizing how the nature of the parents fixes that of their children. *Felix Holt* depends for its climax on a visible resemblance between father and son. The earlier pages of *The Mill on the Floss* are full of the power of family tradition, the manner in which children reproduce and yet modify their parents' characters, and above all, the sense that kinship by blood is the basis of just such a slowly operating, half-inarticulate interdependence between things as George Eliot desires us to recognize everywhere. The reader who responds to this will see an added point when Maggie rescues Tom from the flood. The details of the narrative may leave much to be desired. But Maggie's action shows how a deep sentiment of kinship may overcome years of hostility; and in essence, it is apt in the same way as Aunt Glegg's sudden change to helpfulness when her niece is in trouble. It is not pure melodrama or pure sentimentalism at all. Again, in *Adam Bede*, the author is careful to bring out the partial resemblance and partial contrast between Adam and his mother, or Mr. Irwine and old Mrs. Irwine, or Mrs. Poyser and her niece Dinah the Puritan. There is a sustained sense of continuity by blood decisive in its influence but almost too obscure and subtle for observation. If there were any doubt that this contributes to a general impression of nature, the point is made explicitly in *Daniel Deronda*. When Daniel tells Mordecai, his Jewish future brother-in-law, that he too is a Jew, Mordecai's first words indicate how this kinship adumbrates a wider system: 'we know not all the pathways . . . all things are bound together in that Omnipresence which is the plan and habitation of the world, and events are as a glass where-through our eyes see some of the pathways'. Kinship is an aspect of the system of Nature.

BARBARA HARDY

The Moment of Disenchantment

In almost all George Eliot's novels
there is a crisis of disenchantment described in images which echo, more
or less closely, a passage in one of her letters. On 4 June 1848 she wrote to
Sara Hennell:

> Alas for the fate of poor mortals which condemns them to wake up some
> fine morning and find all the poetry in which their world was bathed,
> only the evening before, utterly gone!—the hard, angular world of chairs
> and tables and looking-glasses staring at them in all its naked prose!

This image of the disenchanted day-lit room is one of the most
important recurring images in her work. It first returns in "Janet's Repentance" though in a context very different from that of George Eliot's
lament. Janet's cold, hard vision of reality is no result of waking from a
dream: it summarizes and freezes a disenchantment with which she has
been living without fully admitting it:

> The daylight changes the aspect of misery to us, as of everything else. In
> the night it presses on our imagination—the forms it takes are false,
> fitful, exaggerated; in broad day it sickens our sense with the dreary
> persistence of definite measurable reality. . . . That moment of intensest
> depression was come to Janet, when the daylight which showed her the
> walls, and chairs, and tables, and all the commonplace reality that
> surrounded her, seemed to lay bare the future too, and bring out into
> oppressive distinctness all the details of a weary life to be lived from day
> to day. . . .
>
> (ch. xvi)

From *The Review of English Studies*, New Series, 19, vol. 5 (July 1954). Copyright © 1954 by
The Clarendon Press.

The clear light on the objects in a room, the definiteness and dreariness, and the suggestion of a prosaic present stretching into an unchanging prosaic future are the unmistakable links with the first image in the letter and the many later repetitions.

With Hetty Sorrel in *Adam Bede* it is the second look at a very new loss of enchantment which makes her feel "that dry-eyed morning misery, which is worse than the first shock, because it has the future in it as well as the present" (ch. xxxi) and so it is with Adam, on whom George Eliot bestows her own image of the well-lit charmless room:

> now that by the light of this new morning he was come back to his home, and surrounded by the familiar objects that seemed for ever robbed of their charm, the reality—the hard, inevitable reality—of his troubles pressed upon him with a new weight.
>
> (ch. xxxviii)

This also echoes faintly the desolation of his mother, Lisbeth Bede, when after her husband's death "the bright afternoon's sun shone dismally" in her kitchen. But for Lisbeth this is no disenchantment marking or making growth while for Adam, as for Janet, the hard impact of reality is a crisis in nurture—he is far less static than is often suggested. It is also a crisis which corresponds to Hetty's and thus brings the two into oblique but organic relation. His joyless vision of the world in which there is "no margin of dreams beyond the daylight reality" recapitulates the common unromantic daylight which drove her, ironically, to him. The dreamless daylight makes the challenge, which he accepts, propelled as he is by the strong inseparable combination of his character and his vocation, and which Hetty rejects in panic.

In "The Lifted Veil," the story published in *Blackwood's Magazine*, July 1859, the image of the lighted room recurs to stamp the crisis, though the crisis is less one of disenchantment than one of discovery. It is rather a melodramatic use of the image, partly because it is a metaphor and not the actual pressure of the seen world, partly because of the feverish fantasy of the narrative:

> The terrible moment of complete illumination had come to me, and I saw that the darkness had hidden no landscape from me, but only a blank prosaic wall: from that evening forth, through the sickening years which followed, I saw all round the narrow room of this woman's soul.

Here is the first appearance of the antithetical image of space which in the later novels puts extra emphasis on the narrowness of the room; but this is the only instance I know where the narrow room is the woman's soul and not the soul's oppressive environment.

Maggie Tulliver's awakening from her dream, in *The Mill on the Floss*, has enormous causal significance. It prepares her for her second dream, made up of an unrealistic renunciation which is both self-abnegation and self-indulgence, but it also prepares the last and real awakening, when the revival of her old dream of love and beauty in her meeting with Stephen leads first to the drifting with the stream and then to the genuine renunciation.

The immediate causes of Maggie's disenchantment are the causes of George Eliot's: family trouble, especially her father's illness, a lasting feeling of separation, and sense of impotence and aspiration. Here, although there is the emphasis of the dull and heavy prosaic routine, we move away from the autobiographical images of light and common objects:

> She could make dream-worlds of her own—but no dream-world would satisfy her now. She wanted some explanation of this hard, real life: the unhappy-looking father, seated at the dull breakfast table; the childish, bewildered mother; the little sordid tasks that filled the hours, or the more oppressive emptiness of weary, joyless leisure.
>
> (Bk. IV, ch. iii)

In *Romola* the images of light return, though not the common objects. Romola's disenchanting illumination is something more dramatic than the cold light of morning, as we might expect from the novel which contains almost nothing of George Eliot's understatement of event and character. Romola loses her dream, the dream of human fellowship and service, and she shrinks from "the light of the stars, which seemed to her like the hard light of eyes that looked at her without seeing her" (ch. lxi). Like the common daylight in the other books the significance of the light is that it forces her to see the indifferent life outside the self.

Here too the image is repeated, and the repetition emphasizes a coincidence of character. Similar light falls on Savonarola, the parallel and the contrast to Romola. When he asks for a sign from Heaven there is a sudden stream of sunlight which lights his face and satisfies the crowd. But the effect is contemporary:

> when the Frate had disappeared, and the sunlight seemed no longer to have anything special in its illumination, but was spreading itself impartially over all things clean and unclean, there began, along with the general movement of the crowd, a confusion of voices.
>
> (ch. lxii)

Two chapters farther on the images of light are repeated. There is the light of common day in Savonarola's cell, contrasted with the colour and radiance of Fra Angelico's frescoes and especially his Madonna's "radiant glory":

The light through the narrow windows looked in on nothing but bare walls, and the hard pallet and the crucifix.

This is the contrast (for the reader and not for the characters) between the glory and the hard reality. In the next chapter, Savonarola himself sees the light, the disenchanting light which is the image of the crowd's disillusion and which returns as the image of his own doubt:

But there seemed no glory in the light that fell on him now, no smile of heaven: it was only that light which shines on, patiently and impartially, justifying or condemning by simply showing all things in the slow history of their ripening.

The images of light in *Romola* stand apart from those in the other books but they are still images of the light which shows a dreamless or unresponsive world outside the self.

In *Felix Holt* the description of brightly lit despair is put into the motto which prefaces chapter xliv:

> I'm sick at heart. The eye of day,
> The insistent summer noon, seems pitiless,
> Shining in all the barren crevices
> Of weary life, leaving no shade, no dark,
> Where I may dream that hidden waters lie.

This fragment introduces Esther's endurance of the dream which comes true, in a different sense, "that state of disenchantment belonging to the actual presence of things which have long dwelt in the imagination with all the factitious charms of arbitrary arrangement" (ch. xliv). There is no place here for the dull and common room. Esther has to feel the oppression of spaciousness, of "a life of middling delights, overhung with the languorous haziness of motiveless ease, where poetry was only literature" (ch. xliv) and the light which shines too brilliantly for her is one she can put out: "she put out the wax lights that she might get rid of the oppressive urgency of walls and upholstery and that portrait smiling with deluded brightness" (ch. xlix). Once more the correspondences of character, the most significant thematic emphasis in the novels, are underlined by the common imagery. Part of Esther's disenchantment is the disenchanted face, in the portrait and outside, of Mrs. Transome, and Mrs. Transome's unbearable reality is also fixed in two images of light. There is the tragic desolation which is more violent than the awakening to prose reality:

all around here, where there had once been brightness and warmth, there were white ashes, and the sunshine looked dreary as it fell on them.

(ch. ix)

And there is the duller impact too, though again strengthened by metaphor:

> Here she moved to and fro amongst the rose-coloured satin of chairs and curtains . . . dull obscurity everywhere, except where the keen light fell on the narrow track of her own lot, wide only for a woman's anguish.
>
> (ch. xxxiv)

In the last novels we come back to the double image of light and common objects. Dorothea's disenchanted room, in *Middlemarch*, is of course the boudoir with the bow-window and the faded blue chairs. She comes back to it after her wedding journey to find a changed aspect:

> The distant flat shrank in uniform whiteness and low-hanging uniformity of cloud. The very furniture in the room seemed to have shrunk since she saw it before: the stag in the tapestry looked more like a ghost in the ghostly blue-green world; the volumes of polite literature in the bookcase looked more like immovable imitations of books. The bright fire of dry oak-boughs burning on the dogs seemed an incongruous renewal of life and glow.
>
> (ch. xxviii)

The emphasis is on disenchantment—"Each remembered thing in the room was disenchanted, was deadened as an unlit transparency"—but the objects recede and grow small rather than strike the vision with their dullness or their hardness. And the light is not a brilliant one, either here or in the dazzling sunlight in a later scene in the same room where the real light is dulled in metaphor: "And just as clearly in the miserable light she saw her own and her husband's solitude—how they walked apart so that she was obliged to survey him" (ch. xlii).

When Gwendolen, in *Daniel Deronda*, meets an unmistakable impact from outside herself which breaks the steady dream of potential brilliance, she comes to realize the shock in a dull room. The image is almost a return to its origin:

> the noonday only brought into more dreary clearness the absence of interest from her life. All memories, all objects, the pieces of music displayed, the open piano—the very reflection of herself in the glass— seemed no better than the packed-up shows of a departing fair.
>
> (ch. xxiii)

And, a little later:

> But this general disenchantment with the world—nay, with herself, since it appeared that she was not made for easy pre-eminence—only intensified her sense of forlornness: it was a visibly sterile distance enclosing the dreary path at her feet.
>
> (ch. xxvi)

There is some interest in following the course of an image which suggested itself in experience or in imagination nine years before George Eliot began to write novels, and the persistent recurrence suggests both the impact of the first experience and the common thematic thread which runs from novel to novel. In order to look more clearly at the common element in these scenes of disenchantment—they are not the only examples but probably the most important—it is necessary to go back to the letter to Sara Hennell. After describing the awakening in the disenchanted room George Eliot writes this:

> It is so in all the stages of life: the poetry of girlhood goes—the poetry of love and marriage—the poetry of maternity—and at last the very poetry of duty forsakes us for a season, and we see ourselves, and all about us, as nothing more than miserable agglomerations of atoms—poor tentative efforts of the Natur Princep to mould a personality.

This disappearance of glamour is an essential part of the process of every novel, and this letter is almost a forecast of what she was to write: the poetry of girlhood vanishes for Janet and Maggie, the poetry of love and marriage for Gilfil, Hetty, Adam, Silas, the poetry of maternity for Mrs. Transome, and the poetry of duty for Romola. Moreover, each conversion of poetry into prose depends on the dispelling of a dream. This poetry is usually not a lost glory, as it is in Wordsworth and Coleridge, and perhaps in Newman. It is a poetry erected on a dream, a dream in which the dreamer occupies the centre, and disenchantment is the waking which forces the dreamer to look painfully at a reality which puts him in his place. Janet, Adam, Maggie, Esther, Romola, and Dorothea all move out of their different dreams into the same clearly lit world where they have to do without the dreamer's drug. The crisis is one of the oblique demonstrations of George Eliot's precept, enunciated as the positivist's challenge to Christianity: "The 'highest calling and election' is to *do without opium.*" George Eliot does not show her own renunciation of opiate, but she shows opiates as various as alcohol, daydream, literature, love, and inexperienced idealism. Most of her heroines need only one disenchantment, though Hetty and Gwendolen withdraw from their disenchanted worlds to find some other temporary opiate. Their failure to find nurture in despair is as significant as the success of Dorothea.

"Nothing more than miserable agglomerations of atoms"—the sense of dislocation within the personality was something which George Eliot felt as strongly as Wordsworth and Coleridge had before her. Her metamorphosis, as she called it, was indeed like Wordsworth's in more ways than one. They were both haunted by a double sense of disintegration: by the break between past and present, and by the break between the heart and the reason.

It is the first break, the loss of continuity in time, the sense of an isolated present snapped off from the past, which she emphasizes most vigorously in the novels. In their very different ways Maggie, Silas, Esther, Dorothea, and Gwendolen all share with their creator this feeling of fragmentariness and unreality. In their lives, as in hers, it was a stage in the metamorphosis. For most of them the break with the past is a break with an opiate, with the exception of Silas, whose opiate was provided by the very isolation of the present. For him exile in place and hence in time was desirable:

> Minds that have been unhinged from their old faith and love, have perhaps sought this Lethean influence of exile, in which the past becomes dreamy because its symbols have all vanished, and the present too is dreamy because it is linked with no memories.
>
> (ch. ii)

George Eliot too had rejected the symbols of her past, and her fear of emotional isolation from the past and from her family is retold, with a difference, in the progress of Silas.

Silas is perhaps not strictly relevant to this discussion since he is one of the very few characters who is not absorbed in the dream of self. This is why his disintegration is a pleasantly unreal state, whereas most of the disenchanted heroines feel clearly and harshly aware of a reality which blocks past from present. It is a blocking which ends the dream of self, which marks the rude and salutary awakening to the world where self is reduced. Gwendolen's awakening stands alone in this respect for it is a slow process, not fairly simply identified with the awakening disenchantment which alters both past and present. Even in her disenchanted moment she is preoccupied with self, and she has to go far before her dread of solitude becomes an acceptance of solitude. Again, the process is given by the repeated images. Just as the dead face in the portrait makes the objective premonition of Grandcourt's death, so the first image of space prepares us for the last. We are told that her fear of

> Solitude in any wide scene impressed her with an undefined feeling of immeasurable existence aloof from her, in the midst of which she was helplessly incapable of asserting herself.
>
> (ch. vi)

This is kept alive in faint echoes throughout the book until it is repeated and justified in the crisis of her parting with Deronda, where we see her for the first time being dislodged from her supremacy in her own world, and getting a sense that her horizon was but a dipping onward of an existence with which her own was revolving.

(ch. lxix)

For Gwendolen, and for many of the others, disenchantment works, slowly or quickly, towards "the state of prostration—the self-abnegation through which the soul must go," as George Eliot described it in the letter to Sara Hennell quoted at the beginning. Gwendolen even shares with George Eliot the sense of physical shrinking. Gwendolen felt that she was reduced to a "speck"; George Eliot says in this same letter:

I feel a sort of madness growing upon me—just the opposite of the delirium which makes people fancy that their bodies are filling the room. It seems to me as if I were shrinking into that mathematical abstraction, a point.

In the feeling of self-annihilation George Eliot is closer to Keats than to Wordsworth or Coleridge.

Whether or not they are reduced to a point, her heroines are certainly forced from the centre of the periphery, from the dream of self which filled the world to a reduced consciousness. The place of the oppressive room in this process is plain. It is the physical enclosure, the daily life, the woman's place. For all the heroines the forcible reduction is in part at least the realization of the woman's lot, and the image of the room is the appropriate feminine image of the shut-in life. The hard reality of the common objects is the only furnishing for the social trap portrayed in The Mill on the Floss, Middlemarch (perhaps to a lesser extent), and Daniel Deronda.

Not that the image is only a plea for the imprisoned woman. It can present Adam Bede's despair of himself and his world, and indeed any crisis in the development of the egoist—and all her characters are egoists—in which self shrinks and vision expands. Three weeks after she wrote to Sara Hennell describing her disenchantment, she wrote, with a backward glance:

All creatures about to moult, or to cast off an old skin, or enter on any new metamorphosis, have sickly feelings. It was so with me. But now I am set free from the irritating worn-out integument.

This is the important thing. The disenchantment marks a stage in metamorphosis: it is the well-lit day which makes George Eliot's dark night of the soul. It is a test and a prelude to change. The idealists, Adam, Romola, and Dorothea, are forced to recognize the egoism in their ideal. The egoists who are successfully nurtured, Maggie and Esther, are forced to abdicate their splendid dreams. But classification is too rough a process. There is all the difference in the world between Maggie's reaction to disenchantment and Esther's: Maggie's prosaic shock leads her into a new dream of theoretical renunciation, Esther's leads her to accept as bitter what had been sweet in the dream. Maggie is roused by the twin shocks of sympathy and helplessness, Esther by the ironical solidifying of her romantic dream. There is also Hetty, caught in the "narrow circle of her imagination," able to do nothing but run desperately from the unbearable daylight. There is Gwendolen, who has to endure a triple disenchantment before she abandons the place of the princess. The pattern remains, the people change. To point to a common image which links character and theme is merely to point to a constant which throws all the variations into relief. George Eliot used the landmarks of her own way of the soul—and this may be one reason why she is sometimes said to use one heroine many times—but it is only the landmarks which are unchanging.

Even the landmarks change in details. The disenchanted objects change. Janet sees ordinary chairs and tables, as George Eliot did, but Adam sees the dressing-table he made for Hetty. Esther sees richer furniture, and Mrs. Transome's portrait, while Dorothea sees the tapestry she had welcomed because it belonged to Casaubon's mother, and, as the one living object, the portrait of Ladislaw's grandmother. Gwendolen, the aspiring amateur rebuked by Klesmer, the beauty whose face is her fatal fortune, sees the piano and the mirror.

What is more, for Esther and Dorothea and Gwendolen there is the movement away from the image of the narrow room. Gwendolen's sense of space has terror in it, but in its implications it is not so very different from the triumph in space which is found in *Felix Holt* and *Middlemarch*. Esther and Dorothea look away from the dead objects and see people: they look at a light which has some promise. Esther wanted "the largeness of the world to help her thought" (ch. xlix) and she turns from the room to the window. Dorothea does the same. She

> could see figures moving. . . . Far off in the bending sky was the pearly light; and she felt the largeness of the world and the manifold wakings of men to labour and endurance.
>
> (ch. lxxx)

What was a single image becomes a significant antithesis. The narrow room marks one stage in metamorphosis, the open window another.

WALTER ALLEN

"The Mill on the Floss"

George Eliot's fiction falls into two parts. *Scenes of Clerical Life, Adam Bede, The Mill on the Floss* and *Silas Marner* were all published between 1858 and 1861. The fiction of her second period was in some respects more ambitious; it opened with *Romola* in 1864, which was followed by *Felix Holt, the Radical* in 1866, *Middlemarch* in 1871–1872 and *Daniel Deronda* in 1876.

What is remarkable is the speed with which, having discovered she could write fiction, she produced her early novels; it shows how accessible was the vein of imagination on which she drew. It was composed very largely of her own memories of childhood and of what may be called family legend. She was to write in *Daniel Deronda*:

> A human life, I think, should be well rooted in some spot of a native land, where it may get the love of tender kinship for the face of the earth, for the labours men go forth to, for the sounds and accents that haunt it, for whatever will give that early home a familiar unmistakable difference amidst the future widening of knowledge: a spot where the definiteness of early memories may be inwrought with affection, and kindly acquaintance with all neighbours, even to the dogs and donkeys, may spread not by sentimental effort and reflection, but as a sweet habit of the blood. At five years old, mortals are not prepared to be citizens of the world, to be stimulated by abstract nouns, to soar above preference into impartiality; and that prejudice in favour of milk with which we blindly begin, is a type of the way body and soul must get nourished at least for a time. The best introduction to astronomy is to think of the nightly heavens as a little lot of stars belonging to one's own homestead.

From *George Eliot*. Copyright © 1964 by Walter Allen. The Macmillan Co.

This deeply rooted, severely localised life of childhood was something Gwendolen Harleth lacked and that her creator had had to the full. To it she returned in *The Mill on the Floss*. It is obviously not an autobiographical novel in anything like a complete sense, as, for example, *David Copperfield* and, especially, *Sons and Lovers* and *A Portrait of the Artist as a Young Man* are. Geographically, St. Ogg's is a considerable distance from Arbury, and a river of the amplitude and power of the Floss is conspicuously missing from the north Warwickshire landscape. And certainly Mr. Tulliver is not a portrait of Robert Evans. On the other hand, however different from George Eliot's are the circumstances in which she is placed, Maggie Tulliver is in all essentials a close projection of the author, so that it is true to see the novel as George Eliot's *A la recherche du temps perdu*. We know that Proust was much influenced by George Eliot, and we see, as Joan Bennett has said, the adult figures in the novel both as the child sees them and as the mature artist comprehends them, as in *Du côté de chez Swann*.

This identification of author with heroine, though it does not at all preclude criticism of the heroine by the author, gives *The Mill on the Floss* a sensuous warmth and a personal urgency beyond anything found in *Adam Bede*. As a rendering of the growth of a girl from early childhood to young womanhood, a girl marked by intellectual distinction, a generously ardent nature and a strong capacity for feeling, Maggie has never been surpassed. She speaks for herself at all times when she says to Philip Wakem: "I was never satisfied with a *little* of anything. That is why it is better for me to do without earthly happiness altogether. . . . I never felt that I had enough music—I wanted more instruments playing together—I wanted voices to be fuller and deeper." She has, indeed, an excess of sensibility, almost an excess of expectation; she is too ardent, swerving passionately from the extreme of desire to the extreme of self-abnegation. As Philip tells her, speaking for George Eliot but speaking all the same in character:

> . . . you are shutting yourself up in a narrow self-delusive fanaticism, which is only a way of escaping pain by starving into dullness all the highest powers of your nature. Joy and peace are not resignation; resignation is the willing endurance of a pain that is not allayed—that you don't expect to be allayed. Stupefaction is not resignation; and it is stupefaction to remain in ignorance—to shut up all the avenues by which the life of your fellow-men might become known to you. I am not resigned: I am not sure that life is long enough to learn that lesson. *You* are not resigned: you are only trying to stupefy yourself.

And again:

"Maggie," he said, in a tone of remonstrance, "don't persist in this wilful, senseless privation. It makes me wretched to see you benumbing and cramping your nature in this way. You were so full of life when you were a child: I thought you would be a brilliant woman—all wit and bright imagination. And it flashes out in your face still, until you draw that veil of dull quiescence over it. . . . It is mere cowardice to seek safety in negations. No character becomes strong in that way. You will be thrown into the world some day, and then every rational satisfaction of your nature that you deny now, will assault you like a savage appetite."

That last sentence is prophetic of the tragic plight into which Maggie is to fall; but what is interesting at this moment is the criticism, which one is bound to see as George Eliot's criticism of herself, made by the only character in the book with sensitivity and intellect enough to understand Maggie. Yet the criticism of her tendency towards excess is implicit, it seems to me, in descriptions of her behaviour from early childhood. She is heart-broken when, as a child, her brother Tom moves away from her, as in the nature of things he must. This tragedy of childhood is beautifully done; and yet one can't help feeling that Maggie's demands on Tom were in their nature excessive. When Philip sees her at Mr. Stelling's, her dark eyes reminded him of the "stories about princesses being turned into animals." He wonders why the thought should come to him, and George Eliot herself gives the answer: "I think it was that her eyes were full of unsatisfied intelligence, and unsatisfied, beseeching affection." What seems clear is that Maggie's affection is of a kind so beseeching in its nature as to be incapable of satisfaction, at any rate in the brutal society in which she must live.

For the society George Eliot describes, that of St. Oggs, and the Tullivers and the ramifications of the Dodson family, is brutal, and Maggie's tragedy is that of the free spirit caught in a blankly materialistic world. It is a world ruled over entirely by the sense of property, by self-regard and by pride in family; but family itself is valued more as a vehicle for the preservation and transmission of property than for any other reason. George Eliot's descriptions of the Dodson ladies and their husbands are probably the high points in her comedy; they are done with a warm appreciation of idiosyncrasy, in which there is certainly affection.

In a chapter of authorial intervention, George Eliot defends the Tullivers and Dodsons, not, it seems to me, too convincingly. "It is a sordid life, you say, this of the Tullivers and Dodsons. . . ." George Eliot does her best for them, but, the fact remains, it is a sordid life, whether one compares it with that of the Poysers in *Adam Bede* or even of the Vincys in *Middlemarch*. It is rendered tolerable, one sometimes feels, only because we see it refracted through the author's humour:

Few wives were more submissive than Mrs. Tulliver on all points uncon-
nected with her family relations; but she had been a Miss Dodson, and the
Dodsons were a very respectable family indeed—as much looked up to as
any in their parish, or the next to it. The Miss Dodsons had always been
brought up to hold their heads very high, and no one was surprised the
two eldest had married so well—not at an early age, for that was not the
practise of the Dodsons. There were particular ways of doing everything
in that family: particular ways of bleaching the linen, of making the
cowslip wine, curing hams, and keeping the bottled gooseberries; so that
no daughter of that house could be indifferent to the privilege of having
been born a Dodson, rather than a Gibson or a Watson. Funerals were
always conducted with peculiar propriety in the Dodson family: the
hat-bands were never of a blue shade, the gloves never split at the
thumb, everybody was a mourner who ought to be, and there were
always scarfs for the bearers. When one of the family was in trouble or
sickness, all the rest went to visit the unfortunate member, usually at the
same time, and did not shrink from uttering the most disagreeable truths
that correct family feeling dictated: if the illness or trouble was the
sufferer's own fault, it was not in the practice of the Dodson family to
shrink from saying so. In short, there was in this family a peculiar tradition
as to what was the right thing in household management and social
demeanour, and the only bitter circumstances attending this superiority
was a painful inability to approve the condiments or the conduct of
families ungoverned by the Dodson tradition. A female Dodson, when in
"strange houses" always ate dry bread with her tea, and declined any sort
of preserves, having no confidence in the butter, and thinking that the
preserves had probably begun to ferment from want of due sugar and
boiling. There were some Dodsons less like the family than others—that
was admitted; but in so far as they were "kin," they were of necessity
better than those who were of "no kin." And it is remarkable that while
no individual Dodson was satisfied with any other individual Dodson,
each was satisfied, not only with him or her self, but with the Dodsons
collectively. The feeblest member of a family—the one who has the least
character—is often the merest epitome of the family habits and traditions; and Mrs. Tulliver was a thorough Dodson, though a mild one, as
small-beer, so long as it is anything, is only describable as very weak ale:
and though she had groaned a little in her youth under the yoke of her
elder sisters, and still shed occasional tears at their sisterly reproaches, it
was not in Mrs. Tulliver to be an innovator on the family ideas. She was
thankful to be a Dodson, and to have one child who took after her own
family at least in his features and complexion, in liking salt and in eating
beans, which a Tulliver never did.

Mrs. Tulliver is the mildest of the Dodson sisters, but it is characteristic of her that, faced with her husband's bankruptcy and the consequences of his stroke, her deepest response should be:

"Oh dear, oh dear," said Mrs. Tulliver, "to think o' my chany being sold i' that way—and I bought it when I was married, just as you did yours, Jane and Sophy: and I know you didn't like mine, because o' the sprig, but I was fond of it; and there's never been a bit broke, for I've washed it myself—and there's the tulip on the cups, and the roses, as anybody might go and look at 'em for pleasure. You wouldn't like *your* chany to go for an old song and be broke to pieces, though yours 'as got no colour in it, Jane—it's all white and fluted, and didn't cost so much as mine. And there's the casters—sister Deane, I can't think but you'd like to have the casters, for I've heard you say they're pretty."

Equally characteristic are the responses of her sisters to this:

"Why, I've no objection to buy some of the best things," said Mrs. Deane, rather loftily; "we can do with extra things in our house."

"Best things!" exclaimed Mrs. Clegg with severity, which had gathered intensity from her long silence. "It drives me past patience to hear you all talking o' best things, and buying in this, that, and the other, such as silver and chany. You must bring your mind to your circum-stances, Bessy, and not to be thinking o' silver and chany; but whether you shall get so much as a flock-bed to lie on, and a blanket to cover you, and a stool to sit on. You must remember, if you get 'em, it'll be because your friends have bought 'em for you, for you're dependent upon *them* for everything; for your husband lies there helpless, and hasn't got a penny i' the world to call his own. And it's for your own good I say this, for it's right you should feel what your state is, and what disgrace your husband's brought on your own family, as you've got to look to for everything—and be humble in your mind."

George Eliot had never been praised enough for her grasp of the property basis of the society she describes in *The Mill on the Floss*. It is a society in which generosity itself is a vice. Mr. Tulliver is not much better than the Dodsons; his downfall is the result of his bull-like obstinacy, but it is made the more certain by his act of generosity to his sister Grittie; and significantly, George Eliot shows how this act is related to his love for his daughter: "It had come across his mind that if he were hard upon his sister, it might somehow tend to make Tom hard upon Maggie at some distant day, when her father was no longer there to take her part; . . . this was his confused way of explaining to himself that his love and anxiety for 'the little wench' had given him a new sensibility towards his sister." Ironi-cally, it is a factor in his undoing. If one wants a personification of spontaneous goodness, uncalculating sympathy in the novel, one has to turn to a character of whom not much is thought by anyone, who scarcely exists in Dodson and Tulliver terms—the pedlar Bob Jakin. The best that can be said of Tom Tulliver is that he will grow up to be a man his Dodson aunts and their husbands can be proud of.

Such, then, are the society and the circumstances in which Maggie must have her being. George Eliot's description of them is masterly, both in detail and in the large set-pieces of family confrontations and conferences. But we see them, of course, always in relation to Maggie:

> Maggie in her brown frock, with her eyes reddened and her heavy hair pushed back, looked from the bed where her father lay, to the dull walls of this sad chamber which was the centre of her world, was a creature full of eager, passionate longings for all that was beautiful and glad; thirsty for all knowledge; with an ear straining after dreamy music that died away and would not come near to her; with a blind, unconscious yearning for something that would link together the wonderful impressions of this mysterious life, and give her soul a sense of home in it.
>
> No wonder, when there is this contrast between the outward and the inward, that painful collisions come of it.

Maggie, since she is the girl she is, living in the society in which she does, is a figure doomed to tragedy.

The resolution of the tragedy, however, is another matter and, since the novel's initial publication, has satisfied no one. The resolution falls into two parts: there is first Maggie's running away with Stephen Guest, only to renounce him, and then the final flood scenes in which she rescues Tom from the mill, only for them to be carried to their death together.

It is obviously right that Maggie should be swept away by the passionate intensity of her nature that she has for too long unnaturally repressed. Indeed, it is prepared for deliberately by Philip Wakem's prediction: "You will be thrown into the world some day, and then every rational satisfaction of your nature that you deny now, will assault you like a savage appetite." It is also obviously right that she should miscontrue her sympathy and fellow-feeling for Philip as love for him and then, having privately committed herself to him, fall in love with another man. The other man, Stephen Guest, who is privately committed to her cousin Lucy, as Maggie knows, has been constantly assailed by critics. "A mere hairdresser's block," Leslie Stephen called him; and he aroused Swinburne's notable powers of denunciation—a "cur" for whom horsewhipping was too good. Admittedly, the first impression he makes on us is of being rather a bounder, certainly of being a too self-satisfied, consciously "superior," facile young man.

George Eliot, in fact, presents him at the beginning in ironical terms. But Stephen's and Swinburne's reactions to him seem excessive; the result, one can't help thinking, of a misreading of Maggie, a failure to heed the criticisms of her made time and again in the course of the novel.

In any case, there is nothing in the nature of things to prevent even so fine a spirit as Maggie falling in love with a spiritually coarse young man. These things happen; and, in fact, Joan Bennett is almost certainly right when she concludes that George Eliot intended Stephen to be changed, "improved," by his love for Maggie, to discover, as a result, a new sincerity, new depths, within himself. If this is not the impression we take away from reading the novel, the fault must lie where I believe it does—in George Eliot's inadequate technique.

Stephen Guest appears very late in the novel, a newcomer almost out of the blue and also of an order different from that to which all the other characters belong. He is of another and higher social class than that which we have met before. We are unprepared for him, and George Eliot, who needed space in which to build up her major characters, has not allowed space or time in which to establish him. We have not been given the necessary opportunity to get used to him, to know him; he is a rush-job.

Maggie's renunciation of him is another matter, and one can only feel that she has become the victim of what may be called an either-or morality that her author has imposed upon her and that denies the facts of experience as known at any time in history. George Eliot has almost gone out of her way to ensure that there has been no public engagement between either Maggie and Philip or Lucy and Stephen. Neither couple, in the eyes of the world, is irrevocably committed. The moral appeal, therefore, is to something beyond the conventional or the legalistic. When she renounces Stephen, Maggie is not sacrificing herself to save a marriage, and her self-sacrifice will not decrease the total stock of the unhappiness of the four people involved. Philip and Lucy will be unhappy in any event; her behaviour merely guarantees that she and Stephen must also be unhappy.

The situation in which Maggie and Stephen find themselves is not, after all, an uncommon one and can never have been. It is one that always involves someone's unhappiness; it is not improved by behaving in such a way as to multiply the unhappiness by two. For the situation is one in which an either-or morality cannot apply, if it can in any situation. George Eliot really sacrifices Maggie to her own doctrine of the virtue of self-sacrifice for its own sake. And the mind revolts against the cruelty implicit in it—and the falsity as well.

On the face of it, the *dénouement*, Maggie's rescue of her estranged brother in the flood and their reunion in death, is well prepared. The Floss flows through the novel from beginning to end. It is there in the title of the novel; it is in the very first sentence as in the last paragraphs. It may be said to encompass and enclose the action. It is closely bound up with the Tullivers' downfall: "There's a story," Mr. Tulliver says, "as when the mill changes hands, the river's angry—I've heard my father say it many a time." As for Mrs. Tulliver: " 'They're such children for the water, mine are,' she said aloud, without reflecting that there was no one to hear her; 'They'll be brought in dead and drowned some day. I wish that river was far enough'." The flood itself may be seen as a retrospective symbol of the flood of passion that has swept Maggie far from the narrow confines of her normal life and conduct.

The flood was obviously in George Eliot's mind from the beginning; we find her writing in her journal, on January 12, 1859: "We went into town today and looked in the 'Annual Register' for cases of *inundation.*" Yet, as the *dénouement* of the novel, it cannot help but strike one as a quite artificial resolution. It is as though Maggie, having made her final act of self-sacrifice, has nothing left for her but death. Even so, the manner of the death is fundamentally unsatisfying, as the very prose in which it is reported, in the last paragraph of the novel, indicates:

> The boat reappeared—but brother and sister had gone down in an embrace never to be parted: lived through again in one supreme moment, the days when they had clasped their little hands in love, and roamed the daisied fields together.

That is sentimentality of the most flagrant kind, as indeed is the notion that Maggie and Tom can ever be united in any real sense again. The return to childhood and to the security of childhood with Tom simply does not work. Yet one sees George Eliot's difficulty. The *dénouement* was forced upon her, one feels, by the falsity of Maggie's renunciation of Stephen. But there is something else implicit in it beyond this. If one looks at later autobiographical novels, Bennett's *Clayhanger,* Joyce's *A Portrait of the Artist as a Young Man,* Lawrence's *Sons and Lovers,* one realizes that in an old-fashioned sense they do not end. There can be no resolution because no action has been completed; a phase of development has been described—no more. Instead of an ending as such, we have a change in direction, as it were, a departure to a new scene: Dedalus's "O life! I go to encounter for the millionth time the reality of experience and to forge in the smithy of my soul the uncreated conscience of my race"; Paul Morel's "But no, he would not give in. Turning sharply, he walked towards the city's gold phosphorescence. His fists were shut, his mouth set. He would not take that direction, to the darkness, to follow her. He walked towards the faintly humming, glowing town, quickly."

But nothing like this was possible for George Eliot at this stage in her career and at the date at which she was writing. She could only fall back, however brilliantly she handled it, on one of the cliché endings of Victorian fiction.

RICHARD ELLMANN

Dorothea's Husbands

A novelist, intent on his art, swallows into it other people along with himself. The living originals of fictional characters are elusive because they have been obliged by the writer to answer purposes not their own. It is as if they were evicted from a universe of free will into a deterministic one. The peril of confusing universes is one to which we have been alerted by fastidious critics and structuralists alike. Yet many novelists are themselves liable to this lapse, and fondly imagine that they have created characters out of people they have known. To follow them a little way is at worst devoted, and at best profitable, since the mode of translating characters from the one universe to the other must be close to basic movements of the mind, and so of critical as well as biographical consequence.

It may be easier to approach George Eliot by way of a writer more patently obsessive. In *Heart of Darkness*, Conrad made avowed use of his own trip to the Congo a dozen years before. Much of the narrative turns out to have an immediate parallel in his experience: Conrad did go to Brussels for his interview, did ship up the Congo River on a steamboat, did rescue a sick agent named Klein who died on the trip back. Yet the story has a quite different feel from the *Congo Diary* and from his letters of the time. And there is an important discrepancy: Klein was no Kurtz, no symbol of spiritual degradation. If anything, he was nondescript. It would seem that the motive power of the story must have come from some other region than the Congo.

This area may be guessed at with the help of a fact first pointed out in Jocelyn Baines's life of Conrad. The correspondence of Conrad's uncle, Thaddeus Bobrowski, discloses that Conrad, at the age of nineteen, did not—as he always said afterwards—fight a duel and suffer a bullet wound. What happened instead was that he gambled away at Monte Carlo some money his uncle had sent him, and then in self-disgust shot himself. This attempted suicide was probably the central event of Conrad's life. In the light of it, the qualities on which Marlow prides himself in *Heart of Darkness*—his rivetlike tenacity, his patience, his coolness under pressure—were the exact opposites of those displayed by the young Conrad. From the moment that he inflicted this wound, Conrad must have regarded it—and its scar—as a sign and symbol of a propensity to give way, to abandon himself. To call his villain Kurtz (German for 'short') was to memorialize this phase of his life when he was not yet Joseph Conrad but still Konrad Korzeniowski—a name prone to be shortened to Korz.

When recovered from his wound, Conrad went to England and sailed on an English coastal vessel. By this time or not long afterwards he had determined to slough off his old life, language, weakness. He decided to present himself no longer as a European but as an Englishman. In the 1880s he took and passed the three examinations which confirmed his navigational skill and executive capacity. If 1875 was the year that he virtually died, 1886 was the year of his virtual resurrection, for during it he qualified as first mate, he became a British subject, and he began to write. Writing was a way of avenging his suicide attempt. Marlow declares, 'mine is the speech that cannot be silenced'. Like Marlow, whose watchword is 'restraint', Conrad must have practised a conscious self-overcoming.

It would seem likely that young Korzeniowski's suicide attempt was extrapolated as the self-abandonment and moral cowardice of the European Kurtz, and that the confrontation with Marlow, captain of English ships and master of English prose, bearer of an indisputably English name, was symbolically rehabilitative. To commit suicide is to yield to the mind's jungle, to write is to colonize with the efficiency so highly regarded by Marlow. Kurtz and Marlow meet in the 'heart of darkness' as in the recesses of Conrad's mind: one dies, the other contrives to be reborn. Conrad did not let this theme rest: his return to it in *Lord Jim* and other works must have been a pricking and stanching of the old wound.

This preliminary example may embolden an inquiry into two characters, and their possible prototypes, in *Middlemarch*. George Eliot, contrary to T. S. Eliot, made no claims for the impersonality of the artist. She confided that her first work of fiction, *Scenes of Clerical Life*, drew upon family reminiscences, and many characters from her other books have been pursued to prototypes in her experience, often with her help. She worked from models then, probably habitually.

Like George Eliot herself, Dorothea had two husbands. Of the two, it is Mr. Casaubon who has deserved and attracted attention. He is a pedant of such Saharan aridity that the temptation to identify him has not often been resisted. Among the proffered candidates, the one most mentioned is Mark Pattison, rector of Lincoln College, Oxford. He had three points of *rapport:* an unhappy marriage with a wife much younger than himself, friendship with George Eliot, and the authorship of a life of the Swiss scholar (of the sixteenth century) Isaac Casaubon. George Eliot obviously borrowed from him the name of his subject, but other resemblances are tenuous, as if the price she paid for the one liberty was not to take others. John Sparrow, the most resolute supporter of Pattison as Casaubon's archetype, has rested his case largely on a passage in Sir Charles Dilke's unpublished autobiography, in which Dilke, later married to Mrs. Pattison, states that Casaubon's marriage proposal and Dorothea's answer were based closely on the equivalent Pattison letters. These letters have not survived. But aside from the flexibility of style and mind so notable in Pattison, so lacking in Casaubon, it is now clear, from a letter of George Eliot published in the *Times Literary Supplement* on 12 February 1971 by Professor Gordon S. Haight, that as early as 1846 she was already diverting her friends by concocting the terms of a pedant's proposal of marriage. Casaubon's letter balances precariously on the questions of whether he is seeking a wife or someone to read to him, and of whether he is actuated by love or myopia; the proposal of 'Professor Bücherwurm', which George Eliot pretends to relay to Charles Bray, similarly hinges on the ambiguity of the Professor's securing as his bride someone to translate his books from German. In 1846 George Eliot did not know Pattison, and evidently she had no need to know him in order to evolve Casaubon's letter.

To consider other possible models for Casaubon is to turn up many of George Eliot's acquaintances. Pedantry was not a scarce commodity among them. Ideally the culprit should combine arid learning with sexual insufficiency. This felicitous blend is unexpectedly hard to find. No doubt the laws of *Middlemarch*, rather than those of experience, demanded that Casaubon's mind symbolize his body, and his body his mind. If George Eliot drew details from models, she used more than one. For sexual low pressure, Herbert Spencer was probably the best example, and Beatrice Webb saw enough resemblance to refer to him as Casaubon. George Eliot knew Spencer well, and may have been perplexed for a time at his failure to marry anyone, herself included. But if his nubility was in doubt for her, his ability was not; it is only a later age that wishes Spencer had been Casaubon enough to finish fewer books. Besides, Spencer came to regard George Eliot as the greatest woman who ever lived, an accolade she would not have so meagrely rewarded.

For the author of the 'Key to all Mythologies', a closer prototype is Dr. R. H. Brabant. It was he whom the novelist Mrs. Eliza Lynn Linton, well acquainted with both him and George Eliot, identified positively as Casaubon. Brabant had similar difficulty in bringing a book to fruition. According to Mrs. Linton, he 'never got farther than the introductory chapter of a book which he intended to be epoch-making, and the final destroyer of superstition and theological dogma'. Under the influence of the German rationalists, Brabant presumably intended to eliminate from all religions that supernatural element which they had eliminated from Christianity. It seems unlikely that he used the word 'key', an inappropriate one for his enterprise. Although Gordon S. Haight, George Eliot's astute and scrupulous biographer, accepts Brabant as the model, there are several obstacles to close identification with him as with Pattison. Brabant's loins were not nearly so exhausted: he did not manifest sexual indifference. He was married, he had a daughter and a son; at the age of sixty-two he squired George Eliot about in a manner which she found happily equivocal in intention, and which his blind wife acutely resented.

Moreover he was a physician, and evidently a good one; his book was a sideline, a token of intellectual community. He had a gift for companionship, and was friends with Coleridge, Moore, Landor, and others. He also had friends in Germany, notably Strauss and Paulus, and it was he who some years later introduced George Eliot, translator of *Das Leben Jesu*, to Strauss, its author. Apparently he could converse more easily in German than she could, and in this respect too he is unlike Casaubon, whose ignorance of German is scored heavily against him. Mrs. Linton describes Brabant as 'well got up and well preserved', while Casaubon is prematurely withered. He was also a man of many interests, in the theatre, art, and science, as references in George Eliot's correspondence and John Chapman's diaries confirm. Most of all, he was a man of enthusiasm, generously tendered to the work of others rather than his own.

George Eliot did feel a brief spell of veneration for Brabant, as Dorothea did for Casaubon, but with more semblance of justification. Whatever Brabant's defects as an idol, he was in the same cultural movement as she was. If he dithered, it was not over 'Cush and Mizraim' like Mr. Casaubon, but over what George Eliot also considered the most pressing spiritual problems of the time. She followed his lead with Strauss, she borrowed his copy of Spinoza. If he was dull, he was dull in the swim. So expert a novelist would not have forgotten him—she may have derived from him not only hints for Casaubon but some for Mr. Brooke, a friend of Wordsworth and everyone else. But she was after other game than the Polonius who benignly called her, as his second daughter, 'Deutera'—an improvement on Mary Ann.

Pattison, Spencer, and Brabant hang upon Casaubon's coattails, but their intellectual interests are far afield. Comparative mythology such as Casaubon's had got off to a heady start in the eighteenth century with Jacob Bryant's *A New System: or, An Analysis of Ancient Mythology.* Mr. Haight has pointed out that George Eliot made use of Bryant's theory of 'Chus and Mizraim', Cush (so respelt by Bryant) being represented as the father of all the Scythian nations, and Mizraim as father of the Egyptians. There are further connections that can be offered: Bryant's theory of the Phoenicians (as sons of Esau), of the ancient priests called the Cabiri, and of Dagon the fish god, whom he identified both with Noah and with the Indian god Vishnu, are all behind Mr. Casaubon's researches. It was as if George Eliot had Bryant ready in case she was suspected of deriding a living comparative mythologist, and she could keep him more easily in reserve because his work was evidently a familiar subject for joking between her and her friend Sara Hennell. Her concocted Professor Bücherwurm had offered the notion that Christianity was merely a late development of Buddhism, which was like making Vishnu a prior version of Noah, and Sara Hennell, in reply to her friend's comic letter about Bücherwurm's marriage proposal, quoted Bryant's favourite Egyptian source, Berosus. Yet George Eliot did have a comparative mythologist of her own day, whom she knew well, to fuse with Bryant. This was Robert William Mackay, the author of *The Progress of the Intellect as Exemplified in the Religious Development of the Greeks and Hebrews,* published by George Eliot's friend John Chapman in 1850, and at his request and Mackay's reviewed by her in her first article for the *Westminster Review.*

That Mackay was connected with Casaubon was proposed, as Mr. Haight recognizes, by Frances Power Cobbe in her 1894 *Life* of herself: 'Mr. Mackay was somewhat of an invalid and a nervous man, much absorbed in his studies. I have heard it said that he was the original of George Eliot's Mr. *Casaubon.* At all events Mrs. Lewes had met him, and taken a strong prejudice against him'. Miss Cobbe is mistaken about George Eliot's feelings towards Mackay, which were always friendly. Perhaps on this account, Mr. Haight dismisses the identification with him as hearsay. But it is not difficult to establish that Mackay contributed a small portion to *Middlemarch.* His book, unlike Brabant's unfinished one, was a revival of comparative mythology. He was more learned even than Bryant, with a dozen footnotes to the latter's one; George Eliot noted his 'industry in research', a virtue constantly claimed by Casaubon. If his search for vegetation gods is difficult to summarize, it is because, as George Eliot complained in her review, much of it seemed mere 'extracts from his commonplace book', rather than results of 'digested study'. It was such a book as Dorothea might have compiled after Casaubon's death. Some of it was manifestly absurd, but George Eliot took a benign view of his objective, which she summarized in this way:

> It is Mr. Mackay's faith that divine revelation is not contained exclusively or pre-eminently in the facts and inspirations of any one age or nation, but is co-extensive with the history of human development. . . . The master key to this revelation, is the recognition of the presence of undeviating law in the material and moral world—of that invariability of sequence which is acknowledged to be the basis of physical science, but which is still perversely ignored in our social organisation, our ethics and our religion.

Here at last is the word 'key', which Mackay himself had not used. It is his kind of locksmith that George Eliot has in mind in Casaubon's Key to all Mythologies.

There are further ties. 'Poor Mr. Casaubon himself was lost . . . in an agitated dimness about the Cabeiri' (chapter 20), and poor Mr. Mackay had followed Bryant to the extent of designating as 'Orphic or Cabiric' the primitive period of mythology. (She noted in her article that this was an older view, but refrained from tracing it to Bryant.) If Mr. Casaubon, in dictating to Dorothea, announces, 'I omit the second excursus on Crete' (chapter 48), it is perhaps because Mr. Mackay had devoted a whole chapter to Crete and its god, 'Minos-Zeus', and Mr. Casaubon may well have felt that this first excursus was enough. If Ladislaw could say of Mr. Casaubon (chapter 22), 'He is not an Orientalist, you know. He does not profess to have more than second-hand knowledge there', it was because Mr. Mackay had conceded in his preface, 'In quoting from Oriental sources the writer is under the disadvantage of ignorance of the languages; but he has taken pains to get the best possible aids'.

Mackay may have had marital designs upon George Eliot; he soon shifted them to another affective object. The resultant marriage obviously interested her. After it he appeared 'rather worse than otherwise', she reported. Following his return from a wedding trip to Weymouth, she asked him how he and his wife had liked it: 'Not at all, not at all', he replied, 'but it was not the fault of the place'. The barrenness of Rome for the honeymooning Casaubons is at least glimpsed here.

Mackay served to update Bryant and to fill in details of Casaubon which other friends could not supply. As ultimate model for the character, he, like Brabant, is disqualified by his positive qualities. What remains to be found is the source of energy which produces both Casaubon's intensity, and the intensity of contempt, mixed with sporadic pity, which his being arouses in author and characters alike in *Middlemarch*. Mr. Haight, sensible of George Eliot's unusual venom, attributes it to her temporary infatuation with Brabant and later disillusionment with him, but so much feeling after twenty-five years of subsequent friendship, and three years after Brabant's death, seems disproportionate. Brabant was at worst one of her own follies.

Her own follies: putting these Casaubons *manqués* aside, we come to George Eliot herself. F. W. H. Myers related in the *Century Magazine* for November 1881, that when asked where she had found Casaubon, 'with a humorous solemnity, which was quite in earnest, nevertheless, she pointed to her own heart'. This remark deserves to be considered. She meant by it exactly what Flaubert had meant when he said, '*Madame Bovary, c'est moi*'. Flaubert too had his Brabants and Mackays, and secured a few useful details from actual events and persons, but in his writing he had other things to think about. What must be sought is not a Casaubon, but casaubonism, and this George Eliot found, as Flaubert found *le bovarysme*, in herself. Casaubonism is the entombing of the senses in the mind's cellarage. As a young woman George Eliot was liable to this iniquity, and all her life she was capable of what Myers calls 'almost morbid accesses of self-reproach'.

Casaubon is the only character in George Eliot's work up to this time to have a sexual problem, in the sense of being aberrant. What the problem may be is not easy to say definitely. Whether his marriage is consummated or not is left obscure. Living when she did, George Eliot had reason to be delicate and reticent about such a matter, but her vagueness had literary as well as Victorian causes. Impotence is a disaster, not a vice; if Casaubon cannot consummate his marriage, he is to that extent as pathetic as Ruskin. Too much sympathy would be out of order. George Eliot's fictional universe never allows her men and women to shirk moral responsibility, and Casaubon is no exception. She said that the idea of Casaubon and Dorothea had been in her mind from the time she began to write fiction, and one reason for her long delay in taking up the theme may have been the difficulty of handling Casaubon's sexual insufficiency. She finally solved the difficulty by blending impotence or near-impotence with a choice of chilliness over warmth, in which his culpability would be clear.

This can be traced in terms of one of those recurrent images which George Eliot used with minute attentiveness. At the centre of Casaubon's situation is the seed. As an image it is evoked three times. One is at dinner at Mr. Brooke's house before Dorothea's engagement. In defence of her not going out to ride, Mr. Casaubon says with sudden fervour, 'We must keep the germinating grain away from the light' (chapter 2). The association of darkness and seed is here fixed, with the residual implication that Mr. Casaubon's grain may not be of the germinating kind. Then in chapter 48 his Key to all Mythologies is unexpectedly rephrased as 'the seed of all tradition'. His inability to construct a key, or make a seed, might seem beyond his control. But his blameableness is established in a passage in chapter 42, to which Barbara Hardy has called attention. Mr. Casaubon's difficulties are here explicitly voluntary, not involuntary; as Dorothea is about to take his arm, he keeps it rigid:

> There was something horrible to Dorothea in the sensation which this unresponsive hardness inflicted on her. That is a strong word but not too strong. It is in these acts called trivialities that the seeds of joy are for ever wasted, until men and women look round with haggard faces at the devastation their own waste has made, and say, the earth bears no harvest of sweetness—calling their denial knowledge.

Mr. Casaubon chooses self-isolation like choosing self-abuse. The image of Onan is invoked to symbolize his spirit, which in turn is reflected in his physical denial.

This passage, while bold, is not quite unique in George Eliot's writings: it has one counterpart, a personal statement, in a letter she wrote in late adolescence (16 March 1839) to her old teacher Miss Lewis. The letter is startling because in it the future novelist repudiates novels, on the grounds of their effect upon her fantasy life. In this burst of candour she declares:

> . . . I venture to believe that the same causes which exist in my own breast to render novels and romances pernicious have their counterpart in that of every fellow-creature.
>
> I am I confess not an impartial member of a jury in this case for I owe the culprits a grudge for injuries inflicted on myself. I shall carry to my grave the mental diseases with which they have contaminated me. When I was quite a little child I could not be satisfied with the things around me; I was constantly living in a world of my own creation, and was quite contented to have no companions that I might be left to my own musings and imagine scenes in which I was chief actress. Conceive what a character novels would give to these Utopias.

Not absence of feeling, but deflection of it, appears to be the charge she is levelling against herself. Mr. Haight in his biography advises against taking these statements seriously, although in his edition of the Letters he notes that J. W. Cross, in *George Eliot's Life*, omitted the sentence that contains 'contaminated', 'diseases', and 'to my grave'. Evidently Cross took them seriously. To use these weighty words lightly is not in character for George Eliot. If they have any serious meaning at all, then she is declaring that she has been contaminated by novels which have aroused in her erotic fantasies, as opposed to the merely megalomaniac ones of childhood. In *Felix Holt* Mrs. Transome reads French novels and so takes a lover. But George Eliot in adolescence found no such requital. Insofar as Casaubon was an expression of her own 'almost morbid accesses of self-reproach'—made vivid by her early evangelicalism—it would seem that his sexual inadequacy was a version of her struggles with adolescent sexuality, and that these struggles stirred in her sensation which remained painful even in memory. The images of darkness which make up Casaubon's mental landscape would then be wincing recollections of 'the mental diseases' which she had predicted she would 'carry to my grave'. Casaubon's sexual insufficiency was an emblem for fruitless fantasies, of which she too felt victim. It was probably in this sense that he drew his strength and intensity from her nature.

The severity with which Casaubon is treated, aside from occasional remissions, would then derive from her need to exorcise this part of her experience. For a woman who prided herself on her plenitude of heart, these early short-circuits of sensual emotion were painful to think on. No wonder that she makes Casaubon die of fatty degeneration of the heart. He is the repository of her inferior qualities, as Dorothea of her superior ones. She instilled her callow misimaginings, suitably shifted in clef, into old Casaubon, and her ripe affirmations into young Dorothea.

The place of Dorothea's second husband, Will Ladislaw, in this drama of George Eliot's mind is not immediately apparent. To a considerable extent Will had to be made congruent with Dorothea, even to the point of sharing or paralleling her traits. Like her, he has a somewhat undirected aspiration to achieve good and useful works, and he has a slight maliciousness to balance her mild vanity. In some ways he too radiates out from George Eliot, even in his person. His rippled nose and strong jaw are an idealization of his creator's features, and are allowed to make him handsome though she felt they made her ugly. In his indictment of Casaubon's mythological researches, he follows closely, as Thomas Pinney has noted, George Eliot's review of Mackay and particularly of her strictures on Mackay's predecessors:

> The introduction of a truly philosophic spirit into the study of mythology—
> an introduction for which we are chiefly indebted to the Germans—is a
> great step in advance of the superficial Lucian-like tone of ridicule

adopted by many authors of the eighteenth century or the orthodox prepossessions of writers such as Bryant, who saw in the Greek legends simply misrepresentations of the authentic history given in the book of Genesis.

Ladislaw says to Dorothea, 'Do you not see that it is no use now to be crawling a little way after men of the last century—men like Bryant—and correcting their mistakes?—living in a lumber-room and furbishing up broken-legged theories about Chus and Mizraim?' Yet if she modelled Ladislaw a little upon herself, she needed and found another model as well. The choice troubled her. She said that the ending of her novel might disappoint, and perhaps the main reason was that, aside from marrying Ladislaw to Dorothea (like Blake fusing Los with Enitharmon), she could not make him inevitable in the Middlemarch terrain.

Prototype hunters have left Ladislaw alone, on the assumption that George Eliot was too happily fixed in her life with Lewes to have anyone else in mind. Her commitment to Lewes was as much beyond suspicion as it was outside law. If she could not take his last name legally, she took both his last and first names extra-legally. When Harriet Beecher Stowe asked if the Casaubon marriage bore any resemblance to her own, George Eliot replied, 'Impossible to conceive any creature less like Mr. Casaubon than my warm, enthusiastic husband, who cares much more for my doing than for his own, and is a miracle of freedom from all author's jealousy and all suspicion. I fear that the Casaubon-tints are not quite foreign to my own mental complexion. At any rate I am very sorry for him'. (She echoes here her comment as author in *Middlemarch* [chapter 20], 'For my part I am very sorry for him'.) Lewes was in fact one of the more engaging minds of his time, willing to tackle scientific, philosophical, and literary subjects, and with a gift of sympathy which George Eliot found indispensable to her existence as well as to her writing. If Thomas and Jane Carlyle could not refrain from calling him 'the ape', or Douglas Jerrold from calling him 'the ugliest man in London', he was not the less likeable; and George Eliot was more indulgent of his ugliness than of her own. He himself sometimes joked about playing Casaubon to his wife's Dorothea, but he had more in common with Ladislaw. He too spent some time as a young man in Germany and knew the language fairly well. He did not have 'a Jew pawnbroker' for his grandfather, an imputation made about Ladislaw, but he had Jewish associations and several times played Shylock on the stage. He had a versatility that smacked of dilettantism, so that he dissected dragonflies one moment and Comtism the next. But like Ladislaw, his variety did not prevent intensity. 'Our sense of duty', says George Eliot in chapter 46, 'must often wait for some work which shall take the place of dilettantism. . . .'

George Eliot was jealous of her husband as well as notably fond of him. Mrs. Linton quotes her as saying, 'I should not think of allowing George to stay away a night from me'. Yet sporadic deflections of erotic feeling are not inconsistent with marital content or vigilance. In her case a superabundance of amorous sentiment, beyond any immediate object, is suggested by the effusively affectionate correspondence she lavished upon women friends even though, as she had to make clear to Edith Simcox, it was men who interested her. The search for Casaubon begins with others and ends with George Eliot; the search for Ladislaw spreads out from her to her husband and beyond. In this character her critical powers, which enabled her to recognize limitations in Dorothea as in heroes outside of fiction such as Luther and Bunyan, are largely suspended. He occupies a special position in her work, because he is the first character of either sex in her novels to be irresistibly handsome and at the same time good. Early reviewers remarked upon him as constituting a new departure in George Eliot's novels. In *Adam Bede* Hetty is beautiful, but is punished for being so; she is not so good as she looks. The same is true of Tito in *Romola*. Only Ladislaw is treated with utter indulgence, even to being encouraged to toss back his curls on numerous occasions, as if George Eliot feared she had not made him fetching enough. It seems possible that she had herself been suddenly captivated by the image of a handsome young man.

The first important meeting of Dorothea and Ladislaw takes place in Rome, and since George Eliot had been to Rome just three and a half months before she began *Middlemarch*, her sojourn may be scrutinized a little. This was the second visit that she and Lewes had paid to that city, and it did not work out as well as the first. On the way there he had suffered from sciatica, and once arrived he was not in the mood to enjoy Rome. He wrote in his journal, 'I have had enough of it and want to be at home and at work again'. Mr. Casaubon had similar thoughts. But George Eliot did not share her husband's impatience. 'Here we had many days of unbroken sunshine . . .' was her summary. It was now she had the meeting which was to prove so momentous in her life, with John Walter Cross, then twenty-nine.

This meeting had long been in prospect. She had met Cross's mother two years before, thanks to Herbert Spencer, who boasted in later life that he had brought George Eliot into touch with both her husbands. At that time Mrs. Cross's other children were in England, but John was in the United States, carrying on the American side of the family's banking business. He must have been a frequent topic of discussion between the Crosses and Leweses.

On an April day in 1869 George Eliot was walking with Lewes in her beloved Pamfili Doria gardens, when she met by accident Mrs. Cross's oldest daughter and her husband, who like the Casaubons took their wedding trip to Rome. Further meetings were arranged, and when, some days later, Mrs. Cross, her son John, and another daughter arrived, they were invited on 18 April to visit the Leweses in their rooms at the Hotel Minerva—the same hotel they had stayed at on their first Roman visit in 1860. John Walter Cross shared the veneration of all members of his family for George Eliot's writings, and must have testified to that. Thanks to him, one bit of the ensuing conversation has survived: 'And I remember, many years ago, at the time of our first acquaintance, how deeply it pained her when, in reply to a direct question, I was obliged to admit that, with all my admiration for her books, I found them, on the whole, profoundly sad'. Her pain carried over into *Middlemarch*. This conversation is closely paralleled in chapter 22 when Ladislaw admonishes Dorothea, 'Would you turn all the youth of the world to a tragic chorus, wailing and moralising over misery?' She replies, as George Eliot must have replied to Cross, 'I am not a sad, melancholy creature', but he is not so easily put down, and eight chapters later has written her a letter which 'was a lively continuation of his remonstrance with her fanatical sympathy and her want of sturdy neutral delight in things as they were—an outpouring of his young vivacity. . . .'

Cross, nothing if not vivacious, had just returned from the United States, and must have been asked about his travels there. His work had been in New York, where he had invested heavily in the railroads, but, as a magazine article he wrote later confirms, he had also been to California. Something of what he said must have put George Eliot in mind of the penultimate project which she attributes to Ladislaw (before his ultimate one of marrying Dorothea), that of promoting a settlement in the 'Far West'. Cross was in fact excited about what he repeatedly called in print the 'New World'; he praised it because it 'rests on the basis of industrialism as opposed to militarism'. He thought his fellow-countrymen wrong to criticize it, and wrote later, 'One thing is certain, namely, that since all gain of *real* wealth in America *must* be of advantage to England it will surely be the first sign of impending decadence if the business men of this country, instead of putting their shoulders to the wheel to carry their chariot over all obstruction, content themselves with cherishing a vindictive feeling to rivals. . . .' This kind of imagery, natural to Cross, is twitted a little in Ladislaw's projected painting of 'Tamburlaine Driving the

Conquered Kings in His Chariot', intended as he says to symbolize 'the tremendous course of the world's physical history lashing on the harnessed dynasties', and to include 'migrations of races and clearings of forests—and America and the steam engine'. Cross's westward travels, the steam engine which drove the trains that carried him, the extension of the railroads to the furthest points of the New World (as he remarked in an article devoted to them), the sympathy for American energy, all found a way into George Eliot's book.

He must have delighted her. The contrast of Ladislaw's youth and Casaubon's age, of the passionate unscholarliness of the first and the uneasy ferreting of the second, would then be an idealized registration of the effect on George Eliot of her meeting with Cross. By implication it promised Dorothea in fiction something better than widow's weeds and good works after Casaubon's death, and so brought the whole of *Middlemarch* into focus. It can only have been a secret tribute to Cross, and one he would have appreciated, that among the misty details of Ladislaw's up-bringing one fact stands out clear and is mentioned twice—he went to Rugby. So did Cross.

Momentarily even the beloved Lewes must have appeared to disad-vantage beside this taller, handsomer, sharper-sighted, younger banker. Cross was to prove his devotion steadily from this time on, and to be rewarded for it by having conferred upon him the title of 'nephew'. In *Middlemarch* Ladislaw, though actually Casaubon's second cousin, is often taken for his nephew. Cross was regularly and affectionately spoken of as Nephew Johnny, and in the letter George Eliot wrote to him after Lewes's death, in which she asked him to call, she addressed him as 'Dearest N.' Not that she considered for a moment infidelity to her husband; for every reason she was bound to him for life. But she was not averse to making renunciation of another cherished object a part of her bond to Lewes. As she remarks of Mary Garth's loyalty to Fred in *Middlemarch*, 'we can set a watch on our affections and our constancy as we can other treasures'. Certainly as a solution to her problems of ending *Middlemarch*, John Walter Cross had much to offer. She banked this banker in her fictional account.

The friendship of the Leweses with Cross grew deeper over the years. After Lewes's death George Eliot would not receive Cross for a time, but indicated she would do so eventually, perhaps before she re-ceived anyone else. And so it was. On the day he was asked to call, her old friend Herbert Spencer was turned away. Since Cross's mother and one of his sisters had died soon after Lewes, he and George Eliot could share each other's grief. As consolation in the next months, they read

Dante's *Inferno* and *Purgatorio* together. There was no need to read the *Paradiso*, for the parallel with Beatrice required no enforcement. Cross felt Dantean about George Eliot; she was 'my ideal', 'the best', and to marry her was his 'high calling'. George Eliot did not reprove this exalted feeling; in a letter to Mrs. Burne-Jones of 5 May 1880, she wrote: 'he sees his only longed-for happiness in dedicating his life to me'.

Ladislaw objects to Casaubon's ignorance of the Germans on comparative mythology, but George Eliot is at pains to indicate that he himself has little more than vague acquaintance with these arcane books. No erudition is allowed Ladislaw, only a general interest in art, poetry, and politics. His reformist political views are close to those of Cross, who espoused a non-revolutionary amelioration of inequity as a liberal goal. A strong hint of George Eliot's sense of Cross as a Ladislaw figure comes in a patronizing (if also matronizing) letter she wrote him on 16 October 1879: 'Best loved and loving one . . . Thou dost not know anything of verbs in Hiphil and Hophal or the history of metaphysics or the position of Kepler in science, but thou knowest best things of another sort, such as belong to the manly heart—secrets of lovingness and rectitude. O I am flattering. Consider what thou wast a little time ago in pantaloons and back hair'. (Back hair was one of Ladislaw's attributes.) By this time Cross was thirty-nine and a settled man in City banking, but he still stood for her as the embodiment of youth, almost of boyhood, with an ignorance that surpassed knowledge. No doubt these feelings had grown in George Eliot over the ten years of their friendship, but the jingled Hebrew of 'Hiphil and Hophal' suggests that from the beginning he had stood as the polar opposite of 'Cush and Mizraim'. He was also the opposite of her husband, and of most of her old friends, in knowing nothing—as she indelicately underlines—of words in ancient languages, in metaphysics, or in science. Marrying Dorothea to Ladislaw had been George Eliot's only adulterous act. Artistically it proved to be a sin. Marrying Cross as Lewes's widow legalized the fantasy. In the same way her own reconciliation with her brother Isaac validated the reconciliation of brother and sister which she had fictionally imagined, in *The Mill on the Floss*.

Now, when they married, there was a strange reversal of roles, with a sixty-year-old Dorothea marrying a forty-one-year-old Ladislaw, a disparity almost as great as that between Casaubon and his bride. Cross's own sentiments could only have been intricate, since he was her nephew, son, pupil, and reader, as well as husband. The sense of being a once independently orbited fragment drawn back now into the parent body must have been immensely disturbing. Perhaps more than sexual awkwardness or disparity of age or health was involved in Cross's pitching himself into the Grand Canal at Venice during their wedding trip. It was a solution which George Eliot had never allowed Dorothea to contemplate. Fished out, and restored to the same bedroom, he gave no further trouble.

A final witness is Eliza Lynn Linton. She had known George Eliot as a young provincial, holding her hands and arms like a kangaroo. She had been invited to call just after the decision to live with Lewes, and she met her later on too. Mrs. Linton was jealous of George Eliot's literary pre-eminence, but she acknowledged it. She also wrote a long essay on George Eliot's works, and had this to say about the second marriage of Dorothea in *Middlemarch:*

> And to think that to her first mistake she adds that second of marrying Will Ladislaw—the utter snob that he is! Where were George Eliot's perceptions? Or was it that in Ladislaw she had a model near at hand, whom she saw through coloured glasses, which also shed their rosy light on her reproduction, as that his copy was to her as idealized as the original, and she as ignorant of the effect produced on the clear-sighted?

In another place Mrs. Linton makes clear that she entirely disapproved of the marriage to Cross, as reducing the first marriage to a house of cards, and it is clearly Cross she has here in mind. She is unkind, but she does suggest the fictional complications for George Eliot of modelling Ladislaw on Cross, a man distinguished more for youthful ardour and amorphousness than anything else. (His skill in investment was hard to idealize.) But George Eliot chose well in making him her husband, for he was impeccably discreet in his *Life* of her, and during the more than forty years that he outlived her.

Cross did not allow his photograph to be taken, and in general he effaced himself. But he was not devoid of ambition, and he published two books. The first and more important had the ragbag title, *Impressions of Dante and of the New World with a Few Words on Bimetallism* (1893). His Dante essays provide a contrast to the worldly report on American railroads, and indicate that like Ladislaw he loved poetry. The preface perhaps gives a sense of his goodhearted and unassuming but garrulous temperament:

> 'Don't shoot the organist; he's doing his level best.' This ancient American story of a notice prominently affixed in a church in the Wild West, as a gentle appeal to the congregation, expresses the mildly deprecatory attitude that I desire to assume to my readers—if I have any—or rather the attitude that I hope they will assume to me. 'Don't shoot the essayist; he's doing his level best'. I confess that it is difficult to find a naked excuse for republishing old magazine articles, and in my own case I

cannot plead that any host of admiring friends has put pressure on me to collect mine. I take it that the real reason for the republication is always the same—a desire on the part of the writer to leave some print of his footsteps, however shallow, on the sands of time.

This is johnnycrossism, abashed yet candid, the reverse of Casaubon's closed room which no key could unlock. After a lifetime with intellectuals, George Eliot chose a simpler love for herself as she had had Dorothea do after Casaubon's death. The Key to all Mythologies was not so hard to find. Her decision may have been sentimental, but it established the verisimilitude of Dorothea's act.

The two husbands of Dorothea have different functions in *Middlemarch*. The one is all labyrinth and darkness, the other all candour and light. George Eliot was dissatisfied with the book's ending, but she committed herself to Ladislaw in a way hard for most readers to follow. Part of the reason lies in the very different histories of the characters in her internal dialectic. To berate Casaubon, and to bury him, was to overcome in transformed state the narcissistic sensuality of her adolescence. Old feelings of self-reproach could be renewed, and the character, once stirred by this motive power, could be furnished out with details adroitly selected from people she had known either personally or through their writings. The result was a triumph, a new creature. In Ladislaw, a fantasy of middle age, indulged because innocuous, the character is deprived of her usual controls. She allows herself to idealize him, his only imperfection being what is also his chief perfection—youth. He remains a surrogate sun, lacking in energy and heat, no fiction but a figment executed in pastel colours. She had had much time to reflect on the implications of Casaubon; but, if these speculations are valid, the new image of Ladislaw took her unawares, as a result of the luxuriantly fantasied encounter in Rome with her young admirer and future husband.

RAYMOND WILLIAMS

Knowable Communities

Most novels are in some sense knowable communities. It is part of a traditional method—an underlying stance and approach—that the novelist offers to show people and their relationships in essentially knowable and communicable ways. The full extent of Dickens's genius can then only be realised when we see that for him, in the experience of the city, so much that was important, and even decisive, could not be simply known or simply communicated, but had, as I have said, to be revealed, to be forced into consciousness. And it would then be possible to set up a contrast between the fiction of the city and the fiction of the country. In the city kind, experience and community would be essentially opaque; in the country kind, essentially transparent. As a first way of thinking, there is some use in this contrast. There can be no doubt, for example, that identity and community became more problematic, as a matter of perception and as a matter of valuation, as the scale and complexity of the characteristic social organisation increased. Up to that point, the transition from country to city—from a predominantly rural to a predominantly urban society—is transforming and significant. The growth of towns and especially of cities and a metropolis; the increasing division and complexity of labour; the altered and critical relations between and within social classes; in changes like these any assumption of a knowable community—a whole community, wholly knowable—became harder and harder to sustain. But this is not the whole story, and once again, in realising the new fact of the city, we must be careful not to idealise the old and new facts of the country. For what is knowable is not only a function of objects—of what is there to be known. It is also a function of subjects, of observers—of what is desired and what needs to be known. And what we have then to see, as throughout, in the country writing, is not only the reality of the rural community; it is the observer's position in and towards it; a position which is part of the community being known.

Thus it is still often said, under the pressure of urban and metropolitan experience, and as a direct and even conventional contrast, that a country community, most typically a village, is an epitome of direct relationships: of face-to-face contacts within which we can find and value the real substance of personal relationships. Certainly this immediate aspect of its difference from the city or the suburb is important; it is smaller in scale; people are more easily identified and connected within it; the structure of the community is in many ways more visible. But a knowable community, within country life as anywhere else, is still a matter of consciousness, and of continuing as well as day-to-day experience. In the village as in the city there is division of labour; there is the contrast of social position, and then necessarily there are alternative points of view. It is to these points of view, in the nineteenth-century country novel, that we must now turn, for while the contrast between country and city is dramatic and important, the intricate developments within country life and country writing are also inescapable and significant.

Look back, for a moment, at the knowable community of Jane Austen. It is outstandingly face-to-face; its crises, physically and spiritually, are in just these terms: a look, a gesture, a stare, a confrontation; and behind these, all the time, the novelist is watching, observing, physically recording and reflecting. That is the whole stance—the grammar of her morality. Yet while it is a community wholly known, within the essential terms of the novel, it is as an actual community very precisely selective. Neighbours in Jane Austen are not the people actually living nearby; they are the people living a little less nearby who, in social recognition, can be visited. What she sees across the land is a network of propertied houses and families, and through the holes of this tightly drawn mesh most actual people are simply not seen. To be face-to-face in this world is already to belong to a class. No other community, in physical presence or in social reality, is by any means knowable. And it is not only most of the people who have disappeared, in a stylised convention as precise as Ben Jonson's. It is also most of the country, which becomes real only as it relates to the houses which are the real nodes; for the rest the country is weather or a place for a walk.

It is proper to trace the continuity of moral analysis from Jane

Austen to George Eliot, but we can do this intelligently only if we recognise what else is happening in this literary development: a recognition of other kinds of people, other kinds of country, other kinds of action on which a moral emphasis must be brought to bear. For just as the difference between Jonson and Crabbe is not the historical arrival of the 'poor laborious natives' but a change in literary bearings which allows them suddenly to be seen, so the difference between Jane Austen and George Eliot, and between both and Thomas Hardy, is not the sudden disintegration of a traditional rural order but a change in literary bearings which brings into focus a persistent rural disturbance that had previously been excluded or blurred.

Thus *Adam Bede* is set by George Eliot in Jane Austen's period: at the turn of the eighteenth into the nineteenth century. What she sees is of course very different: not primarily because the country has changed, but because she has available to her a different social tradition.

> The germ of *Adam Bede* was an anecdote told me by my Methodist Aunt Samuel . . . an anecdote from her own experience. . . . I afterwards began to think of blending this and some other recollections of my aunt in one story, with some points in my father's early life and character.

Thus the propertied house is still there, in the possession of the Donnithornes. But they are now seen at work on their income, dealing with their tenants:

> 'What a fine old kitchen this is!' said Mr Donnithorne, looking round admiringly. He always spoke in the same deliberate, well-chiselled, polite way, whether his words were sugary or venomous. 'And you keep it so exquisitely clean, Mrs Poyser. I like these premises, do you know, beyond any on the estate.'

We have encountered this 'deliberate, well-chiselled, polite' way of speaking before, but it is not now among relative equals, just as the old Squire's way of looking is not now simply an aspect of character but of character in a precise and dominating social relationship. As Mrs Poyser says, it seems 'as if you was an insect, and he was going to dab his finger-nail on you'.

The proposition that is put, through the politeness, is in fact a reorganisation of the tenancy, for the estate's convenience, which will take away the Poysters' corn land; it is accompanied by a threat that the proposed new neighbour, 'who is a man of some capital, would be glad to take both the farms, as they could be worked so well together. But I don't want to part with an old tenant like you'.

It is not a particularly dramatic event, but it is a crucial admission of everyday experience which had been there all the time, and which is now seen from an altered point of view. The politeness of improvement is then necessarily counterpointed by the crude facts of economic power, and a different moral emphasis has become inevitable. This is then extended. The young squire is anxious to improve the estate—as the tenants saw it, 'there was to be a millennial abundance of new gates, allowances of lime, and returns of ten per cent'—and he takes up Adam Bede as the manager of his woods. But in what is essentially the same spirit he takes up Hetty Sorrel as his girl and succeeds in ruining her. A way of using people for convenience is an aspect of personal character—this emphasis is not relaxed—but it is also an aspect of particular social and economic relationships. And then, as George Eliot observes ironically:

> It would be ridiculous to be prying and analytic in such cases, as if one was inquiring into the character of a confidential clerk. We use round, general, gentlemanly epithets about a young man of birth and fortune.

Jane Austen, precisely, had been prying and analytic, but into a limited group of people in their relations with each other. The analysis is now brought to bear without the class limitation; the social and economic relationships, necessarily, are seen as elements, often determining elements, of conduct.

It is more important to stress this aspect of George Eliot's development of the novel than her inclusion of new social experience in a documentary sense. Certainly it is good to see the farmers and the craftsmen, and almost the labourers, as people present in the action in their own right. But there are difficulties here of a significant kind. It is often said about the Poysers in *Adam Bede*, as about the Gleggs and the Dodsons in *The Mill on the Floss*, that they are marvellously (or warmly, richly, charmingly) done. But what this points to is a recurring problem in the social consciousness of the writer. George Eliot's connections with the farmers and craftsmen—her connections as Mary Ann Evans—can be heard again and again in their language. Characteristically, she presents them mainly through speech. But while they are present audibly as a community, they have only to emerge in significant action to change in quality. What Adam or Dinah or Hetty say, when they are acting as individuals, is not particularly convincing. Into a novel still predicated on the analysis of individual conduct, the farmers and craftsmen can be included as 'country people' but much less significantly as the active bearers of personal experience. When Adam and Dinah and Hetty talk in what is supposed to be personal crisis—or later, in a more glaring case, when Felix Holt talks—we are shifted to the level of generalised attitudes or of declamation. Another way of putting this would be to say that though George Eliot restores the real inhabitants of rural England to their places in what had been a socially selective landscape, she does not get much further than restoring them *as a landscape.* They begin to talk, as it were collectively, in what middle-class critics still foolishly call a kind of chorus, a 'ballad-element'. But as themselves they are still only socially present, and can emerge into personal consciousness only through externally formulated attitudes and ideas.

I would not make this point bitterly, for the difficulty is acute. It is a contradiction in the form of the novel, as George Eliot received and developed it, that the moral emphasis on conduct—and therefore the technical strategy of unified narrative and analytic tones—must be at odds with any society—the 'knowable community' of the novel—in which moral bearings have been extended to substantial and conflicting social relationships. One would not willingly lose the Poysers, the Gleggs, and the Dodsons, but it is significant that we can talk to them in this way in the plural, while the emotional direction of the novel is towards separated individuals. A knowable community can be, as in Jane Austen, socially selected; what it then lacks in full social reference it gains in an available unity of language in all its main uses. But we have only to read a George Eliot novel to see the difficulty of the coexistence, within one form, of an analytically conscious observer of conduct with a developed analytic vocabulary, and of people represented as living and speaking in mainly customary ways; for it is not the precision of detailed observation but the inclusive, socially appealing, loose and repetitive manner that predominates. There is a new kind of break in the texture of the novel, an evident failure of continuity between the necessary language of the novelist and the recorded language of many of the characters.

This is not, it must be emphasised, a problem of fact. The consciousness of actual farmers and tradesmen was as strong and developed as that of the established and manœuvring proprietors of Jane Austen's world; these people also are, and are shown as, inclusive, socially appealing, loose and repetitive; it is a common way of talking at any time. But whereas the idiom of the novelist, in Jane Austen, is connected with the idiom of her characters, in George Eliot a disconnection is the most evident fact and the novelist herself is most acutely aware of this. Speech and narrative and analysis, in Jane Austen, are connected by a *literary* convention. While the 'deliberate, well-chiselled, polite' idiom is the product of a particular education and of the leisured, dominating relationships which the education served, it is also idealised, conventionalised; the novelist's powers of effect and precision are given without hesitation to her characters, because, for all the individual moral discrimination, they are felt to belong in the same world. At points of emotional crisis and confrontation this is especially so, and it is the novelist who articulates a personal experience, in a way for the sake of her group, and to give it an idiom. But then it is clear that George Eliot is not *with* anyone in quite this way: the very recognition of conflict, of the existence of classes, of divisions and contrasts of feeling and speaking, makes a unity of idiom impossible. George Eliot gives her own consciousness, often disguised as a personal dialect, to the characters with whom she does really feel; but the strain of the impersonation is usually evident—in Adam, Daniel, Maggie, or Felix Holt. For the rest she gives out a kind of generalising affection which can be extended to a generalising sharpness (compare the Poysers with the Gleggs and Dodsons), but which cannot extend to a recognition of lives individually made from a common source; rather, as is said in that foolish mode of praise, the characters are 'done'. For there is a point often reached in George Eliot when the novelist is conscious that the characters she is describing are 'different' from her probable readers; she then offers to know them, and to make them 'knowable', in a deeply inauthentic but socially successful way. Taking the tip from her own difficulty, she works the formula which has been so complacently powerful in English novel-writing: the 'fine old', 'dear old', quaint-talking, honest-living country characters. Observing very promptly the patronage of economic power— 'deliberate, well-chiselled, polite' in the exercise of its crude controls—she still slips against her will into another patronage: since the people she respects in general (and of course for good reasons) she cannot respect enough in particular unless she gives them, by surrogate, parts of her own consciousness. There are then three idioms uneasily combined: the full analytic, often ironic power; the compromise between this and either disturbed intense feelings or a position of moral strength; and the self-consciously generalising, honest rustic background.

I can feel enough connection with the problems George Eliot was facing to believe I could make these points in her presence; that I am, in a sense, making them in her presence, since her particular intelligence, in a particular structure of feeling, persists and connects. Some years ago a British Council critic described George Eliot, Hardy, and Lawrence as 'our three great autodidacts'. It was one of the sharp revealing moments of English cultural history. For all three writers were actively interested in learning, and while they read a good deal for themselves were not without formal education. Their fathers were a bailiff, a builder, and a miner. George Eliot was at school till sixteen and left only because her mother died. Hardy was at Dorchester High School till the same age and then completed his professional training as an architect. Lawrence went into the sixth form at Nottingham High School and after a gap went on to Nottingham University College. It is not only that by their contemporary standards these levels of formal education are high; it is also that they are higher, absolutely, than those of four out of five people in contemporary Britain.

So the flat patronage of 'autodidact' can be related to only one fact: that none of the three was in the pattern of boarding school and Oxbridge which by the end of the century was being regarded not simply as a kind of education but as education itself: to have missed that circuit was to have missed being 'educated' at all. In other words, a 'standard' education was that received by one or two per cent of the population; all the rest were seen as 'uneducated' or as 'autodidacts'; seen also, of course, as either comically ignorant or, when they pretended to learning, as awkward, over-earnest, fanatical. The effects of this on the English imagination have been deep.

But to many of us now, George Eliot, Hardy and Lawrence are important because they connect directly with our own kind of upbringing and education. They belong to a cultural tradition much older and more central in Britain than the comparatively modern and deliberately exclusive circuit of what are called the public schools. And the point is that they continue to connect in this way into a later period in which some of us have gone to Oxford or Cambridge; to myself, for instance, who went to Cambridge and now teach there. For it is not the education, the developed intelligence, that is really in question; how many people, if it came to it, on the British Council or anywhere else, could survive a strictly intellectual comparison with George Eliot? It is a question of the relation between education—not the marks or degrees but the substance of a developed intelligence—and the actual lives of a continuing majority of our people: people who are not, by any formula, objects of record or study or concern, but who are specifically, literally, our own families. George Eliot is the first major novelist in whom this question is active. That is why we speak of her now with a connecting respect, and with a hardness—a sort of family plainness—that we have learned from our own and common experience.

The problem of the knowable community is then, in a new way, a problem of language.

> In writing the history of unfashionable families, one is apt to fall into a
> tone of emphasis which is very far from being the tone of good society,
> where principles and beliefs are not only of an extremely moderate kind,
> but are always presupposed, no subjects being eligible but such as can be
> touched with a light and graceful irony. But then, good society has its

claret and its velvet carpets, its dinner-engagements six weeks deep, its opera and its fairy ballrooms; rides off its *ennui* on thoroughbred horses, lounges at the club, has to keep clear of crinoline vortices, gets its science done by Faraday, and its religion by the superior clergy who are to be met in the best houses: how should it have time or need for belief and emphasis? But good society, floated on gossamer wings of light irony, is of very expensive production; requiring nothing less than a wide and arduous national life condensed in unfragrant, deafening factories, cramp-ing itself in mines, sweating at furnaces, grinding, hammering, weaving under more or less oppression of carbonic acid—or else, spread over sheepwalks, and scattered in lonely houses and huts on the clayey or chalky corn-lands, where the rainy days look dreary. This wide national life is based entirely on emphasis—the emphasis of want, which urges it into all the activities necessary for the maintenance of good society and light irony. . . .

This striking paragraph from *The Mill on the Floss* is at once the problem and the response. The emphasis of want is undoubtedly central in George Eliot, and she sees work here as it is, without any sentimental contrast between the town and the village labourer. Emphasis as a class feeling: this is what she acknowledges and accepts. But then it has to be noticed that she writes of it with her own brand of irony; she is defensive and self-conscious in the very demonstration of emphasis, so that in this structure of communication the very poor become the 'unfashionable'. Her central seriousness, and yet her acute consciousness of other and often congenial tones, is at once a paradox of language and of community. We find this again in two characteristic passages in *Adam Bede*:

Paint us an angel, if you can, with a flowing violet robe, and a face paled by the celestial light; paint us yet oftener a Madonna, turning her mild face upward and opening her arms to welcome the divine glory; but do not impose on us any aesthetic rules which shall banish from the region of Art those old women scraping carrots with their work-worn hands, those heavy clowns taking holiday in a dingy pot-house, those rounded backs and stupid weather-beaten faces that have bent over the spade and done the rough work of the world—those homes with their tin pans, their brown pitchers, their rough curs, and their clusters of onions. In this world there are so many of these common coarse people, who have no picturesque sentimental wretchedness. It is so needful we should remember their existence. . . .

I am not ashamed of commemorating old Kester: you and I are indebted to the hard hands of such men—hands that have long ago mingled with the soil they tilled so faithfully, thriftily making the best they could of the earth's fruits, and receiving the smallest share as their own wages.

The declaration is again serious, but who is being spoken to in the anxious plea: 'do not impose on us any aesthetic rules which shall banish . . .'? Who made the compact of 'you and I', who must be shown as indebted? Who, finally, provoked the consciousness which requires the acknowledgment 'I am not ashamed' and its associated language of 'clowns' and 'stupid weather-beaten faces', mixing as it so strangely does with the warmth of memory of the kitchens and with the truth about wages, the firm rejection of 'picturesque sentimental wretchedness'?

In passages like these, and in the novels from which they are taken, George Eliot has gone further than Crabbe in *The Village*, and yet is more self-conscious, more uneasily placating and appealing to what seems a dominant image of a particular kind of reader. The knowable community is this common life which she is glad to record with a necessary emphasis; but the known community is something else again—an uneasy contract, in language, with another interest and another sensibility.

What is true of language will be true of action. George Eliot extends the plots of her novels to include the farmers and the craftsmen, and also the disinherited. But just as she finds it difficult to individuate working people—falling back on a choral mode, a generalising description, or an endowment with her own awkwardly translated consciousness—so she finds it difficult to conceive whole actions which spring from the substance of these lives and which can be worked through in relation to their interests. *Adam Bede* is the nearest to this, but it is overridden, finally, by an external interest: Hetty is a subject to that last moment on the road before she abandons her baby; but after that moment she is an object of confessions and conversion—of *attitudes* to suffering. This is the essential difference from Hardy's *Tess of the D'Urbervilles*, which has the strength to keep to the subject to the end. Adam Bede and Dinah Morris—as one might say the dignity of self-respecting labour and religious enthusiasm—are more important, finally. Even the changed, repentant Arthur is more important than the girl whom the novelist abandons in a moral action more decisive than Hetty's own confused and desperate leaving of her child.

Yet still the history she is writing is active: a finding of continuity in the stress of learned feelings. *The Mill on the Floss* is the crisis of just this development and tension. It is an action written from within the emphasis of want: but now of want not as leading to ordinary work but as human deprivation; in the guarded, unattractive rituals of survival of the small farmers, the Dodsons; in the rash independence of Tulliver, broken by the complications of law and economic pressure that he does not understand. In neither of these ways, as George Eliot sees them, can any fullness of life be achieved, but there is no other way through; only the imagined escapes, the reading and the history, and then the unwilled, temporary escape of the trip on the river: a fantasy of comfort. All that can then finally happen is a return to childhood and the river; a return which releases feeling, but as death, not life. From the social history, which had been seen as determining but as narrowly determining, there is a contraction of sympathy to the exposed and separated individual, in whom the only action of value, of any full human feeling, is located. And then what in *The Mill on the Floss* is an active, desperate isolation becomes, in a new way of seeing, a sad resignation.

For in the subsequent works, for all their evidence of growing maturity and control—a control, precisely, based on sad resignation; a maturity construed as that exact feeling—the actions become more external to that common world in which the emphasis of want had been seen as decisive. As if overcome by the dead weight of the interests of a separated and propertied class, the formal plots of the later works are in a different social world. *Felix Holt* is made to turn on the inheritance of an estate, and this is a crucial surrender to that typical interest which preoccupied the nineteenth-century middle-class imagination. Of course Esther rejects the inheritance in the end; George Eliot's moral emphasis is too genuinely of an improving kind, of a self-making and self-made life, to permit Esther to accept the inheritance and find the fashionable way out. The corruption of that inheriting world, in which the price of security is intrigue, is powerfully shown in Mrs Transome and Jermyn. But the emphasis of want is now specialised to Felix Holt: to the exposed, separated, potentially mobile individual. It is part of a crucial history in the development of the novel, in which the knowable community—the extended and emphatic world of an actual rural and then industrial England—comes to be known primarily as a problem of ambivalent relationship: of how the separated individual, with a divided consciousness of belonging and not belonging, makes his own moral history.

This is the source of the disturbance, the unease, the divided construction of the later George Eliot novels (the exception is *Middlemarch*, significantly a novel of a single community again; a small town just before the decisive historical changes). Yet we have only to compare George Eliot with her contemporary, Anthony Trollope, to see the significance of this disturbance. Trollope, in his Barsetshire novels, is at ease with schemes of inheritance, with the interaction of classes and interests, with the lucky discovery and the successful propertied marriage. His interest is all in how it happens, how it is done. An even, easy narrative tone, with a minimum of searching analysis, can then achieve all that is asked of it: a recorded observation, an explanation at that level of social mechanics. To read *Doctor Thorne* beside *Felix Holt* is not only to find ease in Trollope where there is disturbance in George Eliot; to find a level of interest corresponding with the plot instead of struggling to break free of a dutifully sustained external complication; to find the conventional happy ending where property and happiness can coexist and be celebrated instead of an awkward, stubborn, unappeased resignation. It is also, quite evidently, to see the source of these differences in a real social history.

Near the beginning of *Doctor Thorne*, Trollope announces with characteristic confidence the state of his rural England:

> Its green pastures, its waving wheat, its deep and shady and—let us add—dirty lanes, its paths and stiles, its tawny-coloured, well-built rural churches, its avenues of beeches, and frequent Tudor mansions, its constant county hunt, its social graces, and the air of clanship which pervades it, has made it to its own inhabitants a favoured land of Goshen. It is purely agricultural: agricultural in its produce, agricultural in its poor, and agricultural in its pleasures.

Here the extent of realism is the mannered concession that the lanes are dirty. For the rest, what is seen is a social structure with pastoral trimmings. The agricultural poor are placed easily between the produce and the pleasures. And while this easy relationship holds, there is no moral problem of any consequence to disturb the smooth and recommending construction.

> England is not yet a commercial country in the sense in which that epithet is used for her; and let us hope that she will not soon become so. She might surely as well be called feudal England, or chivalrous England. If in western civilised Europe there does exist a nation among whom there are high signors, and with whom the owners of the land are the true aristocracy, the aristocracy that is trusted as being best and fitted to rule, that nation is the English.

As a description of mid-nineteenth-century England this is ludicrous; but as a way of seeing it without extended question it is perfect. It takes the values for granted, and can then study with a persistent accuracy the internal difficulties of the class, and especially the problem of the relation between the inheriting landed families and the connected and rising cadet and professional people. Trollope shares an interest in getting into that class, which is what the inheritance plot had always mainly served, and he can describe its processes without further illusion, once the basic illusion of describing the landowners as an aristocracy has been accepted. George

Eliot, by contrast, questioning in a profoundly moral way the real and assumed relations between property and human quality, accepts the emphasis of inheritance as the central action, and then has to make it external, contradictory, and finally irrelevant, as her real interest transfers to the separated and exposed individual, who becomes sadly resigned or must go away. What happens to the Transomes' land in *Felix Holt*, or to Grandcourt's in *Daniel Deronda*, is no longer decisive; yet around the complications of that kind of interest a substantial part of each novel is built. In this sense, George Eliot's novels are transitional between the form which had ended in a series of settlements, in which the social and economic solutions and the personal achievements were in single dimension, and the form which, extending and complicating and then finally collapsing this dimension, ends with a single person going away on his own, having achieved his moral growth through distancing or extrication. It is a divided consciousness of belonging and not belonging; for the social solutions are still taken seriously up to the last point of personal crisis, and then what is achieved as a personal moral development has to express itself in some kind of physical or spiritual renewal—an emigration, at once resigned and hopeful, from what had been offered as a decisive social world.

The complications of the inheritance plot, with its underlying assumption of a definite relation between property and human quality, had in fact been used in one remarkable novel, significantly based on a whole action rather than on individual analysis. Emily Brontë's *Wuthering Heights* is remarkable because it takes the crisis of inheritance at its full human value, without displacement to the external and representative attitudes of disembodied classes. There is a formal contrast of values between the exposed and working Heights and the sheltered and renting Grange, and the complicated relations between their families are consistently determined by the power and endurance of the Heights. Yet the creation is so total that the social mechanism of inheritance is transcended. It is class and property that divide Heathcliff and Cathy, and it is in the positive alteration of these relationships that a resolution is arrived at in the second generation. But it is not in social alteration that the human solution is at any point conceived. What is created and held to is a kind of human intensity and connection which is the ground of continuing life. Unaffected by settlements, it survives them and, in a familiar tragic emphasis, survives and is learned again through death. This tragic separation between human intensity and any available social settlement is accepted from the beginning in the whole design and idiom of the novel. The complication of the plot is then sustained by a single feeling, which is the act of transcendence. George Eliot, by contrast, working in a more critically realist world, conceives and yet cannot sustain acceptable social solutions; it is then not transcendence but a sad resignation on which she finally comes to rest. As a creative history, each of these solutions has a decisive importance, for each is reworked by the significant successors of George Eliot and Emily Brontë: Thomas Hardy and D. H. Lawrence.

The country action of George Eliot's *Daniel Deronda* takes place in Wessex. But whereas the Loamshire and Stonyshire of *Felix Holt* had been George Eliot's England, the Wessex of *Daniel Deronda* might be Jane Austen's Hampshire or Derbyshire: the great and the less great houses, and the selected 'knowable community', as it is to be found again later in Henry James and in other 'country-house novels' of our own century. *Daniel Deronda* was finished in 1876, but by that time there was a new Wessex in the novel: the country of Hardy. To move from one to the other is to repeat, ironically, the movement from the world around Chawton to the world of *Adam Bede*: a reappearance, a remaking of the general life, with its known community and its hard emphasis of want.

For George Eliot, in writing her only novel set in her own time, had moved significantly away from the full and known world of her earlier works. She had her own clear reasons for this. If the decisive history was that of character and of the frustration of human impulse by an unacceptable and yet inevitable world, she needed to create no more than the conditions for this kind of moral, intellectual and ideal history. The social conditions for a more generally valuing history were in every real sense behind her.

And this is the right way, I believe, to introduce the question of George Eliot's important attitudes to the past, especially the rural past. In *Adam Bede*, for example, she had looked back with a generalising affection to the first years of the nineteenth century, 'those old leisurely times', and concluded:

> Leisure is gone—gone where the spinning wheels are gone, and the pack-horses, and the slow waggons, and the pedlars, who brought bargains to the door on sunny afternoons. Ingenious philosophers tell you, perhaps, that the great work of the steam-engine is to create leisure for mankind. Do not believe them: it only creates a vacuum for eager thoughts to rush in. Even idleness is eager now—eager for amusement: prone to excursion-trains, art-museums, periodical literature, and exciting novels: prone even to scientific theorising, and cursory peeps through microscopes. Old Leisure was quite a different personage: he only read one newspaper, innocent of leaders, and was free from that periodicity of sensations which we call post-time. He was a contemplative, rather stout gentleman, of excellent digestion—of quiet perception, undiseased by

hypothesis: happy in his inability to know the causes of things, preferring the things themselves. He lived chiefly in the country, among pleasant seats and homesteads, and was fond of sauntering by the fruit-tree wall, and scenting the apricots when they were warmed by the morning sunshine, or of sheltering himself under the orchard boughs at noon, when the summer pears were falling. He knew nothing of weekday services, and thought none the worse of the Sunday sermon if it allowed him to sleep from the text to the blessing—liking the afternoon service best because the prayers were the shortest, and not ashamed to say so; for he had an easy, jolly conscience, broad-backed like himself, and able to carry a great deal of beer and port-wine—not being made squeamish by doubts and qualms and lofty aspirations. Life was not a task to him, but a sinecure; he fingered the guineas in his pocket, and ate his dinners, and slept the sleep of the irresponsible; for had he not kept up his charter by going to church on the Sunday afternoons!

Fine old Leisure! Do not be severe upon him, and judge him by our modern standard; he never went to Exeter Hall, or heard a popular preacher, or read *Tracts for the Times* or *Sartor Resartus.*

It is lightly enough written, an ironic rumination on the past which has been extended into a kind of history; a personification, using the simplest devices of fiction, which is significantly very different from the active personifications of Dickens: the shaping contemporary forces. Old Leisure is history, is a time and a period; but with his apricots and his orchard, his single newspaper, his port-wine and his guineas in his pocket, he is a class figure who can afford to saunter, who has leisure precisely in the sweat of other men's work. This foreshortening, this selection, this special indulgence are all characteristic of what has become a main form of the modern rural retrospect.

Yet in being lightly done, conveying a clear picture yet always ready to qualify, to smile, to move on, it seems protected against the very feelings, including the emphasis of want, which it effectively mediates and suppresses. For it was not *Tracts for the Times* or *Sartor Resartus* or the newspapers or science which disturbed Old Leisure as he fingered his guineas. It was—but can one say it, while the smiling reminiscence continues?—men who in just those years were being broken by endless work and by the want of bread; Old Leisure the roundsman, Old Leisure with the pauper's letter on his back, Old Leisure in the workhouse as a reward for fifty years in the fields. Yet there is another leisure, a quiet, of some childhood days, and of a father asleep on a Sunday afternoon, which can suddenly, in inattention, become a whole past and an historical scheme.

George Eliot's most extended rural retrospect—important because it is not given as a dream by the fire but as conscious historical interpretation—is the introduction to *Felix Holt*. It is more persuasive and more substantial than the dream of Old Leisure, but in its whole organisation shows even more clearly the structure of feeling which was being laid over the country. The description of the meadows and the hedgerows has the warmth of observation and of memory; it is the green language of Clare. But the passenger on the box of the stage-coach, through whose eyes we are directed to look, is more than a nature poet; he has, as it were naturally, combined with these perceptions a quite solid set of social presuppositions. When he sees the shepherd 'with a slow and slouching walk', he knows by some alchemy that the shepherd feels 'no bitterness except in the matter of pauper labourers and the bad luck that sent contrarious seasons and the sheep rot'.

What bitterness about the 'pauper labourers'? That he might become one of them, which was always possible and even likely? Or that they troubled the ratepayers? In this moment of watching, when the quiet landscape has 'an unchanging stillness, as if Time itself were pausing', and when 'it was easy for the traveller to conceive that town and country had no pulse in common', there is a sudden conflation, a stereotyping, of 'rural Englishmen' whose 'notion of Reform was a confused combination of rick-burners, trades-unions, Nottingham riots, and in general whatever required the calling-out of the yeomanry'.

Who then, the traveller might ask as Time pauses, were the yeomanry called out to face? Who, always somewhere else, was burning the ricks or combining under the threat of transportation? These others by the conflation of 'rural Englishmen' are effectively abolished.

> The passenger on the box could see that this was the district of protuberant optimists, sure that old England was the best of all possible countries, and that if there were any facts which had not fallen under their own observation, they were facts not worth observing: the district of clean little market-towns without manufactures, of fat livings, an aristocratic clergy, and low poor-rates.

And this is then not the known but the knowable community: a selected society in a selected point of view. The low poor-rates—that index of the emphasis of want: are they an irony or a comfort? For when the poor are suddenly present it is not as people but as 'a brawny and many-breeding pauperism'—that word, 'breeding', that George Eliot so often uses where the poor are in question, as if they were animals; in any case not men but a condition, an 'ism.' And 'brawny'?—getting strong and fat, no doubt, on the poor-rates.

The point of this willing illusion is then suddenly seen: it is manufacturing and the railways which destroy this old England. The full modern myth comes quite sharply into focus.

> The breath of the manufacturing town, which made a cloudy day and a red gloom by night on the horizon, diffused itself over all the surrounding country, filling the air with eager unrest. Here was a population not convinced that old England was as good as possible.

The unrest, that is to say, is a product of industrialisation; in being placed in that way, after the country idyll, it can itself be placed and on the whole rejected. What is then being bought from this view on the box-seat is a political comfort: a position which admits one set of causes for radicalism but in a comfortable contrast with the settled content of the old rural order. The social position of the observer is then quite clear: a whole reality is admitted in the industrial districts; a selected reality in the rural.

> After the coach had rattled over the pavement of a manufacturing town, the scene of riots and trades-union meetings, it would take him in another ten minutes into a rural region, where the neighbourhood of the town was only felt in the advantages of a near market for corn, cheese, and hay, and where men with a considerable banking account were accustomed to say that 'they never meddled with politics themselves'.

Of course; because the visible unrest of the town, in a whole action, is compared not with the whole knowable community of the rural region, but with the condition and point of view of 'men with a considerable banking account'. A willing, lulling illusion of old country life has now paid its political dividends. A natural country ease is contrasted with an unnatural urban unrest. The 'modern world', both in its suffering and, crucially, in its protest against suffering, is mediated by reference to a lost condition which is better than both and which can place both: a condition imagined out of a landscape and a selective observation and memory.

This is then the structure on which we must fix our attention, for it connects crucially with George Eliot's development. A valuing society, the common condition of a knowable community, belongs ideally in the past. It can be recreated there for a widely ranging moral action. But the real step that has been taken is withdrawal from any full response to an existing society. Value is in the past, as a general retrospective condition, and is in the present only as a particular and private sensibility, the individual moral action.

The combination of these two conclusions has been very powerful; it has shaped and trained a whole literary tradition. And this is the meaning of George Eliot's Wessex, in the only novel set in her own actual period: a narrowing of people and situations to those capable, in traditional terms, of limitation to an individual moral action; the fading-out of all others, as most country people had been faded out in that view from the box-seat; the re-creation, after all the earlier emphasis of want, of a country-house England, a class England in which only certain histories matter, and to which the sensibility—the bitter and frank sensibility—of the isolated moral observer can be made appropriate. She is able, conscientiously, to narrow her range because the wide-ranging community, the daily emphasis of want, is supposed past and gone with old England. All that is left is a set of personal relationships and of intellectual and moral insights, in a history that for all valuing purposes has, disastrously, ended.

We can then see why Mr Leavis, who is the most distinguished modern exponent of just this structure of feeling, should go on, in outlining the great tradition, from George Eliot to Henry James. It is an obvious transition from that country-house England of *Daniel Deronda* (of course with Continental extensions and with ideas, like Deronda's Zionism, about everywhere) to the country-house England of James. But the development that matters in the English novel is not to James; it is within that same Wessex, in the return of a general and inescapable history, to the novels of Hardy.

J. HILLIS MILLER

Optic and Semiotic in "Middlemarch"

The most persistent of the structural metaphors [in Middlemarch], as has often been noticed, is the metaphor of the web. One explicit application of the image of a web to the whole range of social relationships in the novel comes in the passage where the narrator distinguishes his enterprise from that of Fielding. Whereas Fielding lived in more spacious times and could allow himself the luxury of the famous "copious remarks and digressions," "I at least," says the narrator, "have so much to do in unravelling certain human lots, and seeing how they were woven and interwoven, that all the light I can command must be concentrated on this particular web, and not dispersed over that tempting range of relevancies called the universe" (chap. 15). The narrator's effort is not merely that of observation. He must, like a good scientist, take apart the specimen being analyzed, unravel all its fibers to see how it is put together, how it has been woven and interwoven. That the texture of Middlemarch society as a whole may be accurately represented in a metaphor of woven cloth is taken for granted throughout the novel. It appears in many apparently casual texts as a reinforcement of more elaborate passages inviting the reader to keep the paradigm of the web before his mind. Lydgate, to give one example from early in the novel, finds himself for the first time "feeling the hampering threadlike pressure of small social conditions, and their frustrating complexity" (chap. 18).

The metaphor of a web, however, is also used repeatedly in *Middlemarch* to describe the texture of smaller-scale entities within the larger social fabric. The lovemaking of Rosamond and Lydgate, for example, is described as the collective weaving of an intersubjective tissue:

> Young love-making—that gossamer web! Even the points it clings to—the things whence its subtle interlacings are swung—are scarcely perceptible; momentary touches of finger-tips, meetings of rays from blue and dark orbs, unfinished phrases, lightest changes of cheek and lip, faintest tremors. The web itself is made of spontaneous beliefs and indefinable joys, yearnings of one life towards another, visions of completeness, indefinite trust. And Lydgate fell to spinning that web from his inward self with wonderful rapidity . . . As for Rosamond, she was in the water-lily's expanding wonderment at its own fuller life, and she too was spinning industriously at the mutual web.
>
> (Chap. 36)

Another important use of the metaphor of a web is made in the description of Lydgate's scientific research. Lydgate's attempt to find the "primitive tissue" is based on the assumption that the metaphor of woven cloth applies in the organic as well as in the social realm. His use of the figure brings into the open the parallelism between Eliot's aim as a sociologist of provincial life and the aims of contemporary biologists. Lydgate's research is based on the hypothesis that all the organs of the body are differentiations of "certain primary webs or tissues": "have not these structures some common basis from which they have all started, as your sarsnet, gauze, net, satin and velvet from the raw cocoon?" (chap. 15). If Lydgate assumes that biological entities may be described as tissues, the narrator of Middlemarch makes the same assumptions about the subjective lives of the characters. Of Lydgate, for example, the narrator says that "momentary speculations as to all the possible grounds for Mrs. Bulstrode's hints had managed to get woven like slight clinging hairs into the more substantial web of his thoughts" (chap. 31). Much later in the novel, basing the generalization again on Lydgate's psychology, the narrator asks: "Is it not rather what we expect in men, that they should have numerous strands of experience lying side by side and never compare them with each other?" (chap. 58). This image of mental or intersubjective life as a reticulated pattern like a grid is implicit when a few pages earlier the narrator says of Rosamond and Lydgate that "between him and her indeed there was that total missing of each other's mental track, which is too evidently possible even between persons who are continually thinking of each other." The image of mental or social life as traveling along tracks which may or may not intersect with others is also latent in an earlier remark about Ladislaw: "There are characters which are continually creating collisions and nodes for themselves in dramas which nobody is prepared to act with them" (chap. 19).

To the metaphor of the web, however, must be added the metaphor of the stream. Collective or individual life in Middlemarch is not a fixed pattern like a carpet. The web is aways in movement. The pervasive figure for this is that of flowing water. This figure is homogeneous with the figure of the web in that flowing water, for Eliot, is seen as made up of currents, filaments flowing side by side, intermingling and dividing. Flowing water is, so to speak, a temporalized web. Casaubon, for example, is said, in a fine series of phrases, to have possessed "that proud narrow sensitiveness which has not mass enough to spare for transformation into sympathy, and quivers thread-like in small currents of self-preoccupation or at best of an egoistic scrupulosity" (chap. 29). Lydgate, after he has met Rosamond, "had no sense that any new current had set into his life" (chap 16). Of his life as a whole when it is in the midst of being lived (in the middle of its march, as one might say), the narrator asserts that it has "the complicated probabilities of an arduous purpose, with all the possible thwartings and furtherings of circumstance, all the niceties of inward balance, by which a man swims and makes his point or else is carried headlong," for "Character too is a process and an unfolding" (chap. 15). In another place, the narrator speaks of the "chief current" of Dorothea's anxiety, (chap. 22), and, as opposed to the egotistic scrupulosity of Casaubon's small soul, "in Dorothea's mind there was a current into which all thought and feeling were apt sooner or later to flow—the reaching forward of the whole consciousness towards the fullest truth, the least partial good" (chap. 20). In the climactic scene of Dorothea's renunciation of her fortune to marry Will, "the flood of her young passion bear[s] down all the obstruction which had kept her silent" (chap. 83).

One final element must be added to complete the description of Eliot's admirable development of a quasi-scientific model to describe the subjective life of the individual, the relations of two persons within the social "medium," and the nature of that medium as a whole. This element has already been anticipated in what has been said about the correspondence, in Eliot's view of things, between small- and large-scale structures. This idea, however, is but one aspect of a larger assumption, that is, the notion that any process in any of the three "scales" is made up of endlessly subdividable "minutiae." Anything that we call a "unit" or a single fact, in social or in mental life, is not single but multiple. A finer lens would always make smaller parts visible. The smaller parts, in turn, are made up of even smaller entities.

One corollary of this vision of things is the rejection of that straightforward idea of single causes which had characterized, for example, *Adam Bede*. In *Middlemarch* Eliot still believes in causality, but in the psychological and social realms the causes are now seen as unimaginably multiple. No fact is in itself single, and no fact is explicable by a single relationship to a single cause. Each fact is a kind of multitudinous node which exists only arbitrarily as a single thing because we happen to have the microscope focused as we do. If the focus were finer, the apparently single fact would subdivide and reveal itself to be made of multiple minutiae. If the focus were coarser the fact would disappear within the larger entity of which it is a part. A single momentary state of mind, for example, exists in relation to all its latent motives, the minutiae of mental life which underlie it, in relation also to its own past and future, and in multiple relation to what is outside it, all the other people to whom the person is socially related. The metaphor of the variable lens of a micro-scope is in fact used by Eliot to make this point:

> Even with a microscope directed on a water-drop we find ourselves making interpretations which turn out to be rather coarse; for whereas under a weak lens you may seem to see a creature exhibiting an active voracity into which other smaller creatures actively play as if they were so many animated tax-pennies, a stronger lens reveals to you certain tiniest hairlets which make vortices for these victims while the swallower waits passively at his receipt of custom.
>
> (Chap. 6)

One might ask, parenthetically, how and why the metaphor of the microscope has been contaminated here by another apparently unrelated metaphor, that of money, taxes, and "custom." This interpretation of one metaphor by another metaphor is characteristic of Eliot's use of figure. An attempt to explain fully this linguistic habit must be postponed, but one can say that the displacement of one figure by another is asymmetrically parallel to the displacement of the weak lens by the strong lens of the microscope. In each case, one vision of things is replaced by another. The optical visions are apparently reconcilable, whereas the two metaphors interfere with one another even if they are not wholly contradictory. The text of *Middlemarch*, in any case, goes on to apply the metaphor of the double-lensed microscope to a particular case in the novel: "In this way, metaphorically speaking, a strong lens applied to Mrs. Cadwallader's match-making will show a play of minute causes producing what may be called thought and speech vortices to bring her the sort of food she needed."

The phrase "play of minute causes" is echoed throughout the novel by similar phrases keeping before the reader the idea that the mental and social events being described are extremely complex. This complexity is essential to their mode of existence. The narrator speaks, for example, of "a slow preparation of effects from one life to another" (chap. 11), or of an ardor which cooled "imperceptibly," like other youthful loves ("Nothing in the world more subtle than the process of their gradual change!" chap. 15), or of "the minutiae of mental make in which one of us differs from another" (chap. 15), or of Lydgate's "testing vision of details and relations" (chap. 16), or of "the suppressed transitions which unite all contrasts" (chap. 20), or of the "nice distinctions of rank in Middlemarch" (chap. 23), or of "the living myriad of hidden suckers whereby the belief and the conduct are wrought into mutual sustainment" (chap. 53), or of a "fact" which "was broken into little sequences" (chap. 61), or of the way Bulstrode's "misdeeds were like the subtle muscular movements which are not taken account of in the consciousness" (chap. 68).

All this family of intertwined metaphors and motifs—the web, the current, the minutely subdivided entity—make up a single comprehensive model or picture of Middlemarch society as being a complex moving medium, tightly interwoven into a single fabric, always in process, endlessly subdividable. This medium can be seen and studied objectively, as if there could be an ideal observer who does not change what he observes and who sees the moving web as it were from all perspectives at once, from close up and far away, with both gross and fine lenses, in a continual systole and diastole of inquiry. The storyteller in *Middlemarch* is in short the ideal observer of Victorian fiction, the "omniscient" narrator. His aim is to do full representative justice to the complexity of the condition of man in his social medium. There are many admirable passages in *Middlemarch* giving examples of what the narrator sees, each a new application of the model I have been describing. None is perhaps so comprehensive an exploitation of the totalizing implications of this family of metaphors as an admirable passage in chapter 11 describing "old provincial society":

> Old provincial society had its share of this subtle movement: had not only its striking downfalls, its brilliant young professional dandies who ended by living up an entry with a drab and six children for their establishment, but also those less marked vicissitudes which are constantly shifting the boundaries of social intercourse, and begetting new consciousness of interdependence. Some slipped a little downward, some got higher footing: people denied aspirates, gained wealth, and fastidious gentlemen stood for boroughs; some were caught in political currents, some in ecclesiastical, and perhaps found themselves surprisingly grouped

in consequence; while a few personages or families that stood with rocky firmness amid all this fluctuation, were slowly presenting new aspects in spite of solidity, and altering with the double change of self and beholder.

"Double change of self and beholder!" I have said that my first family of metaphors in *Middlemarch* does not raise problems or perspective, or that in any case it presupposes the possibility of an ideal observer such as that assumed in much nineteenth-century science, in the days before operationalism, relativity, and the principle of indeterminancy. This is true, but in fact an optical or epistemological metaphor has already introduced itself surreptitiously into many of my examples. The narrator must concentrate "all the light [he] can command" (chap. 15) on his particular web in order to see clearly how it is woven. Study of the web requires constant changes of the lens in the systole and diastole of inquiry. Any conceivable observer in Middlemarch will be changing himself along with all the other changes and so will change what he sees.

A pervasive figure for the human situation in *Middlemarch* is that of the seer who must try to identify clearly what is present before him. This metaphor contaminates the apparently clear-cut objectivist implications of the metaphor of the flowing web. As more and more examples of it accumulate, it struggles with a kind of imperialistic will to power over the whole to replace that objectivism with a fully developed subjectivism or perspectivism. The "omniscience" of the narrator, according to this alternative model for the human condition, can be obtained only because he is able to share the points of view all the characters, thereby transcending the limited vision of any single person. "In watching effects," as the narrator says, "if only of an electric battery, it is often necessary to change our place and examine a particular mixture or group at some distance from the point where the movement we are interested in was set up" (chap. 40). The narrator can move in imagination from one vantage point to another, or from close up to far away. He can be, like the angel Uriel, "watching the progress of planetary history from the Sun" (chap. 41), and at the same time share in that microscopic vision of invisible process, perceptible only to inward imaginative vision, so splendidly described in a passage about Lydgate's method as a scientist. It is a passage which also describes covertly the claims of Eliot's own fictional imagination. Lydgate, the narrator says, is endowed

> with the imagination that reveals subtle actions inaccessible by any sort of lens, but tracked in that outer darkness through long pathways of necessary sequence by the inward light which is the last refinement of Energy, capable of bathing even the ethereal atoms in its ideally illuminated space . . . he was enamoured of that arduous invention which is

the very eye of research, provisionally framing its object and correcting it
to more and more exactness of relation; he wanted to pierce the obscurity
of those minute processes which prepare human misery and joy . . .

(Chap. 16)

The metaphor of the complex moving web, the "embroiled medium" is, one can see, further complicated, or even contradicted, by the
metaphor of vision. Each of those nodes in the social web which is a
separate human being is endowed with a power to see the whole. This
power is defined throughout the novel as essentially distorting. Each man
or woman has a "centre of self, whence the lights and shadows must
always fall with a certain difference" (chap. 31). The "radiance" of
Dorothea's "transfigured girlhood," as the narrator says, "fell on the first
object that came within its level" (chap. 5). Her mistakes, as her sister
Celia tells her, are errors in seeing, of which her literal myopia is a
metonymy. "I thought it right to tell you," says Celia apropos of the fact
that Sir James intends to propose to Dorothea, "because you went on as
you always do, never looking just where you are, and treading in the
wrong place. You always see what nobody else sees; it is impossible to
satisfy you; yet you never see what is quite plain" (chap. 4). Mr. Casaubon, however, is also "the centre of his own world." From that point of
view he is "liable to think that others were providentially made for him,
and especially to consider them in the light of their fitness for the author
of a 'Key to all Mythologies' " (chap. 10). Of the inhabitants of Middlemarch
generally it can in fact be said that each makes of what he sees something
determined by his own idiosyncratic perspective, for "Probabilities are as
various as the faces to be seen at will on fretwork or paperhangings: every
form is there, from Jupiter to Judy, if you only look with creative inclina-
tion" (chap. 32).

Seeing, then, is for Eliot not a neutral, objective, dispassionate, or
passive act. It is the creative projection of light from an egotistic center
motivated by desire and need. This projected radiance orders the field of
vision according to the presuppositions of the seer. The act of seeing is the
spontaneous affirmation of a will to power over what is seen. This
affirmation of order is based on the instinctive desire to believe that the
world is providentially structured in a neat pattern of which one is oneself
the center, for "we are all of us born in moral stupidity, taking the world
as an udder to feed our supreme selves." This interpretation of the act of
seeing is most fully presented in the admirable and often discussed "parable" of the "pier-glass" at the beginning of chapter 27:

An eminent philosopher among my friends, who can dignify even your
ugly furniture by lifting it into the serene light of science, has shown me

this pregnant little fact. Your pier-glass or extensive surface of polished steel made to be rubbed by a housemaid, will be minutely and multitudinously scratched in all directions; but place now against it a lighted candle as a centre of illumination, and lo! the scratches will seem to arrange themselves in a fine series of concentric circles round that little sun. It is demonstrable that the scratches are going everywhere impartially, and it is only your candle which produces the flattering illusion of a concentric arrangement, its light falling with an exclusive optical selection. These things are a parable. The scratches are events, and the candle is the egoism of any person now absent—of Miss Vincy, for example. Rosamond had a Providence of her own who had kindly made her more charming than other girls, and who seemed to have arranged Fred's illness and Mr. Wrench's mistake in order to bring her and Lydgate within effective proximity.

This passage is perhaps more complicated than it at first appears. It begins with an example of what it describes, an example which implicitly takes note of the fact that Eliot's own "parabolic" method, in this text, as in many other passages in *Middlemarch*, is a seeing of one thing in the "light" of another. The word "parable," like the word "allegory," the word "metaphor," or indeed all terms for figures of speech, is of course itself based on a figure. It means "to set beside," from the Greek *para*, beside, and *ballein*, to throw. A parable is set or thrown at some distance from the meaning which controls it and to which it obliquely or parabolically refers, as a parabolic curve is controlled, across a space, by its parallelism to a line on the cone of which it is a section. The line and the cone may have only a virtual or imaginary existence, as in the case of a comet with a parabolic course. The parabola creates that line in the empty air, just as the parables of Jesus remedy a defect of vision, give sight to the blind, and make the invisible visible. In Eliot's parable of the pier glass the "eminent philosopher" transfigures "ugly furniture," a pier glass, by "lifting it into the serene light of science," but also makes an obscure scientific principle visible. In the same way, the candle makes the random scratches on the pier glass appear to be concentric circles, and so Rosamond interprets what happens around her as being governed by her private providence, just as Eliot sees provincial society as like a woven web, or the ego of an individual person in the light of a comparison to a candle. The same projective, subjective, even egotistic act, seeing one thing as set or thrown, parabolically, beside another, is involved in all four cases.

At this point the reader may remember that the narrator, in a passage I earlier took as a "key" expression of Eliot's use of a model of objective scientific observation, says "all the light I can command must be concentrated on this particular web." With a slight change of formulation this could be seen as implying that the subjective source of light not only illuminates what is seen but also, as in the case of the candle held to the pier glass, determines the structure of what is seen. Middlemarch society perhaps appears to be a web only because a certain kind of subjective light is concentrated on it. The passage taken in isolation does not say this, but its near congruence with the passage about the pier glass, a slightly asymmetrical analogy based on the fact that the same metaphorical elements are present in each allows the contradictory meaning to seep into the passage about the web when the two texts are set side by side. Each is seen as a modulation of the other. The same key would not open both, though a "master key" might.

In spite of the disquieting possibilities generated by resonances between two similar but not quite congruent passages, the narrator in various ways throughout Middlemarch is clearly claiming to be able to transcend the limitations of the self-centered ego by seeing things impersonally, objectively, scientifically: "It is demonstrable that the scratches are going everywhere impartially." This objective vision, such is the logic of Eliot's parable, shows that what is "really there" has no order whatsoever, but is merely random scratches without pattern or meaning. The pier glass is "minutely and multitudinously scratched in all directions." The idea that reality is chaotic, without intrinsic order or form, and the corollary that any order it may appear to have is projected illicitly by some patterning ego, would seem to be contradicted by the series of totalizing metaphors I have explored—web, flowing water, and so on—as well as by the generalizing, rationalizing, order-finding activity of the narrator throughout the book. It would seem hardly plausible, at this point at least, to say that reality for Eliot is a chaotic disorder. It might seem more likely that this is an irrelevant implication of the parable, an implication which has by accident, as it were, slipped in along with implications which are "intended." A decision about this must be postponed.

Among the "intended" implications, however, may be one arising from the fact that a pier glass is a kind of mirror, while the examples of the "flattering illusion" Eliot would have encountered in Herbert Spencer or in Ruskin lacked this feature. Ruskin, for example, speaks of the path of reflected moonlight seen across the surface of a lake by a spectator on the shore. The pier glass would, after all, reflect what was brought near it, as well as produce its own interfering illusion of concentric circles, and the candle is a displacement of parable for the ego, of Rosamond or whomever. Rosamond would of course see her own image in the mirror, Narcissus-like. This implication of the parable links it with all those other passages, not only in Middlemarch but also in Adam Bede, for example, or in *Daniel Deronda*, where egotism is symbolized by the admiration of one's image in a mirror, or where the work of representation is expressed in the traditional image of holding a mirror up to reality. A passage in chapter 10, for example, apropos of the low opinion of Mr. Casaubon held by his neighbors, says that even "the greatest man of his age" could not escape "unfavourable reflections of himself in various small mirrors." This apparently uses the figure of the mirror in a way contradicting the parable of the pier glass. The mirror is now the ego rather than the external world. In fact, however, what is always in question when the mirror appears is narcissistic self-reflection. This may be thought of as seeing our own reflection in the mirroring world outside because we have projected it there. Or it may be thought of as our distortion of the world outside in our reflecting ego, so that it takes the configurations of our private vision of things. Any two subjectivities, according to this model, will face one another like confronting mirrors. If Casaubon was "the centre of his own world," had "an equivalent centre of self, whence the lights and shadows must always fall with a certain difference," the people in whom he seeks the reflection of his own sense of himself are not innocent mirrors, but are themselves instruments of distortion: "even Milton, looking for his portrait in a spoon, must submit to have the facial angle of a bumpkin" (chap. 10). The projection of one's selfish needs or desires on reality orders that random set of events into a pattern, the image of the mirror would imply. This pattern is in fact a portrait of the ego itself, an objective embodiment of its subjective configurations. The terrible isolation of each person, for Eliot, lies in the way each goes through the world encountering only himself, his own image reflected back to him by the world because he (or she) has put it there in the first place, in the illusory interpretation of the world the person spontaneously makes.

The narrator of *Middlemarch*, it would seem, can escape from this fate only by using perspective to transcend perspective, by moving from the microscopic close-up to the panoramic distant view, and by shifting constantly from the point of view of one character to the point of view of another. Such shifts will give a full multidimensional picture of what is "really there," as when the narrator, after a prolonged immersion within the subjective experience of Dorothea, asks: "—but why always Dorothea? Was her point of view the only possible one with regard to this marriage? I protest against all our interest, all our efforts at understanding being given to the young skins that look blooming in spite of trouble . . . In spite of the blinking eyes and white moles objectionable to Celia, and the want of muscular curve which was morally painful to Sir James, Mr. Casaubon had an intense consciousness within him, and was spiritually a-hungered like the rest of us" (chap. 29).

The word "interpretation," however, which I used just above, will serve as a clue indicating the presence within the optical metaphors of an element so far not identified as such. This element contaminates and ultimately subverts the optical model in the same way that the optical model contaminates and makes more problematic the images of the web or of the current. All the optical passages in fact contain elements which show that for Eliot seeing is never "merely" optical. Seeing is never simply a matter of identifying correctly what is seen, seeing that windmills are windmills and not giants, a washpan a washpan and not the helmet of Mambrino, to use the example from *Don Quixote* cited as an epigraph for chapter 2. Seeing is always interpretation, that is, what is seen is always taken as a sign standing for something else, as an emblem, a hieroglyph, a parable.

Superimposed on the models for the human situation of the objective scientist and the subjective perspectivist, interlaced with them, overlapping them in each of their expressions, is a model for the situation of the characters and of the narrator which says all human beings in all situations are like readers of a text. Moreover, if for Eliot all seeing is falsified by the limitations of point of view, it is an even more inevitable law, for her, that we make things what they are by naming them in one way or another, that is, by the incorporation of empirical data into a conventional system of signs. A corollary of this law is the fact that all interpretation of signs is false interpretation. The original naming was an act of interpretation which falsified. The reading of things made into signs is necessarily a further falsification, an interpretation of an interpretation. An important sequence of passages running like Ariadne's thread through the labyrinthine verbal complexity of *Middlemarch* develops a subtle theory of signs and of interpretation. Along with this goes a recognition of the irreducible figurative or metaphorical nature of all language.

I have elsewhere discussed George Eliot's theory of signs, of interpretation, and of figurative language in *Middlemarch*. Limitations of space would in any case forbid discussion of this third model for the human situation here. It is possible, however, to conclude on the basis of what I have said about two families of metaphors in *Middlemarch* that the models are multiple and incompatible. They are incompatible not in the sense that one is more primitive or naive and gives way to a more sophisticated paradigm, but in the sense that any passage will reveal itself when examined closely to be the battleground of conflicting metaphors. This incoherent, heterogeneous, "unreadable," or nonsynthesizable quality of the text of *Middlemarch* jeopardizes the narrator's effort of totalization. It suggests that one gets a different kind of totality depending on what metaphorical model is used. The presence of several incompatible models brings into the open the arbitrary and partial character of each and so ruins the claim of the narrator to have total, unified, and impartial vision. What is true for the characters of *Middlemarch*, that "we all of us, grave or light, get our thoughts entangled in metaphors, and act fatally on the strength of them" (chap. 10), must also be true for the narrator. The web of interpretative figures cast by the narrator over the characters of the story becomes a net in which the narrator himself is entangled and trapped, his sovereign vision blinded.

George Eliot's insight into the dismaying dangers of metaphor is expressed already in an admirably witty and perceptive passage in *The Mill on the Floss*, published over a decade before *Middlemarch*, in 1860. Here already she formulates her recognition of the deconstructive powers of figurative language, its undoing of any attempt to make a complete, and completely coherent, picture of human life. This undoing follows from the fact that if we can seldom say what a thing is without saying it is something else, without speaking parabolically, then there is no way to avoid the ever present possibility of altering the meaning by altering the metaphor:

> It is astonishing what a different result one gets by changing the metaphor! Once call the brain an intellectual stomach, and one's ingenious conception of the classics and geometry as ploughs and harrows seems to settle nothing. But then it is open to some one else to follow great authorities, and call the mind a sheet of white paper or a mirror, in which case one's knowledge of the digestive process becomes quite irrelevant. It was doubtless an ingenious idea to call the camel the ship of the desert, but it would hardly lead one far in training that useful beast. O Aristotle! If you had had the advantage of being "the freshest modern" instead of the greatest ancient, would you not have mingled your praise of metaphorical speech, as a sign of high intelligence, with a lamentation that intelligence so rarely shows itself in speech without metaphor—that we can so seldom declare what a thing is, except by saying it is something else?
> (Book 2, chap. 1)

ELIZABETH WEED

The Liquidation of
Maggie Tulliver

With the drowning of Maggie Tulliver in the arms of her brother Tom, the story of *The Mill on the Floss* comes to an end. All that remains is the narrator's "Conclusion," closing the book with the words that form the epitaph on the tomb of the sister and brother—words that circle around to meet the book's epigraph: "In their death they were not divided." One might expect the reader to be satisfied with such a conventional Victorian ending, to find in it the resolution that follows conflict, the repose that follows catharsis. This is not, of course, the case. Critical readers have long debated the meaning of the novel's final scene and the success or failure of its closure. Regardless of the arguments, the debate inevitably focuses on the story of Maggie. Why is such an attractive character, so rich in strengths and weaknesses, abandoned to a death by flood, a catastrophe which, however well or poorly integrated it may be in the novel, precludes all possibility of Maggie's resolving her dilemma in exclusively human terms?

In order to answer such questions, the reader turns to the novel for guidance. What he finds there is an authoritative omniscient narrator who seems to convey a clear Feuerbachian message of the necessity of nurturing a humanistic social ethic, based on altruism and achieved through the cultivation of sympathetic bonds among people. Persons of "broad, strong sense," he tells us, are those who (unlike the "men of maxims") follow the "promptings and inspirations that spring from growing insight and sympathy," and who achieve this insight through "a life vivid and intense

From *Genre* 11 (Fall 1978). Copyright © 1978 by University of Oklahoma.

enough to have created a wide, fellow-feeling with all that is human."
(The *Mill on the Floss*, ed. Gordon S. Haight. Boston: Riverside Editions,
1961. Bk. IV, ch. ii, p. 435. Subsequent references will be to this edition
and will be given in the text). The society of St. Ogg's is characterized,
however, by its "oppressive narrowness," and the reader is invited to
sympathize with the effect this narrowness has on the lives of Tom and
Maggie and "on young natures in many generations, that in the onward
tendency of human things have risen above the mental level of the
generation before them, to which they have nevertheless been tied by the
strongest fibres of their hearts" (IV, i, 238–39). The thematic dilemma of
the novel is thus clear: if, as Feuerbach says, "the relations of child and
parent, of husband and wife, of brother and friend—in general, of man to
man . . . are per se religious" in that they contribute to the ethical
development of the individual, then in order to achieve a life of "wide
fellow feeling with all that is human," the young person of St. Ogg's must
learn and cultivate his sympathy for others through the very fibers that
bind him to narrowness.

The moral function of the novel is also clear: by participating in
the experience of the novel, the reader will receive an education of his
own. As Eliot wrote in a letter to Clifford Allbutt, "the inspiring principle
which alone gives me courage to write is that of so presenting our human
life as to help my readers in getting a clearer conception and a more active
admiration of those vital elements which bind man together and give a
higher worthiness to their existence." Guided by the narrator, the reader
can see into hearts which would otherwise remain closed to him. Moreover, the narrator assures the reader that the story he is relating, the story
of Maggie and Tom, is, no matter how insignificant it may seem, related
to the larger question of human development: "and we need not shrink
from this comparison of small things with great; for does not science tell
us that its highest striving is after the ascertainment of a unity which shall
bind the smallest things with the greatest? In natural science, I have
understood, there is nothing petty to the mind that has a large vision of
relations, and to which every single object suggests a vast sum of conditions. It is surely the same with the observation of human life" (IV, i,
239). And within the novel it is surely, by implication, the narrator who
possesses the large vision of relations, which can perceive the vast sum of
conditions, and who invites the reader to share in his omniscience.

For Eliot, the writing of the novel is, then, a performative enterprise: by portraying the "small things" of St. Ogg's, she wants to enlarge
the understanding and sympathies of the reader, and thereby to contribute
to the realization of her ethical principles. That enterprise is facilitated by

the author's adoption of an authoritative male narrator. Her Feuerbachian ethic, which rejects all transcendent grounding, is, in a sense, regrounded by her assumption of the quasi-divine narrative authority that grounds the novel, and the value of her performative endeavor is legitimized by the conventionalized system of logocentric values that supports her fiction.

An examination of the economy of values governing the formal construction of Eliot's fiction reveals a fundamental analogical relationship between the function of language on the one hand and the functioning of "real" society on the other. Just as the language or languages of the novel are denied an absolute guarantee of significance but remain to varying degreees meaningful and potentially useful, so are societies to varying degrees meaningful and ameliorable even though they are deprived of a transcendent moral base. An illustration of this analogy may be found in the characters' relationships to language. In the first place, much of the action of the novel, much of what happens, is experienced by the characters themselves through the medium of language. The children understand the truth of Mr. Tulliver's bankruptcy by confronting words and phrases from their childhood: to "have the bailiff in the house," "to be sold up," to "fail" (III, ii, 178). Mr. Tulliver learns of his financial disaster through a letter. His curse against Wakem is inscribed in his family Bible, and this inscription becomes, for Tom, the law, and for the family, a source of much of its suffering. Tom attacks Philip with words; and Maggie is denied reentry into St. Ogg's society by the obloquy fashioned by the "world's wife."

Moreover, the human experience of virtually every character in the book is presented through the metaphor of language: life itself is seen as a language to which one must gain access, and success or failure in life is seen as a function of one's command of one or various languages. For Mr. Tulliver, "this is a puzzling world," and all sufferings are a result of lacking the clue, the key to the enigma. From his perspective, the problem is not so much with the world of the Creator, but with the world of men: "if the world had been left as God made it, I could ha' seen my way, and held my own wi' the best of 'em; but things have got so twisted round and wrapped up i' unreasonable words, as aren't a bit like 'em, as I'm clean at fault, often an' often. Everything winds about so—the more straightforrard you are, the more you're puzzled" (I, iii, 18–19). For the more intelligent Maggie, life begins as a joyful exploration, a delighted discovery of etymologies and of the English keys at the end of Tom's Latin books, which open up to her a whole magical world. As she gets older she searches with less joy but as much energy for the "key that would enable her to understand, and, in understanding, endure, the heavy weight that had fallen on her young heart" (IV, iii, 251).

Once the languages of life are deciphered, they must be used in order to survive. Mr. Tulliver invests a considerable sum of money in Tom's education so that the boy can avoid the linguistic handicaps of his father and better outwit the lawyers of the world. He wants Tom " 'to know what folks mean, and how to wrap things up in words as aren't actionable. It's an uncommon fine thing, that is,' concluded Mr. Tulliver, shaking his head, 'when you can let a man know what you think of him without paying for it' " (I, iii, 21). After a false start, Tom does, in fact, learn the language he needs to succeed in the world. It is not Latin, which he quickly forgets (and which Mr. Dean considers to be such a luxury that it ought to be taxed), but the language of commerce that affords him an entry into the lucrative world of trade of St. Ogg's.

For Maggie the problem is not so simple. As a girl, she is unable to learn the languages that guarantee access to the larger world of men. Nor has she completely learned her "life-lessons" in the "very trivial language" of women (VI, vii, 366). Denied a coherent language of her own, Maggie is forced to search among foreign languages for one that will help her survive. And in her search she looks not only for a language, but for a full-blown narrative model that will help her to read the fiction of her own life, a fiction that will offer her control and a way of making her experience intelligible. When she is very young she is attracted to stories about witches and gypsies and women warriors. As she gets older she ceases to find female models and simply adapts herself to whatever promising male authority she encounters, such as St. Thomas à Kempis, whom she looks to as the "secret of life that would enable her to renounce all other secrets" (IV, iii, 254). After reading St. Thomas à Kempis, Maggie immediately fashions for herself a life of ascetic self-sacrifice, just as she had earlier created "wild romances of a flight home in search of something less sordid and dreary" (IV, iii, 252).

Whereas Tom is rather successful in realizing the fictions he invents for his future, the unfortunate Maggie resembles her father in her inability to create the narrative of her life. For Mr. Tulliver, the threads of the narrative forever form a tangled skein. For Maggie, the problem is one of becoming trapped somehow, not only in the fictions fashioned by others, such as the obloquy of the world's wife, or Philip's playful prediction as to how she will revenge the dark haired women of the novels, but in the intersection of her own narratives with the force of events.

The characters' fictions are, in fact, all tested in one way or another by the strength they show against the forces of life. To use the figures frequently used in the book, the narratives that can best withstand the onrush of life's forces are those that are strongly woven fabrics. The fabric of Maggie's fictions is weak. Not only is she forced to choose her authorities at random, but cut off as she is from a truly performative language, and unable to invent a satisfactory ending to her own story, she fabricates incomplete and fragile fictions. Her method of reading Tom's Latin grammar is illustrative: "she delighted in new words, and quickly found that there was an English Key at the end, which would make her very wise about Latin, at slight expense. She presently made up her mind to skip the rules in the Syntax—the examples became so absorbing. . . . The most fragmentary examples were her favorites" (II, i, 131).

An illustration of the positive function of the strong narrative fabric is found in the scene where Tom tells his father of the money he has saved to pay off the family debts. Overjoyed by the news, Mr. Tulliver wants to hear the whole story of Tom's commercial ventures and his dealings with Bob Jakin. It is at this point that the narrator comments: "It was well that there was this interest of narrative [on Mr. Tulliver's part] to keep under the vague but fierce sense of triumph over Wakem, which would otherwise have been the channel his joy would have rushed into with dangerous force. Even as it was, that feeling from time to time gave threats of its ultimate mastery, in sudden bursts of irrelevant exclamation" (V, vi, 309). In this instance it is Tom's narrative, made up of the threads of his story, that contains the force of Mr. Tulliver's emotion, or diverts that emotion from the channel it would have otherwise taken.

The reader has only to pursue this tension between the figure of the narrative thread on the one hand and that of the channel of unrestrained force on the other to discover the way in which one of the major dramas of the novel is metaphorically enacted. For the threads that are woven into the tissue of the character's personal fictions are not merely the threads of fiction, but also—by an association through which the metaphor of language circles back around to meet the thematic concern with society—the fibers that bind men's hearts. In one Proustian passage the narrator underlines this metaphorical relationship of the fibers of the heart to language, a relationship that is repeated and strengthened throughout the novel. Referring to the familiar wood in which he is walking, the narrator comments on the happiness derived from the known: what exotic sights, is asked, "what strange ferns or splendid broad-petalled blossoms, could ever thrill such deep and delicate fibres within me as this home-scene?" For him, the familiar flowers, birdsongs, sky, and fields, "such things as these are the mother tongue of our imagination, the language that is laden with all the subtle inextricable associations the fleeting hours of our childhood left behind them" (I, v, 37–38).

If the fibers are the threads that tie the heart to the things and people of childhood and, hence, by sympathy and imagination to other people, the currents, streams, tides, and waves, all of which insistently recur in the novel, represent the flow of unleashed forces. These forces can be both good and bad, both external—such as the force of destiny or the inexorable tide or flow of events—and internal, such as Mr. Tulliver's violent hatred for Wakem or Maggie's passion for Stephen. The important difference is that the fibers represent containment, whereas the currents represent the opposite, the absence of restraint.

An important locus in the novel for the conflict between these two figures is the river Floss itself. On the one hand, the river means home to Maggie and Tom, the privileged place of childhood to which they are bound by the fibers of their memory. On the other hand, it remains a river, a flow of water that holds within it the ever-present danger of flood and of the unleashed forces of death and destruction. Significantly, the word "floss" itself contains both elements of the tension. A "floss" is a silky fiber, such as twisted embroidery thread and, at the same time, it is the preterite of the German verb *fliessen*, meaning to "to flow." When, in the first sentence of the novel, the narrator introduces the reader to the Floss, it is described as follows: "A wide plain, where the broadening Floss hurries on between its green banks to the sea, and the loving tide, rushing to meet it, checks its passage with an impetuous embrace" (I, i, 7). The two elements of the fiber/current tension are present in the description, but the narrator assures us that although the tide "checks the passage" of the Floss, it is a "loving" tide and does so with an embrace.

The reader who enters the novel for the first time may be somewhat troubled by this sentence, in spite of its reassuring tone. One problem is that the sentence is syntactically incomplete, unclosed. Accepting this anomaly as part of the narrator's technique for presenting the landscape to one's imagination, the reader moves on with the story. However, once he has completed the novel, he finds, if he returns to the first sentence, that its unsettling elements are somewhat more problematic. The reader now knows that the loving embrace is an obvious foreshadowing of Maggie and Tom's embrace in death, and that the point at which the tide meets the Floss—a point of indetermination, where it is impossible to tell which direction the tide is flowing and which direction the Floss—can also be the point at which the destructive forces of the flood are set loose. Finally, for the reader whose interrogation of the passage extends to its etymological sources, there is the additional knowledge that just as the name "floss" contains both current and fiber, so, concealed beneath the image of the loving embrace of the tide, is the word "tide" itself, which carries with it its Indo-European root, "dā," meaning "to divide" or "cut up."

Although one is clearly invited by the author to join the first sentence to the ending of the novel in a closure of circular symmetry, the juxtaposition of beginning and ending may increase one's doubts about the resolution of the novel rather than assuage them. On the one hand, the narrator assures us, through direct statement and a formally satisfying closure, that the deaths of Maggie and Tom in some way represent a resolution of tensions and a union, on various levels perhaps, of warring elements. Since it is the narrator's assurance that counts in the novel, since he serves as the grounding authority of the work, one wants to believe his assurances. On the other hand, the disturbing aspects of the first sentence remain and seem to be reinforced by the epigraph-epitaph, "In their death they were not divided." Do the litotes formed by the two negative terms, "not" and "divided," strengthen the positive force of the statement as litotes generally do, or do they in this case, attenuate it? Are Maggie and Tom, who were never truly joined in life except in Maggie's desire and imagination, meaningfully joined in death? The question, closed by their drowning, seems nevertheless to be permanently open to debate.

A similarly problematic passage is found in the middle of the novel, at the low point of the Tulliver family's story of bankruptcy, in the first chapter of the book entitled, "The Valley of Humiliation." It is here that the narrator steps as far away from the narrative as he ever does, in order to contrast two European rivers, the Rhone and the Rhine, and to draw comparisons between the Rhone and the Floss. The latter two rivers are seen to share the same sordidness, the same vulgarity, the same lack of energy. Just as the floods have already swept away the "feeble generation" of the Rhone, so will the "gross sum of obscure vitality" remaining to it (and by association to the Floss) "be swept into the same oblivion with the generations of ants and beavers" (IV, i, 238). In contrast, there is the Rhine:

> Strange contrast, you may have thought, between the effect produced on
> us by these dismal remnants of commonplace houses [along the banks of
> the Rhone], which in their best days were but the sign of a sordid life,
> belonging in all its details to our own vulgar era; and the effect produced
> by those ruins on the castled Rhine, which have crumbled and mellowed
> into such harmony with the green and rocky steeps, that they seem to
> have a natural fitness, like the mountainpine: nay, even in the day when

they were built they must have had this fitness, as if they had been raised by an earth-born race, who had inherited from their mighty parent a sublime instinct of form. And that was a day of romance! If those robber-barons were somewhat grim and drunken ogres, they had a certain grandeur of the wild beast in them—they were forest boars with tusks, tearing and rending, not the ordinary domestic grunter; they represented the demon forces for ever in collision with beauty, virtue, and the gentle uses of life; they made a fine contrast in the picture with the wandering minstrel, the soft-lipped princess, the pious recluse, and the timid Israelite. That was a time of colour, when the sunlight fell on glancing steel and floating banners; a time of adventure and fierce struggle. . . .

(IV, i, 237)

In his comments on both the Rhone and the Rhine, the narrator first describes the ruins along their banks, then, taking the ruins as a "sign" or "trace" of the lives of the people who constructed and inhabited them, points to similarities between those lives and the edifices. In the case of the Rhine, the castle ruins are seen to have a fitness with nature, "as if they had been raised by an earth-born race who had inherited from their mighty parent a sublime instinct of form." In the passage that follows, the life of the period is characterized by a strong contrast between the destructive but energetic robber-barons on the one hand, and the civilized elements of the courtly romance on the other. If one follows the logical development of the passage, one may then assume that the "tearing and rending" of the forest boars, as well as the elements of civilized courtly romance, are reflected in the "sublime" form of the castles. This assumption leads to a kind of dionysian-apollonian synthesis, a synthesis reinforced by the joining of the words "sublime" and "instinct," and again by the word "sublime" itself. The reader who pursues the same etymological interrogation that revealed the tensions contained in the words "Floss" and "tide" discovers that "sub" is a double antithetical prefix which can mean, among other things, in its Indo-European form, "under," "underneath," and "below," as well as "from below," "up," "up to," and "away." When joined to the Latin *līmin*, meaning "threshold," which is related to *līmes*, meaning "boundary" or "limit," it forms such words as "sublime," and "sublimate," but *also* "subliminal." The synthesis of the dionysian and apollonian is reinforced, finally, by the word "raze," homonym of the word "raise," whose hidden function becomes quite plausible when one remembers that the castles were, after all, always open to attack by outlaws and enemy knights and that they are now in ruins.

Located at the very center of the book, the passage is a significant one in that the narrator interrupts the story line in order to establish a set of correspondences and contrasts designed to help the reader interpret the novel. As in the opening lines, the narrator here assures the reader, though in a more complicated, hence more covert way, that "the demon forces forever in collision with beauty, virtue, and the gentle use of life" can be contained in a synthesis or resolution. If one were to carry that assurance to the last chapter, one might interpret the ending as a synthesis within Maggie of her darker demon forces and her more sublime impulses, the two extremes represented by the rage with which she once drove nails into the head of her fetish and the enthusiasm with which she imitated the abnegation of Thomas à Kempis. At the same time, one might also see the ending as a union of the opposing personalities of Maggie and Tom, a union admittedly problematic, but possible according to some interpretations. A reader such as Laura Comer Emery, for example, explains the final scene in Freudian terms. For her, the embrace of the sister and brother can be seen to offer a satisfying closure in several ways: it affords Maggie a way of reuniting with her mother through Tom, who is very much a Dodson and a rival sibling preferred by the mother; it permits a regression to the Oceanic state anterior to the sexual differentiation of the fetus; and it enables Maggie to participate in Tom's maleness, thus alleviating castration anxieties.

The most satisfactory reading is probably the one that understands the ending not as a neat, closed synthesis, but rather as part of a permanent dialectic in which the author places some small hope in the possibility of ethical advancement of society. In such a reading, one sees that although Maggie's impulses and intentions are sound, she is too limited by her particular condition and environment to resolve her dilemma on her own. Thus, true to her nature, she renounces Stephen because "she had made up her mind to suffer" (VI, xiv, 416), welcomes the flood with relief and energy, and rushes to her death as to the only possible fiction remaining to her.

The problem with all of these readings is that none of them really accounts for the flood itself, an event considered by many to be a flaw in the novel, a device unworthy of Eliot. However unresolvable the human and social conflicts of the book, the formal elements are clearly intended to achieve an harmoniously ordered, closed structure. And if it is difficult to be satisfied with the way Eliot disposes of Maggie, it is perhaps even more difficult to accept fully the author's efforts at formal resolution, particularly her often heavy-handed use of foreshadowing. But it is precisely at this point—where the book seems to "fail"—that the reader can find the fundamental conflict of the novel, the conflict between the centered text offering the consolation of "meaning," and the decentered one permanently subverting that meaning.

One has seen how the narrator attempts to assure the reader that violence can be contained within the synthesis represented by sublime form. In order to accept that notion, however, one must also fully accept the whole economy of equivalences that guarantees the potential resolution of antitheses. And in order to do that, one must accept the authority of the narrator as grounded in a logos, albeit an ersatz one. In order to accept that authority, finally, one must accept the fiction of George Eliot the male novelist, a fiction which, in turn, permits the fiction of the (male) omniscient narrator. It is possible, then, to say that the narrator's assurances as to the containment of the violence of the novel hold only to the extent to which the fictions of the author and narrator hold.

The difficulty the reader has accepting these fictions stems from the fact that he knows and remembers that behind George Eliot there is a woman. Moreover, he may know that behind the fiction of Maggie Tulliver there is the life of Mary Anne Evans with which it shares certain characteristics. If he knows this, he finds that the already ambiguous stance of the narrator in the first chapter becomes even more ambiguous. As Lynne Roberts comments in her analysis of the opening scene, the emphasis on memory in the first chapter "suggests that the narrator is going to tell her [sic] own story, the story of her childhood and her past," but unexpected spatial and temporal shifts put that conventional narrative use of memory into question. In the first pages the narrator moves, by means of a Proustian legerdemain, through several levels of time and space, with the result that at the end of the chapter the reader remains uncertain of the precise relationships existing between the narrator and the setting he (she?) has just described and between him (her?) and the little girl standing by the water.

The ambiguities regarding gender, in particular, are never really clarified. As the novel progresses and the narrator takes on a masculine identity, the reader may either forget the questions raised by the opening scene, or assume he has misread the chapter. The problem does not go away, however, for just as Mary Anne Evans remains behind George Eliot and the narrator, so does the first chapter remain anterior to the rest of the book.

Not only does one have difficulty at times *not* remembering that George Eliot is a fiction, and not only does one have trouble at times accepting the convention of the male narrator, but one also has problems with the author's use of Maggie as heroine of the book. Although Eliot gives considerable attention to the character's particular problems as a female, it is clear nonetheless that Maggie's experience is meant to be seen as generally analogous to the experiences of the other characters in

the novel, male as well as female. In other words, Maggie has a synecdochic function in the novel: she, a young girl, stands for man, for human
beings in general. When Maggie cuts her hair in anger and then immediately regrets her act and bursts into sobs, the narrator takes the opportunity to comment on the generality of the experience of adults forgetting
the importance of the tragedies of childhood, thereby reinforcing Maggie's
synecdochic role. It is at this point, however, that he chooses to express
himself as an unequivocally male (human) narrator who addresses himself
to a male (human) reader by referring to "our youth and manhood," and
common problems with frocks, trousers, and tails (I, vii, 59). Following as
it does Maggie's very particular act of defiance against her female condition, this passage from the particular to the "general" seems a jarring one.

Another, related, reason why Maggie does not function with complete success as a synecdochic character is simply that the limitations she
faces as a female set her too far apart from the male characters of the
book. If language is the currency of the economy of human experience in
the novel, then Maggie is cut off by her inability to find a performative
language of her own. Whereas in the first part of the book she is eager to
teach Tom, or the gypsies, or anyone who will listen, in the later sections
her energies are more and more directed toward her search for an authority, a Teacher. The only male character with whom she can share a truly
analogous experience is Philip, who is described as androgynous and who
is, like Maggie, excluded from the real world of men by his deformity.

Fundamental to Maggie's failure in her synecdochic role is the
logocentric, logical system on which the novel's economy of equivalences
is grounded, for that system, which permits the functioning of synecdoche, is an exclusively male domain. As Luce Irigaray demonstrates in her
reading of Western attitudes toward women from Freud backwards through
Plato, metaphysics is not only logocentric but also phallocentric. Since, in
the male paradigm, the opposite of male is not female, but nonmale, the
woman is deprived of all grounding in presence. As a result, she functions
as a kind of *charnière* or hinge, a kind of "reserve of negativity," as Irigaray
says, which assures the reproduction of the male, both biologically and
within the closed logo-/phallocentric system of representation. It is in this
context that the woman is a victim of foreclosure—shut out or barred *from
the beginning*—and that Maggie's role as a synecdochic character is doomed
to failure.

This foreclosure, this exclusion of the woman from the book's
system of equivalences, can be read clearly in the economic story of the
novel. Regardless of how one interprets its role in the book, the whole
story of Mr. Tulliver's bankruptcy and loss of the mill, and Tom's payment

of the debts and repossession of the property, is an exclusively male one. It is the father who plunges the family into bankruptcy and debt, the father who inscribes his curse against Wakem in the Bible, and the son who observes the curse, who restores the value of the Tulliver name, and regains the mill. Throughout these events, Maggie and her mother are merely passive observers and victims of the whole commercial drama. When Mrs. Tulliver falls into pathetic confusion and misery over the loss of her beloved household goods, she is distressed chiefly at the thought that her linen with the name "Elizabeth Dodson," her "maiden mark" (I, ix, 87), embroidered on it, will all "be sold, and go into strange people's houses, and perhaps be cut with the knives" (III, ii, 179). What she is losing with her name is, in fact, nothing, for although much is made of the "Dodsons and Tullivers," there is no living Dodson in the book. As Wakem reminds his son, "We don't ask what a woman does—we ask whom she belongs to" (VI, viii, 372), and all of the Dodson women belong to men. Although they frantically defend the Dodson identity, their attempt is futile; the Dodson name is part of a paternal hegemony and poor Mrs. Tulliver's identity has already been lost in the trade of commodities.

Just as Maggie's early self-styled role as teacher—as active, influential, esteemed transmitter of language—must be abandoned for the passive role of recipient, so are all the women of St. Ogg's forced into passivity or ersatz activity. The men of St. Ogg's conduct the business of the world; the "world's wife" spreads false rumors. The Mrs. Deans and Mr. Wakems possess the keys to worldly success; the Mrs. Tullivers and Mrs. Pullets possess the keys to linen cabinets. The men create, control, and exploit the networks of trade; the women sew the fabrics.

On one level, the commercial drama of *The Mill on the Floss* might be seen to provide an interesting allegory of the whole. In this context, one might play a rather fanciful game and suggest that George Eliot's somewhat problematic relationship to Maggie be understood in terms of "liquidation." According to the dictionary, the word "liquidate" comes from the late Latin *liquidāre*, meaning "to make clear," "to melt," from the Indo-European root meaning "to leave." The word can mean 1) "to pay off or settle (a debt, claim, or obligation)"; 2) "to wind up the affairs (of a business, a bankrupt estate, or the like) by determining the liabilities and applying the assets to their discharge"; 3) "to convert (assets) into cash"; 4) "to abolish"; and 5) "to kill." It is possible to find in the play of these definitions the narrative of Eliot's creation and destruction of her character Maggie.

Her writing of the novel is (1) a settling of her debt or a fulfillment of her obligation to the Feuerbachian ethic she has espoused. In introducing the character into the economy of the novel, she (3) gives her a meaning, a value. The problem is, however, that in order to insert the character into the novel's economy of equivalences, she must (Indo-European root) create a distance between her female self and her narrator, and between her female self and her character Maggie, just as George Eliot must partially abandon Mary Anne Evans. What remains are oscillations between autobiography and fiction, and between female and male—oscillations that the writer cannot entirely control. The character of Maggie is thus written into an impasse from which she is (4 and 5) rescued by death. The final balancing of the character's assets and liabilities (2), the summing up of her value, is both achieved by the grounded novel and left unachieved by the ungrounded, decentered one. Maggie is thus liquidated in the flood, but her liquidation is read both as (3) a conversion into value and (4 and 5) an obliteration.

Although it is difficult to take such a game seriously, it is possible to speculate about some of the problems Eliot might have had with the novel, and particularly with the application of her Feuerbachian principles to the character of Maggie. In the first place, the humanistic notion of a god made in the image of man is merely the converse of the whole Christian play of mirrors among God and his Son, God and man, and Christ and man, a game in which all of the actors—and the stakes—are masculine. In the second place, the Feuerbachian ethic, which makes positive moral integration into the community dependent on a movement away from egoism toward selflessness, seems to place excessive demands on the woman. For the Victorian woman who, like Maggie, had to wage a great battle to achieve any sense of self, abnegation and altruism may be seen as a return to zero.

Whatever the value of such speculation, *The Mill on the Floss* is uncontestably the battleground for remarkable conflict and violence. Throughout the novel there are instruments of penetration, tearing, cutting, and reading. In thematic terms, these scissors, nails, knives, swords, and thorns serve to threaten the fibers that bind men's hearts; and in the world of St. Ogg's, to cut the threads of the fabrics of human relation is to expose oneself to chaos and perhaps destruction. For Mrs. Tulliver, bankruptcy and disaster mean the loss of her hand-woven, monogrammed cloths to strangers who may "cut them with the knives"; for Maggie, the sense of transgression comes through the realization that "she had rent the ties that had given meaning to duty, and had made herself an outlawed soul" (VI, xiv, 413); and for the Tulliver family, at the lowest point in their fortunes (at the center of the book), home is "a torn nest pierced with thorns" (IV, ii).

If the instruments of violence serve to evoke the disorder and danger perpetually menacing the order of St. Ogg's, they also function as figurative elements of the novel's story of its own dismantling. Clearly the most dramatic moment of that story is the flood scene. As Roberts demonstrates in her essay on the book, the whole of the novel—indeed, the very process of the creation of the novel—is reenacted in that scene, where Maggie, desperately searching for home, tries to make order out of the undifferentiated landscape, "much as the narrator does in the opening pages." Her effort is not entirely successful, of course, but for the reader who looks for the consolation of closure, Maggie's return to the mill and her embrace of Tom in death represent at least a formally satisfying movement of circularity. In a deconstructive reading, however, the "masses" and "huge fragments" that appear in the last scene and cause the death of the sister and brother can be seen as the dismantled pieces of the novel itself. And underlying that scene of dismantling, in which the crisis of the fiction becomes, *en abîme*, the crisis of the text, are the many instruments of violence.

These instruments are, in a sense, allegorical equivalents of simultaneous construction and deconstruction, for they are—these pointed objects—analogues of the authorial pen. On the one hand, the pen is the symbolic instrument of the creation of all literary order. On the other, it is the instrument of writing (*écriture*), the very operation, as Derrida argues, that deconstructs the Western logocentric myth of full presence, for in the scene of writing, the signified loses its "formal essence of presence," and "always already functions as a signifier," the inscription of meaning being always the play of differences among signifiers.

When Mary Anne Evans takes the pen name of George Eliot and sets out to construct an edifying fiction through the medium of an omniscient male narrator, she assumes the "phallogocentric" power of language to appropriate meaning. And as Derrida says in his discussion of Nietzsche's "styles," such a function of language is both aggressive and defensive: "In the question of style [or form] there is always the weight or *examen* of some pointed object. . . . Such objects might be used in a vicious attack against what philosophy appeals to in the name of matter or matrix, an attack whose thrust could not but leave its mark, could not but inscribe there some imprint of form. But they might also be used as protection against the threat of such an attack, in order to keep it at a distance, to repel it. . . ." What style is protecting is "the presence, the content, the thing itself, meaning, truth—on the condition at least that it should not *already* (*déjà*) be that gaping chasm which has been deflowered in the unveiling of the difference." That condition cannot be met, of course. In the world of George Eliot/Mary Anne Evans, a world deprived of absolute grounding, the pen defends order, but it *also* tears and rends, and the covering-over of the abyss, like the containment of violence, can only be a convention, a fictional construction.

In his discussion of Nietzsche, Derrida observes that if, for that philosopher, the woman is so dangerously seductive, it is perhaps because for him "the 'woman' is not a determinable identity. . . . Perhaps woman—a non-identity, a non-figure, a simulacrum—is distance's very chasm, the outdistancing of distance. . . . Out of the depths, endless and unfathomable, she engulfs and distorts all vestige of essentiality, of identity, of property." And if, as Derrida says, the philosophical discourse founders on the shoals of woman, it is because woman is the "abyssal divergence of the truth," the untruth that is "truth." The narrative discourse, identical in this context to the philosophical discourse, flounders on the same shoals. To use Derrida's language, any writing that puts "truth" into question, that inscribes the untruth of truth, "is indeed the feminine 'operation.' Because woman is (her own) writing, style must return to her. In other words, it could be said that if style were a man . . . then writing would be a woman."

In *The Mill on the Floss*, the ordered and meaningful discourse, with its conventional logocentric grounding, its fictitious male author and fictional male narrator, finds itself ungrounded, decentered, by its female elements. Style is indeed dismantled by writing, as George Eliot is dismantled by Maggie Tulliver and Mary Anne Evans. And if the author takes such pains to assure us that the destructive and violent elements of the novel can be contained within it, it is perhaps because she herself is aware that containment is impossible. "Because, indeed," to quote Derrida once more, "if woman *is* truth, *she* at least knows that there is no truth. . . ." The narrator who speaks to the reader so fraternally of "our youth and manhood," and who guides that reader to the resolution and closure of the novel, is *also* the narrator of the first chapter, that elusive figure of indeterminate gender who, far from establishing discrete categories, puts the temporal, spatial, and narrational elements of the novel into question and declares his/her love of fluidity and "moistness" (I, i, 8).

At the end of "The Last Conflict," the final chapter of the novel, we are told that Maggie and Tom go down "in an embrace never to be parted." It seems here as if Maggie has managed—as on the day she ran away and encountered the gypsies—to transgress boundaries, to break limits, and to return, in a final synthesizing embrace, to her origin. But the embrace of Tom and Maggie, like that of the Floss and the tide, is not one of resolution but of indetermination. One can read that indetermination in the "Conclusion" that serves as an epilogue not only to the novel but to the novel's story of itself. There we are told that on Tom and Maggie's tomb are written the words "In their death they were not divided." At first appearance, the epitaph reinforces the closure of the embrace; but if we wish to go to the source of those words, to II Samuel 1:23, we find that they refer not to the union of a man and a woman, but to the union in death of Saul and his son Jonathan. Once again, even in her death, Maggie is excluded from the closed system of logocentric representation. What severs, then, as the novel's resolution, its closure, is also its point of permanent interrogation, for Maggie, deprived of full presence, is always there to tear it and rend it and open it anew.

ROBERT CASERIO

"Felix Holt" and "Bleak House"

Dickensian plot seems to be always a search for a way whereby "the novelistic real" and the "purely" nominal may be imagined to be and may become operable as action; story in Dickens insists that it represents the real world in order that it can ultimately comment on and honor its own code of acts—as it comments on and honors acts in the world outside the text—as more significant than the *maya* activity of nomination, [as Roland Barthes terms it]. But there is no doubt that a shift away from just this featuring of acts, from an interest in their defining capacity or their paramount importance for the instruction and consummation of narrative reasonings, caused Dickensian plot in its author's last ten years to decline in the estimate of readers and other novelists. We find a novelist like D. H. Lawrence, for example, pointing to George Eliot as the major revisionist of the senses of plot and action because she *internalizes* action: "You see, it was really George Eliot who started it all. . . . It was she who started putting all the action inside. Before, you know, with Fielding and the others, it had been outside. Now I wonder which is right?"

It is perhaps by the internalization of action, a step that ultimately makes action imponderable or makes it at best an arbitrary and unfixed sign in an unending series of metonymies, that George Eliot most undermines Dickens's sense of plot. Of course the impulse originating this internalization is an appeal to reality. Is there "really" and plausibly, George Eliot wonders, any one way of truthful narrative reasoning about charac-

From *Plot, Story, and the Novel: From Dickens and Poe to the Modern Period.* Copyright © 1979 by Princeton University Press.

ter, action, experience? Are narrative reasonings not always infinite and arbitrary, incapable of resolution either by thought or action? Indeed, George Eliot also wonders if there is a genuine difference between action and suffering, doing and refraining from doing. Is the difference itself not nominal (as narrative reasonings are nominal); is it not inexact and misleading to call action in both the real world and in novelistic representation creative or the only measure of creativity? And it is not only action that is imponderable. Are the characters of real or fictive men and women significantly differentiated or not? Is there not an internality of experience, an always constrained potential or intensity of feeling not expressed by action that is most synonymous with life? Because of its insistence upon such questions, the Eliotic plot, we might say, constrains itself from reaching (certainly from enacting) an answer. And this self-constraint has a powerfully ironic result: George Eliot makes such questionings the ground of the plausible "realism" of her novels, yet the persistent cultivation of the questions verges on an unintended result for the realist tradition. It results in an emphasis upon the novel as preeminently a special kind of discourse which, as Barthes puts it, "has no responsibility" to the real after all. George Eliot's questionings of Dickens's stories for the sake of realism brings the novel to the brink of the dissolution of realism, to "the *maya* activity" of linguistic classification we find later in Stein, in Woolf, and in the Joyce of *Finnegans Wake.*

Now "which *is* right," Dickens or George Eliot? Even in *this* age of criticism let us risk repeating Lawrence's naive question. Are the acts and the rescuing power of acts represented by the Dickensian sense of plot unrealistic, implausible, merely an unfolding of names—"right" only as such? If we cannot establish scientific exactitude on this point, perhaps we can at least recover Dickens's intentions for featuring acts as fruitful arbiters of meaning and happiness; perhaps we can keep his sense of plot distinct from that which is now more in vogue. To do this we shall compare two roughly complementary sequences from *Bleak House* and *Felix Holt the Radical.* I suggest *Felix Holt the Radical* documents—much better at least than "The Natural History of German Life" or than any of G. H. Lewes's criticism—George Eliot's quarrel with Dickens's way of plotting life and meaning and of featuring act. This novel exhibits similarities to *Bleak House* which indicate that George Eliot set out to rewrite Dickens's story as a way of confronting his sense of plot with her own. Her motive for the confrontation is like Carlyle's and Pater's or Stein's and Orwell's—an opposition to traditional plotted form for the sake of fiction's claim to truthfulness. She seems to have intended to illuminate by her work's contrast Dickens's narrative sensationalism and his inability to control his "*animal* intelligence, restricted to perceptions" with any plausibly plotted experience.

The resemblance between these novels is not limited to the prominence in both of a disputed inheritance mired in Chancery. The study of Mrs. Transome seems most closely to connect George Eliot's novel with that of Dickens, for like Lady Dedlock this proud and aristocratic lady needs to suppress a guilty past and suffers at the mercy of a cold and unscrupulous Chancery lawyer. George Eliot seems especially to want to criticize the implausibility of Dickens's Lady Dedlock, particularly on the grounds of an absence of credible and normative psychology in her. We can imagine Eliot criticizing the pure fictitiousness of Dickens's story in the following way: "Dickens makes Lady Dedlock all but innocent of her own sin, first by stressing her continued fidelity to a lover who deserted her twenty years before—and by asking us to believe in her continuing remorse for an incident so long buried; then by conveniently keeping her ignorant of the fact that her innocent child by her lover still lives; and finally by portraying the lawyer who tortures her as a morality-play fiend without humane affections or connections. I will not so manipulate the story of my version of Lady Dedlock. Realistically I imagine her living in full knowlege of her illegitimate child; plausibly I imagine the lawyer to be both her former lover and her present neighbor and business manager. I see their passion, true to the nature of things, as long since over. In this I have a more lifelike donnée and more potential genuine pity and fear than Dickens could achieve."

Yet there are deeper motives for an appeal to lifelikeness and plausibility than those revealed by this monologue. To clarify and illustrate the differences between Eliot and Dickens, I will now give summaries of segments of plot from each of the novels. These summaries will reproduce in detail how the stories unfold purely as sequences of act in order later to discriminate Dickens and George Eliot as imitators of action. In saying that I present "pure" sequences of act, I mean that I am presenting what happens without any appeal to theme, since we want to see if acts in Dickens and Eliot are presented as agents of meaning in themselves. This is in line with my assumption that action may initiate meaning as well as consummate it. We will want to see how the acts are featured by their authors, how and to what extent they are made to represent the rescue of life's meanings from indeterminacy, from confusion and inhibition of utterance, from unhappiness. Both sequences dramatize rescue as action and act as rescue. Here then—with apology for its necessary length—is what happens in chapters 54 through 59, the three installments of *Bleak House* that narrate the last days of Lady Dedlock's life:

Inspector Bucket of the London detective force must reveal Lady

Dedlock's past to her husband because a crowd of blackmailers, threatening to expose her to the public, demand that the old baronet pay to keep them quiet. The blackmailers include: a usurer who once was a creditor to Lady Dedlock's long-lost lover, Captain Hawdon, and who has now discovered Hawdon's love letters in the rubbish of a rag-and-bone shop where Hawdon had been living; an absurd independent minister now married to the nurse of Lady Dedlock's bastard child Esther Summerson; and a Mrs. Snagsby, the wife of a stationer to the Courts, who participates in all this to spite her husband, since she believes Hawdon's old friend, Jo, the crossing-sweep, was Mr. Snagsby's illegitimate son. Bucket has also had to prepare Sir Leicester for the suspicion that his wife has murdered the family lawyer, Tulkinghorn, because he knew her past. But the detective can now relieve Sir Leicester of this suspicion; he has lured Lady Dedlock's discharged French maid, Hortense, to the house; and once the blackmailers go, he arrests *her* as the murderess. These exposures stun Sir Leicester. Left alone in his library, he suffers a stroke and collapses.

Another suspect has already been arrested for the Lawyer's murder: George, a former army officer, and once an intimate friend of Hawdon's. Long ago George ran away from home and never returned, and it turns out that his mother is Mrs. Rouncewell, who keeps house for the Dedlocks at their country estate. The mother has steadily hoped to be reunited with her son; but George, ashamed of his youth, has refused to return. In prison he also refuses to be represented by any lawyers because Tulkinghorn has tried (unsuccessfully) to extort from him information about Hawdon's love affair and because George has also seen the fruits of Chancery practice: he runs a fencing and shooting gallery in Soho, and two victims of the Court's legal fraudulence have died on his premises. But his friends will not allow him to go unaided. The wife of an old army mate has done her own detective work, and has found out George's mother. She brings her to London from the country house, and reunites mother and son. Yet George remains in prison, since all this occurs just before Bucket arrests Hortense.

It so happens that Mrs. Rouncewell has received an unsigned letter (sent by Hortense) accusing Lady Dedlock of the crime. From the jail she has gone to her mistress, showing her the letter and asking her—without making any accusation—to help secure the release of the returned prodigal. And Lady Dedlock has endured another upsetting visit. The first man to notice a similarity between Lady Dedlock and her bastard daughter was a silly lawyer's assistant named Guppy. Gambling on the resemblance and expecting eventual profit from it, Guppy proposed to Esther. She rejected him. He did not really accept the rejection until he saw her disfigured by an attack of smallpox. Stirred by shame at his own behavior, Guppy has now turned up to tell Esther's mother that her past is public: he has just seen the blackmailers leave the house. In despair, Lady Dedlock runs away without attempting to see her husband.

Not until hours later does an old maid cousin discover Sir Leicester's stunned body in the library. He regains consciousness, but is frenzied. He cannot speak, yet wants desperately to see his wife. He tries to write inquiries about her on a slate, but learns he is partially paralyzed. Finally Bucket returns from committing Hortense and freeing George. He understands he must follow Lady Dedlock and rescue her—perhaps from suicide. Looking for a helpful clue, he stops in her bedroom, where he finds a handkerchief with Esther's name on it; he realizes she must be the illegitimate daughter (he has not heard her name, even from the blackmailers). Esther may help in winning Lady Dedlock back to her home, so Bucket sets out to find her. He succeeds, although in doing this he loses more time.

Waked out of sleep, Esther goes with Bucket first to the police station where he files a description of Lady Dedlock as a missing person and then to a Thameside spot where the river is dragged for drowned bodies. This check turns up nothing, and Bucket and the girl set off for St. Albans, the village outside London and the site of Bleak House, the home of Esther's guardian. Bucket surmises that Lady Dedlock wants to see her daughter. But there is a complication here connected with the handkerchief. Near Bleak House are located a miserable band of brickmakers, who are from time to time the objects of avowedly charitable evangelical missions. Very early in the story Esther found herself dragged along on one of these missions by a particularly outrageous do-gooder. She had at that time left her handkerchief in a brickmaker's hut, and this handkerchief had later come into the hands of Lady Dedlock. It may be, Bucket thinks, that Lady Dedlock went first to the brickmakers rather than to Bleak House to learn of Esther's whereabouts. And she has been there. But the brickmakers sullenly refuse to be helpful; they will only say that Lady Dedlock has proceeded north. Bucket and Esther move ahead as day dawns in heavy snow, sleet, and fog; with Esther close to collapse, they push through this bad weather until past nightfall. Then Bucket begins to lose his confidence. He announces in the middle of the night that they must turn around and go back to London, following the track not of Lady Dedlock but of one of the brickmaker's wives who was missing from the cottage and whom they first thought had been sent by Lady Dedlock back to London with a message for Sir Leicester or for Esther.

But Sir Leicester has received no message. Mrs. Rouncewell's reunion with her son encourages his hopes. He regains enough speech to declare to the household his forgiveness of his wife. As his daylong watch stretches into the early hours of the next morning, Esther and Bucket reenter London. The track of the brickmaker's wife has led them to Chancery Lane and the vicinity of the courts. Esther, terrified by being farther from her mother than before, recognizes Allan Woodcourt, a young surgeon, in the street; she allows him to join the search. Esther really loves Woodcourt, but she has refused to admit this to herself, especially now that she is disfigured; she has decided, instead, to marry her old benevolent guardian, Jarndyce.

The surgeon, who has just come from tending wards of the court, accompanies Esther and Bucket to Snagsby the law-stationer's, for a policeman has seen the brickmaker's wife with Snagsby's servant Guster. It happens that Guster periodically falls into violent fits of hysteria, and she is in one at the moment. The jealous Mrs. Snagsby, thinking that the visit had something to do with the infidelities she ascribes to her bewildered husband, has made the girl senseless with fear of punishment or dismissal. Woodcourt manages to calm her, and secures the message Guster has in fact received. It is a statement of remorse, and it announces Lady Dedlock's intention to be lost to the world. Where then is the brickmaker's wife? She has asked directions to a wretched burial ground nearby—the place in fact where Esther's father (though this is unknown to Esther) is buried in a pauper's grave. The pursuers follow her there, and they see a woman lying in the snow and refuse on the steps of the graveyard. Yet it is not the brickmaker's wife but Lady Dedlock. She had the day before changed clothes with the other woman in order more effectively to lose herself. Esther recognizes her mother, but Lady Dedlock is dead—as we are told—"of terror and her conscience."

So much then for a summary of the content of six chapters of Dickens's novel—six chapters out of sixty-seven. These chapters do not unravel the plot to its end, since the novel has yet to narrate the close of the monumental case of Jarndyce and Jarndyce, the death of Richard Carstone, and the resolution of Esther's love for Woodcourt.

Now the parallel sequence of chapters 44 through 50 in *Felix Holt the Radical* gives us Lady Dedlock's "descendant," Mrs. Transome, meeting her nemesis:

Felix Holt the Radical is in prison, awaiting trial on a charge of manslaughter. He had tried to control an anarchic riot of workingmen on a national election day, but his attempt had in fact made him appear as one of the leaders of the uproar. The riot issued in two deaths. One of the dead men was the last of a line of claimants to the estate of Harold Transome, a Radical candidate in the election. His death makes way for the rightful claimant to the estate from a collateral line: a poor Dissenting minister's daughter, Esther Lyon, who has fallen in love with Felix, though she scarcely acknowledges this to herself.

While Felix is in prison, Esther has gone to live in Transome Court. Harold and his mother know they must resign their estate to her, and have chosen to befriend her. Esther has always dreamed of such an inheritance. When Harold begins to fall in love with her it seems that Esther will have the opportunity to become a great lady without, after all, needing to turn the Transomes out of their hereditary home. But a prison interview with Felix reminds her sharply of her love, especially since Felix remains undaunted in the social and moral idealism she loves him for. At the trial Felix defends himself (he distrusts the honesty of the legal system, and he has distrusted the honesty of the elections); Harold Transome, hoping to please Esther, gives testimony in Felix's favor; and Esther suddenly and dramatically steps forward to testify to the goodness of Felix's intentions. But he is found guilty and sentenced to four years in prison.

However, a number of the county leaders, including Transome, have been stirred by Felix's predicament, and they put aside political differences to meet and to secure him a pardon. Transome is followed to this meeting by the family lawer, Jermyn, against whom Harold has started a Chancery suit for mismanagement of the Transome estates. Harold is prosecuting this suit partly out of spite because Jermyn has not helped him win the election. Now Jermyn has in fact mismanaged the estate, and has lined his pockets with income from it. But frustrated and violent, Jermyn intends to goad Harold into giving up the suit, if need be, by revealing Mrs. Transome's past. At the close of the public meeting Harold, infuriated by Jermyn's pursuit of him, strikes Jermyn in the face with a whip. Jermyn blurts out that he is Harold's father. Harold, Jermyn, and Mrs. Transome are now publicly exposed.

Returned to Transome Court, Harold tells Esther that a family disgrace makes it necessary for him to resign the estate at once; he also resigns any personal claims he has made upon her, if that is her desire. To Esther the great estate now represents only an inheritance of pain and moral mediocrity; she can think only of Felix. She has no assurance of a life with him in the future, but although she makes her choice in the dark, she chooses to give up her claim. Her choice is reinforced by a last interview with Mrs. Transome. "The dimly-suggested tragedy of this woman's life, the dreary waste of years empty of trust and affection, afflicted [Esther] even to horror." With this, Esther returns to her father's humble house.

Where shall we begin to discriminate assumptions about story, plot, and rescuing action as they appear in these two novelistic sequences? Three things strike us immediately. First, on the surface at least, Dickens's sequence seems to dramatize a defeat of rescue, whereas Eliot's dramatizes a success—the pardon that rescues Felix. How does this appearance square with our thesis that the rescue is a positive for Dickens and at best a wary ambivalence for Eliot? Second, there appears to be no equivalent in Eliot's story of Buckets and French maids, Snagsbys and Gusters, stray handkerchiefs and similar confusing particulars. Dickens seems to be simultaneously insisting upon the relevance of every detail to his plot and to his characters' actions and upon the allowance of no arbitrariness of detail. Thirdly, Eliot seems far more plausible than Dickens; in her we see the apparently greater normativeness of psychology and experience. To have Lady Dedlock, in clothes underlining her degradation, end at the grave of the lover she has thought dead for twenty years: is this not a most strained coincidence, a manipulation of Lady Dedlock's meaning, and a forcing of action to speak authoritatively and without arbitrariness about her? If Dickens wants to feature the place of action in plot, should he not at least make his action plausible?

Since we come back to the issue of plausibility, perhaps we can best examine the phenomenon of action in both writers by focusing on their plotting of coincidences—for coincidences seem, at least to many readers, the greatest strain upon plausibility in the summarized chapters from *Bleak House*, where they stare out at us far more obviously than in the chapters from *Felix Holt the Radical*. Both novelists seem to make use of coincidence to argue that human connection and interrelation are life's most important facts. But Dickens seems to want to exaggerate integrations by making his story complexly bristle with coincidences; of course he would have defended his practice by claiming he modelled it on life. On the other hand, George Eliot appears to play down or to oppose coincidence and plotted complexity even at the same time as she uses them, for this seems to her to be more responsible to what is real. *Up to a point*, this strategy or responsibility to reality in George Eliot is a featuring of action. For action is purposive creative motion, and when Eliot presents coincidences at first sight as accidents but upon reflection as intellectually and morally purposeful motions and relations, she is using plot's representation of action as an agent that rescues life's appearances from their lack of connection and their arbitrariness of meaning.

But there is a curious, emphatic, and highly characteristic qualification of this featuring of the rescuing agency of plot in Eliot. She gives with one hand and takes away with the other. She plots to reveal accidents as somehow purposefully creative, but she also makes them seem incapable of being principal or enduring agents of meaning. In Eliot there is an arbitrary relation between what is done and narrative reasonings about what is done that always threatens to return action to the form of accident. And this constant threat to the significance of action, which in its turn threatens to return meaning itself to the form of accident or to mere nomination, is also offered by Eliot as most plausibly representative of "the real." Although we may not see much of accident and coincidence in the summarized chapters, their content is deeply threatened by accident and coincidence. The realism of George Eliot ultimately depends upon periodic strenuous exertion against this threat and also upon periodic capitulation to it. Those who find her representation of life most plausible find it so because she presents actions and the narrative reasonings they stimulate as unclear, unresolved problematics of experience.

Whenever Eliot uses plot, narrative reason, or action she uses them to mean something that humbles them, something that means the resistance of life to imitation, explanation, or consummation. Even the normative psychology we associate with Eliot is a form of narrative reasoning about life; and Eliot uses this, but also casts it in doubt. Perspectives on or of the self do not *consummate* themselves in the certainty of a normative psychology in Eliot any more than life-perspectives consummate themselves in clearly definable action in her work. In Eliot's sense of plot there is a connection between praxis in general and practical jokes—a connection that is ominous because the practical joke, though purposeful, is also dangerously close to contingency and seems invariably to become accident. Through the practical joke Eliot can portray experience itself as a prank, an intention "to mean" that is co-opted by resistance to meaning. For example, the riot that leads to Felix's imprisonment is the result of a prank. Workmen at the election cuff and goad each other: it is "fun . . . in danger of getting rather serious." The ensuing uproar *is* serious, and accidentally overtakes Felix to whom

> pressed along with the multitude into Treby Park, his very movement seemed . . . only an image of the day's fatalities, in which the multitudinous small wickednesses of small selfish ends, really undirected towards any larger result, had issued in widely-shared mischief that might yet be hideous.

The passage implies that movement directed purposefully and unselfishly towards larger results is not fatal but creative, and that it is hence significant action. In Eliot meaning results—is rescued from indeterminacy—when coincidences or "sports" are disclosed as the adjuncts of purposes and deeds that make a significant and certain difference to their contexts. But how truly and lastingly is this significance established?

If we examine the roots of the revelatory explosion between Harold and Jermyn, we will find at first a chain of events that Eliot demonstrates is accidental and coincidental in appearance but purposeful in fact. The conflict between the unknown father and the bastard son begins with Esther's knowledge of her right to the Transome estate. This knowledge is caused by the accidental discovery by Felix of a lost wallet and the accidental discovery of another heir to the Transome estate by the man who loses the wallet. The wallet belongs to the valet of a local Tory landowner; the valet is (by the way) an old friend of Esther's dead unknown father, a captain named Maurice Christian Bycliffe. At the captain's death the friend received tokens of Bycliffe's marriage to Esther's mother, a Frenchwoman. For his own personal reasons the valet now calls himself Maurice Christian, and he carries Bycliffe's mementos on his person. Christian belongs to a large, boorish retinue of servants addicted to pranks. He has been sarcastic about his fellow servant the butler, and the butler wants revenge. One afternoon the butler discovers Christian asleep on the estate grounds, and he thinks it a good practical joke to cut off part of the sleeper's coat. In this part, which he tosses into the shrubbery, are the mementos and a wallet belonging to Christian's master, who is the Tory candidate for parliament. Felix finds this fragment and its contents; he brings them to Esther's foster-father Lyon because as a Radical Felix does not want to visit a Tory household. Subsequently, the minister's questioning alerts Christian to the possibility that Bycliffe's heir is alive and has a claim to the Transome estate. But yet another accident and prank must intervene before the Bycliffe heir is found. Christian happens to play a joke on the other heir, Tommy Trounsem, the idiot who will die in the riot. In the course of the joke he learns that Jermyn employed a second lawyer to help administer the Transome estate. Christian looks up this lawyer, puts information from him together with what he already knows about Bycliffe, and then sells what he knows to Harold. The information frees Harold from dependence on Jermyn, and frees him, besides, to start the law suit against the man who is his father.

Now we may certainly accept this as George Eliot's elaboration by means of coincidence of the rich interconnections of experience's threads; and we can certainly see that she is attempting to show that whatever happens, even sheer accident, is pervaded by an intellectual and moral purposiveness that will bend coincidences to its own ends. This purposiveness is natural and plausible, not mysterious; the natural political divisions of the county, for example, get mixed up with the return of the wallet, and hence ordinary politics reveal Esther's background. We may say that George Eliot attempts to *naturalize* coincidence by rescuing it from its arbitrary accidental quality. By naturalizing coincidence, she makes it plausible—real—in essence continuous with genuine action.

But once her plot has moved forward to rescue life from indeterminacy of relation, Eliot's story moves back on itself, humbling its shaping and reasoning power, returning what it represents to indeterminacy. The meaningful agency of action is threatened, for Eliot presents it as a purposive motion that bears no discernible fruit, that creates no defining, fixed transformations. Uncertain in its effects, action again becomes unknowable and indefinable; it seems to make even less a difference to life than coincidences or pranks. When Felix is being rescued from prison, Eliot pointedly makes this genuine act of rescue (purposeful, deliberated, not a practical joke) merely the background of the undoing of the Transomes. Just when Harold and the landowners are repeating their author's form of naturalizing coincidence by making sense out of the nonsense that has engulfed Felix, Eliot shows their action broken in upon by the meaningless, wasted, and hence "coincidental" life that Mrs. Transome's old relation to Jermyn represents. What looks like a creative rescue action for Felix is also uncertain. Liberated from imprisonment, Felix—as we shall see—is delivered over to another form of constraint, as if the rescue made no difference, was not meaningful. And whereas the accidental revelation of kinship between Harold and Jermyn seems creative in itself—the making or re-making of an important relation—the tie is made only to be at once unmade. Harold Transome discovers his real father, but the discovery intensifies Harold's immobility and isolation. Esther, newly seeing the connection between the Transome estate and the Transomes' misery, resigns her inheritance. But what she exchanges the inheritance for is nothing as definite as action: it is the hope of uncertain future creativity and satisfaction. This is also Felix's "gain" in exchange for prison. As for Lady Transome, she becomes more isolated and more dreary and immobilized than she has yet been.

The actions of Eliot's characters do not express what they are intended to express. In compensation for this, it appears that an inhibition of action is accompanied by an enlargement of vision: it makes the characters see more than they saw previously. Harold sees his relation to Jermyn; Esther sees in Lady Transome a person she may come to resemble. But what is seen impresses us as relations that are virtual rather than real. The reader, like Eliot's characters, sees a sign of relation and its referent, but does not see a further actual relation that realizes the connection between the two. In Eliot's world relations are more virtual than actual: they are glimpsed or named, hypothesized rather than substantiated. And this is true of relation in two senses: as connection among persons and events and as narrative reason. Like relation, action and meaning in Eliot are evanescent glimpses, hypotheses whose substantiation seems now imminent, now receding. This virtuality of action and meaning is emblematized in Eliot's way of presenting the self as also a curiously virtual rather than actual nature or identity. She wonders how the self establishes its characteristics and its meanings: Is it through deeds, through feelings, through externalizing utterances and expressions, through identity with others? And she asks, in what way is the self identical with others? Certainly not through its acts, since, in general, acts in Eliot are no more determinately meaningful than those we have described. In Eliot, the self is (at the very least) double, and it is always anxiously constrained from an imagined full utterance: if it expresses itself in sympathy, it cannot express itself in action; if it commits its meaning to action, it loses the meaning of its feelings. As an internalized arena of reflection, the self repeats the condition of action and meaning as Eliot usually presents them: as a continuous interweaving of significance and arbitrariness, a paradoxical indeterminate or virtual determination.

The self in Eliot is "plausible"—and "normative"—because it is an unclear, unresolved problematic. We can see this in Chapter 49, in Esther's interview with Harold just before she leaves Transome Court. Esther wants to know if the public meeting has rescued Felix; but she must restrain her curiosity, since her love for Felix in effect injures Harold. She feels herself very different from Harold, so different that he repels her. Yet *is* she, the Transome heir, different from Harold? And is *he* so different from Felix, especially since he has just done more practical good for Felix than Felix has in fact yet done for anyone? Does action define the differences between the two selves meeting each other? Are Esther and Harold not identical in their inner potential for action and feeling, for bearing good and bad fruit? Why then is each self—as an arena of sympathy and of anxious restraint of sympathy, of simultaneously determined and indeterminate character—not identical with the other but rather its antagonist? The questions are not to be resolved.

> As Esther sat . . . along with the empty chair which suggested the coming presence, the expectation of his beseeching homage brought with it an impatience and repugnance which she had never felt before. . . . Harold appeared.
>   He had recovered his self-possession since his interview with his

mother. . . . He had been occupied with resolute thoughts, determining to do what he knew that perfect honour demanded, let it cost him what it would. . . . It is true he had a glimpse . . . of reward; but it was not less true that he would have acted as he did without that hope or glimpse. It was the most serious moment in Harold Transome's life: for the first time the iron had entered into his soul, and he felt the hard pressure of our common lot, the yoke of that mighty resistless destiny laid upon us by the acts of other men as well as our own.

When Esther looked at him she relented, and felt ashamed of her gratuitous impatience. She saw that his mind was in some way burdened. But then immediately sprang up the dread that he had to say something hopeless about Felix.

They shook hands in silence, Esther looking at him with anxious surprise. He released her hand, but it did not occur to her to sit down, and they both continued standing on the hearth.

This scene epitomizes George Eliot's sense of plot, her curious way of featuring act and of internalizing action in the self. The silence and constraint in which both figures remain standing typifies how George Eliot presents action and self as at best the stress of a potential—a possibility or virtuality of meaning or realization rather than a definite, externalized release or "rescuing" fulfillment of them. Moreover, the act "realized" is described as a hard pressuring yoke: an act, then, is scarcely more valuable or creative than an accident. Action also seems to obstruct the sympathetic identification of one self with another, for Esther and Harold can be intimate only in a speechless and motionless state of restraint. In the preceding passage it is action and definition of self—exteriorization of self through action—that is being held at bay as a threat. Consequently, in silence and stillness, in internality, there is perhaps as much meaning, and more, as in externalizing articulation and motion.

The difficulty this virtuality and internality poses for meaning, for any narrative reasoning that does not check meaning's confident motions, may be exemplified by a comparison of the final states of Mrs. Transome and Felix. The two characters are supposedly different, since we can call the first a failure, the second a success. Yet this difference is indeed nominal—for what meaning can we assign it? Why is Felix happier in *his* hap than Mrs. Transome in hers? Mrs. Transome's last punishment is the lonely and monotonous existence that finds no outlet in action. Her life is ultimately no more significant than a prank, an arbitrary purposeless happening. The older woman's entrapment "afflicts Esther to horror." Surely a significantly active life would rescue Mrs. Transome from despair. Yet the wisdom of the novel, identified with Felix's speeches, is to accept this horror as identical with the fruitful order of things. If Eliot's characters believe that they can enact their lives and rescue them from indeterminacy of meaning and of fulfillment according to plots they willfully fashion and execute, their stories show that this belief must be modified or given up by even the best of them. The plotting motion of consciousness is an arbitrary actor and signifier; its externalizations meet an arbitrary fate and do not consummate perspectives and meanings. Felix understands this, and knows that, in spite of his virtue, his future will be brought to birth as an immobilization rather like Mrs. Transome's. So his plan and plots do *not* feature acts, only the constraint and doubtfulness of acts. They also feature the virtuality rather than the realization or consummation of meaning. He will do work that is "small" and "close at hand." He tells Esther:

> As to just the amount of result [a man] may see from his particular work—that's a tremendous uncertainty. I put effects at their minimum, but I'd rather have the minimum of effect, if it's of the sort I care for. . . .
> Where great things can't happen, I care for very small things, such as will never be known beyond a few garrets and workshops.

So much for the result of action. Is the cause not the same as the result? The initiation of action, whether it be the riot, the rescue, Esther's resignation, or Felix's work, is also "a tremendous uncertainty"—in its own way an accident or coincidence. Among the small things close at hand is another uncertainty, the self. Felix's garrets and workshops, like the silent room in which Esther and Harold speechlessly face each other, are symbols of the interior space of the self, an at once damnable and blessed uncertainty for Eliot similar to that of action. The presentation of life as such uncertainty is the final fruit of Eliot's attempt to naturalize coincidence and to put the action "inside"—her attempt to rescue life from meaninglessness by featuring act and her undoing of the rescue simultaneously by featuring the reality of arbitrariness and indeterminacy. Barthes tells us that the novelistic real is not operable, cannot be put into practice; *Felix Holt the Radical* leaves us wondering whether practice is operable or other than arbitrarily significant within the real itself.

But we must turn back now to Dickens, for what George Eliot presents as reality and what she makes of action and its creative rescuing agency is shaped by her antagonism to his rendition of life and to his plotting of life's form. Dickens does *not* naturalize coincidence in his story; he points up strikingly grotesque accidental interrelations in order to stress the literal nature of coincidence because for him this will make it possible to feature action and rescue. For Dickens, coincidence simply does not

threaten action, plausibility, or meaning. But what is especially coincidental in Dickens? In his kind of story, coincidence (however it may
appear in our summary), has less to do with action, with accidental
events, than with character. Dickens's sense of plot relies upon a notion
that small groups of separate characters or persons are somehow all the
same character or person. Dickens sees character as an aspect of literal
coincidence; and his characters themselves, in shock and wonder, recognize the ways in which they are practically each other.

To speak of coincidence in Dickens is thus to speak of exact
agreements among events or persons rather than, as in Eliot, of accidental
agreements. Where there are exact agreements we feel the presence of
meaning—a realizing rather than a virtualizing of significance. Dickens
uses the coinciding of identity to represent movement towards the realization of meaning in the lives of his characters. We may consider the
apparently individuated or differentiated character of Esther Summerson
in order to see how her differences from others break down. In a chapter
prior to those summarized, Lady Dedlock searches out Jo, so that he will
show her her former lover's grave. In doing this she disguises herself as her
maid Hortense. Tulkinghorn sees her in this disguise and to make sure he
has seen rightly, once she is discharged, he pays Hortense to undergo a
meeting with Jo. Jo identifies Hortense as the lady he showed the grave
to. Then Hortense speaks and shows Jo her hand, and Jo has to admit she
is different. Yet he remains rather obstinate about his impression: "It is
her and it ain't her," he says.

A little later he falls sick. Under Tulkinghorn's direction, Bucket
has been moving Jo out of London; in a delirium caused by disease Jo has
wound up at the brickmakers' cottages in St. Albans. Esther hears of this,
and she and her maid, Charley, go to help him. On the way Esther feels
something uncanny: "I had for a moment an undefinable impression of
myself as being something different from what I then was." In Jo her
feeling finds an immediate response:

> The boy staggered up instantly, and stared at me with a remarkable
> expression of surprise and terror.
>
> "The lady there. She's come to get me to go along with her to the
> berryin ground. I won't go to the berryin ground. I don't like the name on
> it. She might go a-berryin me." His shivering came on again, and as he
> leaned against the wall, he shook the hovel.
>
> "He has been talking off and on about such like, all day, ma'am,"
> said Jenny the brickmaker's wife softly. "Why, how you stare! This is *my*
> lady, Jo."
>
> "Is it?" returned the boy. . . . "She looks to me the t'other

one. It ain't the bonnet, nor yet it ain't the gownd, but she looks
to me the t'other one."

Jo goes on to ask Charley, "Ain't the lady the t'other lady?" And he then
exclaims: "If she ain't the t'other one, she ain't the forenner. Is there *three*
of 'em then?" Intentionally or not, Esther has already partly answered Jo's
question by feeling that she is both herself—and a different being.

Esther is in fact at least "three." When she sees her mother's body,
she is asking in her own way, "Ain't the lady the t'other lady?" "I saw
before me, lying on the step," she insists, "the mother of the dead child."
She means the brickmaker's wife, whose dead baby she had covered with
the significant handkerchief. But these words suit Lady Dedlock as well,
for part of her tragedy had been the belief that her child died at birth. And
in a very damaging way Esther has taken to heart her godmother's
conviction that she would have been better off unborn. Esther lives as a
kind of self-repressing spectre, as if she had survived the end of her own
life. So Esther does discover the mother of the dead child (herself) at the
end of the chase. And the uncanny interidentity of Lady Dedlock, Hortense,
and Esther extends itself: Esther is also like Jo, the diseased orphan, and
like Guster, the Snagsby's hysterical orphan maid. It is arguable that there
is a similar interidentity for each of the characters in *Bleak House*.

This literalizing of coincidental identity in Dickens means that
Dickens plots in order *not* to "put all the action" inside. If the Dickens
characters feel the need to resolve conflicts within themselves, they
discover—as the reader discovers—that the conflicts are not imponderable
and inexpressible but defined in others who are outward personifications
of the conflicts they feel within. For Dickens individuation is in effect
illusory, and thus the only way for persons to resolve conflicts among the
"others" who are simultaneously themselves is through an action that
represents in a literal external event—a rescue event—any one individual's attempt to rescue his life from a predicament. If this predicament is,
for example, that the character cannot establish his purposes, cannot
mean in life what he intends fully to mean, then the rescue can effect this
meaning; for Dickens insists that action, what we do, is not imponderable, not merely arbitrary naming but is the field in which we can bring
arbitrariness to an end, in which we can clarify and actualize meaning,
connecting signs with referents and consummating perspectives. Whereas
in reaction to Dickens Eliot ends by stressing the problematic nature of
identity and action, Dickens begins with this problematic and ends with
at least half of it resolved. For Dickens sees his characters as an arbitrary
metonymic chain, whose links come to accept—without any Eliotic con-

tradiction or qualification—their purely nominal differences (differences that make no difference) in exchange for the sake of making a clear and definite difference for each other on the level of action. Dickens's responsibility to the real is manifested in his belief that reality is preeminently an urgent and practicable desire for a liberation from arbitrariness and indefiniteness of action, from doing's entanglement with undoing.

Is this object of Dickens's representation less plausible or verisimilar than the indeterminacy that Eliot represents? The rescue is Dickens's version of the romance quest, which once had its basis in experience and which Dickens attempts to return to the same basis. He wants to make it appear probable that what we ordinarily do or what we can do has undeniable and operable creative efficacy. Whether or not we agree that he succeeds in making this plausible, we must remember that if the plots of Dickens's delegated agents, his characters, had no fulfilling or defining issue as action, chaos and despair would reign in their world. The prevailing sense of life in *Bleak House* is of a waking nightmare described by Esther during her disfiguring illness: "Strung together somewhere in great black space, there was a flaming necklace, or ring, or starry circle of some kind, of which I was one of the beads! . . . It was . . . inexplicable agony to be part of the dreadful thing." The possibility of plot, of creatively willful and purposeful action, is for Dickens and his characters the hope of rescue and release from this circle of pain. The hope of rescue and release is not confined, as we might say it is in Eliot, to making the dreadful thing explicable by means of defining articulations that come and go or remain virtual; the release here is tied to the possibility of an action that will explain the thing—and that will realize the explanation by consummating it as a clear, enacted rescue from what is dreadful.

How one self acts out the rescue from the circle of pain of another self with which it coincides is made possible in part by the fact that the self is situated in time, which for Dickens does not close down opportunity but continually renews it. If a Dickensian character has missed an opportunity to solve a predicament for himself in *his* time, the crucial time returns in the present predicament of a double. Lady Dedlock's earlier maid, Rosa, is a double of her mistress in her youth, especially since Rosa, in loving the industrialist's son, Watt, repeats the dilemma between spontaneous love and class distinctions that victimized Lady Dedlock. Lady Dedlock helps Rosa overcome those distinctions, thereby contributing to her own self-redeeming rescue. Similarly, we can assume that both Richard Carstone and Captain George duplicate the self-dislike and indolence of Hawdon in his last years, when he went by the name of Nemo. But although Richard sinks along with Nemo, we are made to feel that something of both is saved in the rescue of George by Mrs. Bagnet. Doubles of the past selves of unhappy characters suffering from some choice made or not made in an earlier time can thus be rescued from their past choices by the help of those whose present problems duplicate the past's. In George Eliot's "little world of man or woman" the time of significant opportunity does not return with the same clearly discernible possibility of rescuing transformation.

But how can we speak of successful and creative rescue-acts in the face of the example of Lady Dedlock's loss and death? In answer we can say that even the apparently unsuccessful rescue attempt shows how the actions of men and women speak a definitive truth or meaning about themselves and their inner feelings. Attempting to evade her rescuers, Lady Dedlock's evasion itself spells out what the rescue can accomplish: it makes the dynamic structure of social reality fully and unequivocally visible; it brings some aspect of ultimate truth and interrelation into sight. Hence the rescue-act is meaningful—it constitutes meaning as well as consummates it; it is not only a saving of persons but a rescue of truth from illusions and obscurities. For example, Lady Dedlock's assumed prole-tariat disguise acts out a truth concerning social relations and morality: worn by an aristocrat, the worker's costume has the effect of showing how little sexual "sin" weighs in contrast to the general human exploitation on which privileged social order is founded. The rescue and the sense of plot that imitates the rescue transform life's potential or secret relationships and values into clarified and openly enacted and acknowledged ones. This revelation of relations and their meaning would not come about other-wise: indeed many of the "worst" characters in Bleak House would rather not share their identities with others, would rather evasively speculate on or "feel" truth than enact it, but we can see in Skimpole how little this kind of evasion triumphs or counts!

Unsuccessful in delivering Lady Dedlock from death, the rescue attempt and action succeeds nevertheless in bringing into definitive light the complex truth of the characters' relations. And at the same time there is a way in which Lady Dedlock rescues herself. Dying of terror and remorse, she also fulfills her life as she wants to fulfill it. She ends by uttering as action, without arbitrariness, her love for Hawdon. Exactly equating her self with her passion, she uses action to establish what she wants definitively to mean to herself and the world. Thus her end is not tragic as was the previous internalization of her passion. And personal issues aside, if only because of the challenge to society's repressions made by the release of Lady Dedlock's passion, her act and even her death are creative. They illustrate both the torture of repression by which society partly functions and the ultimate victory, in spite of the torture, of what is repressed.

In contrast, it is interesting to note how George Eliot tends to equate the externalizing of intense passion with destruction: in *Felix Holt the Radical* Mrs. Transome's old passion for Jermyn is a prototype of the novel's riot. In the Dickensian version of enacted passion, all personal intensities of feeling work their way purposefully and creatively into external form; they are also not potential or virtual, not closed within the silent inexpressible nature of self. What one character may be prevented from acting out, another just like him will succeed in acting out; in effect this makes both characters active agents. And Dickens even countenances the creativity of violent deeds for the truth and feeling that violence rescues from repression or inhibition. For example, the hatred for Tulkinghorn that Lady Dedlock suppresses and that Esther would refuse to recognize in herself must issue as a force and an act in their story. Hortense has no right to eliminate Tulkinghorn, yet his murder is—in relation to the characters for whom Hortense doubles—creative by virtue of its transla-tion of their righteous hatred into an event. In the end, Lady Dedlock's death acts out her love for Hawdon, her defeat of her enemy, and the social truth of her life. Can we possibly feel this as a loss, as a defeat of the rescue? Whereas Felix Holt is only nominally rescued, Lady Dedlock rescues her own life from its nominal status, unshakeably differentiating its reality from its appearance.

On the surface, then, a comparison of our summaries seems to show Felix saved and Lady Dedlock lost and Eliot's story less accidental and coincidental than that of Dickens, but in fact the opposite is true because Dickens's plotting does not undermine action. To do so would be for Dickens a humbling of his form. It is not pride, however, that makes Dickens refuse this humbling. Dickens synonymizes rescue, plot, and labor: the rescue of life's meaning from arbitrariness and indeterminacy is the novelist's work, and it is also apparently Dickens's way of seeing all work. We have already noted George Eliot's own attention to a possible identification of rescue, plot, and labor by considering the efficacy of action through Felix's dedication to the work of small garrets and work-shops. In Esther Summerson's nightmare vision of the circle of pain, the agony results as much from the way work in the nightmare counts for nothing—rescues no fruit from chaos—as from the way Esther feels herself to be three separate identities:

> While I was very ill, the way in which . . . divisions of time became confused with one another, distressed my mind exceedingly. At once a child, an elder girl, and the little woman I had been so happy as, I was

not only oppressed by cares and difficulties adapted to each station, but by the great perplexity of endlessly trying to reconcile them.

In my disorder—it seemed one long night, but I believe there were both nights and days in it—. . . I labored up colossal staircases, ever striving to reach the top, and ever turned, as I have seen a worm in a garden path, by some obstruction, and laboring again. I knew perfectly at intervals, and I think vaguely at most times, that I was in my bed; . . . yet I would find myself complaining "O more of these never-ending stairs, Charley—more and more—piled up to the sky, I think!" and laboring on again.

The rescue action reconciles the apparently differing selves; the rescue is the labor that breaks down factitious differences and overcomes obstructions to the realization of life as unqualifiedly coherent form. Esther's persistence in labor shows a sense of plot like Dickens's own, working on to resolve obstructions and to enact the formative and definite release of what is obstructed. The dignity and necessity of the attempt is to be measured by the intense desire for reconciliation and by the strong resistance that it meets: we note "the great perplexity of endlessly trying to reconcile" the large disparities of experience as well as its minute details. For Dickens, labor is this attempt at reconciliation—and its successful achievement. To point up his characters' urgent dedication to plot as the featuring of act and to feature enacted plot in life as the labor that rescues life's meaning from indeterminacy (and even its minutiae from insignificance), Dickens reproduces Esther's nightmare staircases during Mrs. Bagnet's rescue of George in Chapter 50. Mrs. Bagnet is bringing George's mother to London by coach, and Dickens describes the landscape through which the coach passes:

Railroads shall soon traverse all this country, and with a rattle and a glare the engine and train shall shoot like a meteor over the wide night-landscape, turning the moon paler. . . . Preparations are afoot, measurements are made, ground is staked out. Bridges are begun, and their not yet united piers desolately look at one another over roads and streams, like brick and mortar couples with an obstacle to their union; fragments of embankments are thrown up, and left as precipices with torrents of carts and barrows tumbling over them; tripods of tall poles appear on hilltops, where there are rumours of tunnels; everything looks chaotic, and abandoned in full hopelessness.

This landscape repeats the landscape of Esther's dream. But the work being done here looks chaotic only because it is interrupted. It urgently needs completion. The rescue is labor that finally does make the staircases lead somewhere. In the six chapters of *Bleak House* that we have summarized, labor is not only the attempt to rescue Lady Dedlock and George; it is also the baronet's willed recovery of his lost speech, the attempt to allay Guster's fears, and Esther's struggle against the return of the dissociated sensations of her disease. For Dickens, each of these struggles is heroic, since each opposes a disease and paralysis that is communal as well as personal. The social and historical community represented in *Bleak House* is founded on deliberate dissociations. It is committed to a collective self-deceiving and self-punishing evasion of the need to reconcile the disparities and details of experience. In the labor of their rescues Dickens's actors bring to birth a new vision and enactment of community. Plot dramatized as a rescue action by Dickens represents the full humanization of work: a purposive and practicable exertion to liberate, renew, and make significant the total life of its agents.

. . . We need to consider, at least more explicitly than we have so far, the bearing of each writer's sense of plot on the writer's ideas about moral conduct. Narrative intellectual reason merges imperceptibly but undeniably with moral reasoning, with ethical generalizations about action. Clearly in *Nicholas Nickleby* Dickens uses plot not only as a rescue of meaning but as an encouragement to the moral dimension in relational thought. In speaking of the interrelations of plot, labor, and the rescue, we have been treating the relation of plot to representations of ideal conduct as well as of meaningfulness. The labor that reconciles contradictory perspectives in experience is for Dickens a model of the activity that makes us good as well as happy.

The rightness or goodness of conduct that is underwritten by George Eliot's storytelling is more difficult to formulate. We see in Esther Lyon and Felix a desire for reconciliations of the Dickensian kind, and this desire appears as a moral guide to conduct; but Eliot suggests it is also good that this desire be checked. For if it is not checked, there is the chance that Esther Lyon will reconcile her perspectives with Lady Transome's by an uttering and enacting of passion—even if it is asocial in tendency or intensity—in the way Esther Summerson reconciles her internal conflicts by acting out her violences of feeling through her mother and Hortense. Perhaps for Eliot what is most right for conduct, in a way that directly complements her sense of plot, is a form of passivity or quiescence resulting from a vigilant skepticism towards the self's plots, towards their motives and ends, towards their possible manipulations of life and intrusions upon the lives of others. The scene in the library epitomizes the restraint of conduct as a good of conduct: the good of conduct is an intense and passionate inward feeling rather than an overt passionate doing. In its moral dimension the Dickensian rescue plot becomes in Eliot a rescue-passion, an ideal of conduct understood as a particular kind of intense but quiescent feeling rather than a rescue-act.

Nevertheless, at the end of her career George Eliot, in a wonderfully curious artistic reversal, published *Daniel Deronda*, a novel whose "male" half at least—Deronda's story—is pervaded by memories of a Dickensian sense of plot, by the rescue action. Some attention to *Daniel Deronda's* plot, then, is especially in order in an examination of Eliot's relation to Dickens. It is my belief that what induced Eliot to take up the structure of the plot that she had deliberately subverted was the moral dimension she wanted finally to give to "the rescue." Now for Dickens and Eliot the moral value as well as the truth of "the rescue" has a relation to the "conduct" of passion—especially of sexual passion—and also to their sense of the possibilities of personal development and maturation. If we briefly examine these subjects in each of these novelists, we can more cleary grasp Eliot's *moral* revision of the Dickensian rescue.

In *Bleak House* Dickens is concerned to show that plot is not only synonymous with purposeful, willed labor and action but with passion as well. For Dickens thinks that what is done purposefully, even the rescue itself, will be ineffectual and sterile or at the very least weighted down with melancholy if it is not reconciled with passion. If Esther, for example, were to "submit" to her nightmare, she would marry Jarndyce and not Woodcourt; she would thus divorce passion from her activity. This would be a disaster for her, a masochistic evasion of her desire, a self-punishment of the very kind that her upbringing and the normative way of life in *Bleak House* have imposed on her. Jarndyce's moral heroism is that he refuses to allow her to submit to his desire rather than to her own, for he rescues Esther from the self-deprecating and inhibiting evasion of her passion for Woodcourt. Yet for poor Jarndyce this rescue demands that he plot against his own passion. And Dickens is unhappy with this, for he would like to show that the rescue action is compatible with passion, that the passion *for* creative action generally is as strong as, indeed even stronger than, sexual passion and yet can be a perfect ally of it. Paradoxical as it is to speak of passion as action, Dickens allies Bucket, Esther, and Woodcourt in the quest for Lady Dedlock in order to emblematize in their conduct a reconciliation of passion with purposive moral will and plotting work. Bucket himself is an emblem of work, of rescuing action, married to passion: Dickens goes out of his way to imagine him in bed with his spouse; indeed it is Mrs. Bucket who captures Hortense for the police. Connected with Bucket, Esther stands for the need of child for parent, a no less importunate passion than the sexual one. And of course Woodcourt, who rescues others from disease and even shipwreck, whose work is a vocation of passion and whose love for Esther is also a sexual passion, is the type of actor whose conduct Dickens values as most moral.

. . . George Eliot knows as well as Dickens the fearful nature of passion; Mrs. Transome's desire for Jermyn usurped all other realities, blinded her to consequences, to life's inevitable developments and transformations. Even Esther's fosterfather, the sober minister Rufus, has been blinded by passion—indeed has been driven by it to a kind of insanity. In the first stage of his love for Esther's mother, Rufus enters "a spiritual convulsion. . . . These mad wishes [to become Annette's lover and husband] were irreconcilable with that conception of the world which made his faith." But irreconcilable or not, for four years Lyon gives up his vocation for this woman. Eliot admits that the passion satisfies him the way his purposeful moral work in the world should have satisfied him. Suspended in obsessed passivity, turned in upon himself and Annette, Lyon cannot recover the goal of his work, cannot rescue himself from immobility, until the woman dies. What then, is the possibility for conduct, Eliot wonders, of wedding passion to personal development or to creative and active labor? In *Felix Holt the Radical* the union of Esther and Felix represents the tenuous hope that passion will find for itself a plot and an action that transcend stasis and an exclusively sexual goal. But it is as if by the time of *Daniel Deronda* Eliot's hope for something far more than a tenuous wedding of passion and act has grown beyond the possibility of constraint. Apparently it has also grown beyond the need to oppose Dickens by emphasizing internality and by making the rescue a matter of minimal effects and of nominal or imponderable meanings. In no other novel, except perhaps *The Mill on the Floss*, does George Eliot, on the surface at least, allow the rescue plot a fuller rein or a more optimistic bearing than in *Daniel Deronda*.

The results of this return to the rescue plot have always caused justifiable complaints by readers who are used to George Eliot's more characteristic sense of probability and story . . . Given Eliot's natural sense of plot, why did she bother to return at all, even if only in appearance, to a sense of plot anterior to her own? D. H. Lawrence again gives us a possible clue by reminding us in *Fantasia of the Unconscious* that "the great sex goal . . . always cries for the something beyond: for . . . the man disappearing ahead into the distance of futurity, that which his purpose stands for, the future." I have already said that the rescue plot in *Daniel Deronda* belongs to the "male" half of the novel; and this fact, coupled with Lawrence's remark, is perhaps most significant. The Dickensian rescuing action may have seemed to Eliot a peculiarly male production or fantasy of "the beyond"; she turns to this male structure of story both to honor it and to place it critically within a female narrative perspective and moral sense. . . . Eliot is reviving the Dickensian rescue story for the sake of advancing a female narrative sense and of rebuking the male's identification of "beyond" or of personal development with action. For the truth and for its bearing on conduct, the female sense of plot values, in the face of the Dickensian male assurances about action and its significance, the indeterminacy of allegedly liberating deeds, the unresolved problematic of self and other and of meaning; and although the female sense in *Daniel Deronda*, like the male sense in Dickens, is concerned that sexual and cultural goals not be at odds and not stultify maturity, it sees reconciliation of the cultural-sexual conflict emblematized in the familial *passion.* As Eliot sees this passion, it is a quiescent, submissive yielding to experience, to a beyond out of which "the rescue" can come from an agency that transcends will. Thus in the end it may be a female sense of plot in Eliot that sees the necessary redemption of men like Deronda and of plots like Dickens's in the intellectual and moral value of indeterminate meaning, of passive and nonexternalized states of feeling, and of inhibited action.

NEIL HERTZ

Recognizing Casaubon

About half-way through *Middlemarch*, after having described one more manifestation of Mr. Casaubon's preoccupying self-concern, the narrator goes on to add a more general reflection:

> Will not a tiny speck very close to our vision blot out the glory of the world, and leave only a margin by which we see the blot? I know no speck so troublesome as self.
>
> (George Eliot. *Middlemarch*. Ed. by Gordon S. Haight. Boston: Houghton Mifflin, 1956. Page 307. Subsequent references will be to this edition.)

The remark is characteristic of George Eliot in a number of ways, most obviously in its ethical implications: egotism in her writings is almost always rendered as narcissism, the self doubled and figured as both the eye and the blot. But equally typical is the care with which a particular image is introduced and its figurative possibilities developed. The speck blots out the glory of the world: that in itself would have enforced the moral. But the trope is given a second turn: the glory of the world illuminates the margin—the effect is of a sort of halo of light—but only so as to allow us all the better to see the blot. The intelligence at work extending a line of figurative language brings it back, with a nice appropriateness, to the ethical point. This is an instance of the sort of metaphorical control that teacher-critics have always admired in *Middlemarch*, the sign of a humane moral consciousness elaborating patterns of action and imagery with great inventiveness and absolutely no horsing around. Many a telling demonstration—in print and in the classroom—of the extraliterary value of formal analysis has been built around passages like this.

From *Glyph*, vol. 6 (1979). Copyright © 1979 by Johns Hopkins University Press.

But what about that blot and its margin? Is the figurative language here so firmly anchored in a stable understanding of the moral relations of the self that it can't drift off in the direction of other margins and other blots?

I have in mind two specific citations, both associated with Mr. Casaubon early in the novel. At one point George Eliot's heroine, Dorothea, is seen in her library "seated and already deep in one of the pamphlets which had some marginal manuscript of Mr. Casaubon's" (28); at another, Casaubon's pedantically accurate memory is compared to "a volume where a *vide supra* could serve instead of repetitions, and not the ordinary long-used blotting-book which only tells of forgotten writing" (19). It might be objected that the blot we've been considering is clearly not an inkblot, the margin clearly not the margin of a printed page; that indeed it is only by ruling out those meanings as extraneous to this particular context that we can visualize the image at all—this image of vision, of obstructed vision, of some small physical object coming between one's eyes and the world. Of course: the image, to remain an image, must restrict the range of figurative meaning we allow to the words that compose it. And, given that restraining function, it seems all the more appropriate that the image here is operating to clarify an ethical point about the self, just as it is appropriate that the tag "the moral imagination" has been so popular a way of referring to George Eliot's particular powers as a writer.

And yet, between themselves, those words *blot* and *margin* work to encourage just such a misreading of the image they nevertheless define and are defined by: *blot* helps us hear a rustle of paper in *margin*, *margin* makes *blot* sound just a bit inkier. And both, as it happens, are easily drawn out of their immediate context by the cumulative force of a series of less equivocal allusions to handwriting, printing, writing-in-general, all clustered about the figure of Casaubon. One character refers to him as a "sort of parchment code" (51), another wisecracks "Somebody put a drop [of his blood] under a magnifying glass, and it was all semi-colons and parentheses" (52), his own single lugubrious attempt at a joke turns on "a word that has dropped out of the text" (57), and there are more serious and consequential allusions of the same sort. Early in their acquaintance, when Dorothea is most taken with her husband-to-be, George Eliot writes: "He was all she had at first imagined him to be: almost everything he had said seemed like a specimen from a mine, or the inscription on the door of a museum which might open on the treasure of past ages" (24). Later, in Rome, after the first quarrel of their marriage, Dorothea accompanies him to the Vatican, walking with him "through the stony avenue of inscriptions" and leaving him at the entrance to the library (150). Back in England, in their own library, after another quarrel, Mr. Casaubon tries to resume work, but "his hand trembled so much that the words seemed to be written in an unknown character" (209).

In the past, when critics have directed attention to such passages it has been either to comment on the general appropriateness of these images to Mr. Casaubon—who is, after all, a scholar—or on the particular finesse with which one image or another is adjusted to the unfolding drama of the Casaubons' marriage. More recently Hillis Miller, citing a pair of similar passages, both about Dorothea's wildly mistaken first impressions of her husband, has stressed the non-dramatic value of these allusions: Casaubon, he notes, "is a text, a collection of signs which Dorothea misreads, according to that universal propensity for misinterpretation which infects all the characters in *Middlemarch.*" Miller is right about Casaubon, but the point he would make is still more inclusive: he is arguing for a reading of the novel that would see every character as simultaneously an interpreter (the word is a recurrent one in *Middlemarch*) and a text available for the interpretations (plural, always partial, and often in conflict) of others. It is with reference to Lydgate, he could have pointed out, and not to Casaubon, that George Eliot writes that a man may "be known merely as a cluster of signs for his neighbors' false suppositions" (105).

Miller's argument is persuasive, and the reading of the novel he sketches is a bold and attractive one: he takes *Middlemarch* to be simultaneously affirming the values of Victorian humanism which it has been traditionally held to affirm—for example, a belief in the consistency of the self as a moral agent—and systematically undercutting those values, offering in place of an ethically stable notion of the self the somewhat less reassuring figure of a focus of semiotic energy, receiving and interpreting signs, itself a "cluster of signs" more or less legible. Miller's movement towards this poised, deconstructive formulation, however, is condensed and rapid, and may still leave one wondering how those two notions of the self are held in suspension in the novel, and what the commerce is between them. In the pages that follow I propose to take up that question by dwelling on the figure of Casaubon, and by asking what it might mean, if *all* the characters in *Middlemarch* may be thought of as texts or as clusters of signs, for the signs of textuality to cluster so thickly around one particular name. Or, to put it another way, why is Mr. Casaubon made to seem not merely an especially sterile and egotistical person, but at moments like a quasi-allegorical figure, the personification of the dead letter, the written word? Personifications exist somewhere in the middle ground between realistically represented persons and configurations of signs: that would seem to be ground worth going over. But I want to approach it obliquely, by first considering some passages where it is not Casaubon, but George Eliot herself—not the blot but the eye—around whom are clustered the signs of egotism and of writing.

Reading through George Eliot's early letters one comes across—not on every page, but often enough to catch one's attention—a particular kind of apology. In one, for example, written when she was nineteen, she concludes with these lines:

> I have written at random and have not said all I wanted to say. I hope the frequent use of the personal pronoun will not lead you to think that I suppose it to confer any weight on what I have said. I used it to prevent circumlocution and waste of time. I am ashamed to send a letter like this as if I thought more highly of myself than I ought to think, which is alas! too true.
>
> (*The George Eliot Letters.* Ed. by Gordon S. Haight, 7 vols. New Haven: Yale University Press, 1954–1955. I, 23–24. Volume and page numbers are given in the body of the text.)

And then, beneath her signature, as a second-thought, a post-script:

> In reading my letter I find difficulties in understanding my scribble that I fear are hopelessly insurmountable for another.
>
> (I, 24)

Typically, apologies for what she fears may seem like egotism are accompanied by apologies for her handwriting:

> I . . . hope that you will be magnanimous enough to forgive the trouble my almost undecipherable letter will give you. Do not, pray, write neatly to me, for I cannot undertake to correspond with any one who will not allow me to scribble, though this precious sheet has, I think, an extra portion of untidiness. . . .
>
> (I, 8)

> I have written an almost unpardonably egotistical letter to say nothing of its other blemishes. . . .
>
> (I, 52)

> Tell me if you have great trouble in making out my cabalistic letters; if you have, I will write more deliberately next time.
>
> (I, 134)

The feeling behind these apologies need not be either particularly strong or particularly sincere: often they're perfunctory, or positively comical, as in this passage, where jokes about handwriting oddly prefigure the language that will be associated with Casaubon thirty years later:

> You will think me interminably loquacious, and still worse you will be ready to compare my scribbled sheet to the walls of an Egyptian tomb for mystery, and determine not to imitate certain wise antiquaries or anti-quarian wise-acres who "waste their precious years, how soon to fail?" in deciphering information which has only the lichen and moss of age to make it more valuable than the facts graphically conveyed by an upholsterer's pattern book.
>
> (I, 64)

What's curious is the stress not simply on the messiness of what she calls her "scribble," but on its cabalistic or hieroglyphic indecipherability. The point might be that language turns opaque and resistant when it is too purely in the service of the self, when self-expressive scribbles replace legible communicating signs. In that case apologies for sloppy handwriting might be read as slight nervous displacements of the apologies for egotism they accompany. But there is more going on here than that: writing, like the self-doubling of narcissism, is disturbing not simply because it may seem "self-centered" but because it is both that and self-dispersing at once.

When handwriting is legible it becomes not only available to others but transparent—and attractive—as self-expression, seemingly adequate in its relation to whatever it is the self would exteriorize. At such moments one's sense of the distance between one's self and the signs one produces can be cheerfully ignored or even enjoyed. And in fact an instance of just such enjoyment—narcissistic through and through, and thoroughly engaging—can be discerned in what is, by a happy accident, the earliest bit of George Eliot's writing to have survived. It is to be found on the cover of a school notebook she used when she was fourteen, a notebook which contains some arithmetic exercises, on essay on "affectation and conceit," the beginnings of a story in the manner of Sir Walter Scott, some poems she'd copied out, some drawings, and so forth. But on its cover, in a large, flourishing, ornate script, is a date—"March 16th 1834"—and a name: "Marianne Evans." It is her signature, but not quite her name, for she was christened Mary Anne, not Marianne. Gordon Haight, who reprints parts of the notebook in an appendix to his biography, remarks that she was learning French at the time, as well as being trained, as was the custom in girls' schools, in elegant penmanship: the combination seems to have produced this striking emblem of a writer's beginnings, the schoolgirl's slight, slightly romantic alteration of her name, written out large and with care, there to be contemplated on the cover of her book, the space of musing revery opening up between herself and her signature, a space in which a certain play of transformation becomes possible.

Sometimes that space is welcomed as "breathing-space," or, in a favorite image of George Eliot's, as "room" into which she can "expand"; at those moments the writing which structures that space stops being "scribble" and becomes what she likes to call "utterance," drawing on the Pentecostal associations of that word:

> It is necessary to me not simply to *be* but to *utter*, and I require utterance of my friends. . . . It is like a diffusion or expansion of one's own life to be assured that its vibrations are repeated in another, and words are the media of those vibrations. How can you say that music must end in silence? Is not the universe itself a perpetual utterance of the One Being?
>
> (I, 255)

But these moments of expansive utterance, where neither the distance between the self and its signs, nor the difference between selves is felt as a problem, are commonly followed in George Eliot's texts by moments of anxious "shrinking" and remorse:

> I feel a sort of madness growing upon me—just the opposite of the delirium which makes people fancy that their bodies are filling the room. It seems to me as if I were shrinking into that mathematical abstraction, a point—so entirely am I destitute of contact that I am unconscious of length and breadth.
>
> (I, 264)

This alternation between exuberance and apology, expansion and shrinking, utterance and scribble, was to govern George Eliot's literary production throughout her life: she lived it as a rhythm of fluctuating excitement and discouragement while she was working on her novels, followed by deep gloom when each was completed. More interestingly, she inscribed that alternation into her novels, but curiously transformed. At a number of climactic moments the play of expansion and shrinking reappears, but the rhythm is broken, lifted out of the interior life of a single character and distributed to a pair of characters, one of whom is seen expanding in loving recognition of the other, who is commonly figured as shrunken or shrinking from contact. Late in *Middlemarch*, for example, when Mrs. Bulstrode, humiliated by the revelations of her husband's past, but loyal to him nevertheless, goes to join him, we are told that "as she went towards him she thought he looked smaller—he seemed so withered and shrunken" (550). Elsewhere in the novel, when Dorothea touches her husband's arm, only to be horrified by his unresponsive hardness, the narrator adds: "You may ask why, in the name of manliness, Mr. Casaubon should have behaved that way. Consider that his was a mind which shrank from pity" (312).

These are instances of a distribution of attributes operating within the fictional world of the novel: images that we have seen George Eliot, in letters, applying to her own inner life are attached, as in a medieval psychomachia, to separate characters in her narratives. But at times this distributive activity may be seen operating across the boundary that separates the lives of the characters—the ways they conduct themselves and engage with one another—from the sensed activity of an author, the ways George Eliot conducts the plotting of her novels. For example, Dorothea's loving acknowledgement of her husband is followed, after not too long an interval, by his death; or again, when Mrs. Bulstrode goes to her husband's side, he is a permanently broken man. Within the world of *Middlemarch*, neither Dorothea nor Mrs. Bulstrode can be held responsible for the turns of fate that crush their husbands, but it is nonetheless true that certain recipients of moral generosity don't fare well in that world. Seeking an explanation, a critic might wish to read such scenes as unwittingly playing-out their author's preoccupations in some wishful and compensatory fashion. Richard Ellmann, for example, has found in the language associated with Casaubon echoes of images linked, in an early letter, with the novelist's fears of her own erotic fantasizing. "The severity with which Casaubon is treated," Ellmann speculates, "would then derive from her need to exorcise this part of her experience. . . . To berate Casaubon, and to bury him, was to overcome in transformed state the narcissistic sensuality of her adolescence." To seek an author's personal allegory behind the realistic surface she has woven is often as unrewarding as it is methodologically dubious, but in the case of George Eliot's works, because they are explicitly about the imagining of others—about the status of the image of one person in the imagining mind of another—the play between the imaginer and the imagined, between author and character, and the possibility of a narcissistic confusion developing between the one and the other, has already been thematized and made available for interpretations such as Ellmann's. If anything, his claims are too modest: what he presents as a contingent psychobiographical detail—an author's uneasiness about her own "narcissism"—may be read as neither contingent nor primarily biographical, but as part of a sustained and impersonal questioning of the grounds of fiction. Nowhere is that questioning more energetically in evidence than in the pages (in Chapters 20 and 21) that recount the Casaubons' experience in Rome. If we turn to them now, beginning with the final paragraphs of Chapter 21, we shall find another instance of the bifurcated activity characteristic of Eliot's writing:

> Today she had begun to see that she had been under a wild illusion in expecting a response to her feeling from Mr. Casaubon, and she had felt

the waking of a presentiment that there might be a sad consciousness in his life which made as great a need on his side as on her own.

We are all of us born in moral stupidity, taking the world as an udder to feed our supreme selves: Dorothea had early begun to emerge from that stupidity, but yet it had been easier to her to imagine how she would devote herself to Mr. Casaubon, and become wise and strong in his strength and wisdom, than to conceive with that distinctness which is no longer reflection but feeling—an idea wrought back to the directness of sense, like the solidity of objects—that he had an equivalent centre of self, whence the lights and shadows must always fall with a certain difference.

(156–57)

These lines have been rightly admired, both as a powerful presentation of Dorothea's experience and as an epitome of the moral imagination at work, a text exhibiting the links between generous conduct, literary creation and the reading of novels. For Dorothea's exemplary action would seem to be easily assimilated to the activity of a novelist and to that of a reader: to conceive Mr. Casaubon as different from oneself, and to do so "with that distinctness which is no longer reflection but feeling" sounds like a display of the same imaginative power that created the character of Casaubon in the first place, and the same power that *Middlemarch* would quicken in its readers. And indeed this view of the novel, and of the use of novels generally, was one George Eliot had already endorsed: "A picture of human life such as a great artist can give," she wrote, "surprises even the trivial and selfish into that attention to what is apart from themselves, which may be called the raw material of moral sentiment." We shall want to pause to ask where Mr. Casaubon fits into this set of beliefs about literature and conduct, than as the passive (and not altogether grateful) object of Dorothea's (and George Eliot's, and the reader's) regard. But first, let us look more closely at how George Eliot elaborates this view of the moral imagination. The notion that literature calls attention to unnoticed aspects of life, to its intricacies or simply to its variety, is certainly not peculiar to her; more characteristic, however, is the stress she places on the reader's (or the character's) reluctance to attend: in the sentence just quoted, it is the element of surprise that counts—even "the trivial and selfish" are to be shocked into noticing what is apart from themselves. Typically her plots present someone jolted into the consciousness of others, with the jolt all the more forceful because of the resistance encountered, a resistance which is generally figured as a powerfully narcissistic investment in an image of the self, the blot that obscures the glory of the world. Or—still more generally—an investment in *some* image, for the notion of narcissism in these novels is deepened to include other sorts of imaginative fascination.

Thus the "moral stupidity" which Dorothea must emerge from can be presented as a clinging to a mistaken idea of her marriage: "Today she had begun to see that she had been under a wild illusion in expecting a response to her feeling from Mr. Casaubon. . . ." Later in the novel, echoing the encompassing turn of phrase of the earlier passage—"We are all of us born in moral stupidity"—George Eliot writes "We are all of us imaginative in some form or other, for images are the brood of desire" (237). She is writing there of the old miser Featherstone, who never emerges or even begins to emerge from what she names as "the fellowship of illusion." But the repetitions of syntax and cadence suggest an equivalence: to be born in moral stupidity is to be born imaginative; and it is against the inertia of this mode of imaginative activity, the narcissistic dwelling on and in an image, that the moral imagination has to both define itself and defend itself.

Define itself first, for the differences between these two kinds of imagination—one supposedly turned outward and hence moral, the other self-enclosed and narcissistic—may not, under scrutiny, be all that clear. Both activities, whatever their outward effects, would seem to originate within the same enclosure: it becomes important to be able to distinguish them at their source, and not merely in terms of their consequences. George Eliot is here engaging the same problem that led Romantic theorists like Coleridge to insist on a sharp and essential difference between the mental activities they named Imagination and Fancy, and her solution—if we now look back at the paragraph on moral stupidity—will be seen to resemble theirs. For what is most remarkable in that passage is the fact that Dorothea's exemplary action, the acknowledgement of an irreducible difference between persons, is accompanied by—is accomplished in—the flashing reduction of another sort of difference, that between "reflection" and "feeling," "idea" and "sense." To recognize Casaubon as possessing "an equivalent centre of self, whence the lights and shadows must always fall with a certain difference" is, for Dorothea, to overcome not merely her own egotism, but also what another Eliot has called a "dissociation of sensibility," a troublesome interior difference. And, oddly, what she achieves is made to sound very much like what Mr. Casaubon, at another point in the novel, is pitied for never having experienced, that "rapturous transformation of consciousness" into "the vividness of a thought, the ardour of a passion, the energy of an action" (206–7). If we now ask what Mr. Casaubon is doing in this scene, we can see that he is presented both as a character, another person, the object of Dorothea's recognition, and as a figure, an exteriorized embodiment of a mode of imagination threateningly antithetical to hers—and to George Eliot's. For Dorothea to recognize him "as he is" is, for the author, to cast out what he may be taken to represent.

But what, exactly, may he be taken to represent? At times he would seem to be the personification of the written word, at others the personification of the narcissistic imagination; the connection between the two can be made in a more systematic way in terms of an economy of anxiety, by suggesting that the dislocation implicit in narcissism, the doubling of the self into an eye and an image, an eye and a blot, is a more manageable and comforting fiction than the more open and indeterminate self-dispersion associated with a plurality of signs or with the plurality of interpretations that writing can provoke. In Chapters 20 and 21 of *Middlemarch* one can follow a movement towards the more reassuring fiction. They begin with the superb paragraphs in which Mr. Casaubon is associated with a vision of Rome as "stupendous fragmentariness" (143), an unintelligible plurality that baffles Dorothea with "a glut of confused ideas" (144); they then move through a complicated and uncertain grappling—on George Eliot's part—with the threat of narcissism, the threat that her own imaginative activity is nothing but narcissistic, to the exteriorization of that disturbing possibility in the figure of Casaubon, a personification now no longer of "writing" but of "narcissism" who can be "recognized" and banished from the novel. . . .

Chapter 20 opens with Dorothea in tears, with "no distinctly shapen grievance that she could state, even to herself" (143). We might wish to say that it soon becomes clear what is distressing her, that she has been hurt by her husband's cold and pedantic behavior, and overwhelmed by what she has seen of Rome, but that would be to travesty the experience of reading these paragraphs, to turn aside from the subtlety with which Dorothea's psychological state is rendered, as well as from the deft intermingling of the causes of her distress. From the chapter's third paragraph on, it becomes impossible to separate Dorothea's response to her husband from her response to the city, and just as impossible to allow the one noun—Casaubon—to stand in some flatly symbolic equivalence to the other noun—Rome. Certain likenesses are taken for granted: Casaubon is old, he is a historian and an interpreter, he is (to Dorothea, at least) a center of authority; but these paragraphs don't exactly dwell on this analogy or spell out its terms. Instead, the words associated earlier in the novel with Mr. Casaubon, the images that had been clustered around his name, are allowed to drift free of that center and to disperse themselves through the urban landscape: allusions to Mr. Casaubon himself, or to Dorothea's role as his wife, practically disappear. This disappearance, the withdrawal of Casaubon from the foreground of this prose, is marked by an odd figure, a sort of "dissolve" that displaces the couple's relation onto the seasons:

Dorothea had now been five weeks in Rome, and in the kindly mornings when autumn and winter seemed to go hand in hand like a happy aged couple one of whom would presently survive in chiller loneliness, she had driven about at first with Mr. Casaubon, but of late chiefly with Tantripp and their experienced courier.

(143)

While Mr. Casaubon retires to the Vatican Library, Dorothea is left alone with Rome and with her own life, and both are figured to her as enigmas: her confused and disorganized feelings are assimilated to the fragmentary nature of the scene around her, a scene now made up as much of the bits and pieces of language associated with Casaubon as of the "broken revelations of that Imperial and Papal city":

> The weight of unintelligible Rome might lie easily on bright nymphs to whom it formed a background for the brilliant picnic of Anglo-foreign society; but Dorothea had no such defence against deep impressions. Ruins and basilicas, palaces and colossi, set in the midst of a sordid present, where all that was living and warm-blooded seemed sunk in the deep degeneracy of a superstition divorced from reverence; the dimmer yet eager Titanic life gazing and struggling on walls and ceilings; the long vistas of white forms whose marble eyes seemed to hold the monotonous light of an alien world: all this vast wreck of ambitious ideals, sensuous and spiritual, mixed confusedly with the signs of breathing forgetfulness and degradation, at first jarred her as with an electric shock, and then urged themselves on her with that ache belonging to a glut of confused ideas which check the flow of emotion. Forms both pale and glowing took possession of her young sense, and fixed themselves in her memory even when she was not thinking of them, preparing strange associations which remained through her after-years. Our moods are apt to bring with them images which succeed each other like the magic-lantern pictures of a doze; and in certain states of dull forlornness Dorothea all her life continued to see the vastness of St. Peter's, the huge bronze canopy, the excited intention in the attitudes and garments of the prophets and evangelists in the mosaics above, and the red drapery which was being hung for Christmas spreading itself everywhere like a disease of the retina.

(143–44)

I have quoted this passage at length both in order to recall its intensity and to draw attention to its organization. The persistent emphasis on the scene's at once soliciting and resisting comprehension, linked to the rhythms in which these sentences accumulate layer on layer of plural nouns, until that accumulated charge is released in a "shock," a "glut of confused ideas which check the flow of emotion"—these elements mark this experience of Dorothea's as an experience of the sublime, in the specific sense that term took on in the writings of Kant or of Wordsworth.

I mention this not simply to identify a literary tradition—though I have enough of Casaubon in me to take an intense, bleak pleasure in interrupting a passionate moment with a scholarly gloss—but because to recognize the rhythm of the sublime in these sentences is to anticipate where the text might go from here, what one might expect to follow after that abrupt shock. At one point, for instance, Kant describes the feeling of the sublime as a pleasure that arises only indirectly, produced "by the feeling of a momentary checking of the vital powers and a consequent stronger outflow of them." Elsewhere, explaining the "bewilderment or, as it were, perplexity which it is said seizes the spectator on his first entrance into St. Peter's in Rome," he writes: "For there is here a feeling of the inadequacy of his imagination for presenting the ideas of a whole, wherein the imagination reaches its maximum, and, in striving to surpass it, sinks back into itself, by which, however, a kind of emotional satisfaction is produced." We might, with this model in mind, ask if there will be an outflow of vital powers in this passage, or a sinking back of the imagination into itself. Or, if what we have in mind is the language of "Tintern Abbey," we might wonder if Dorothea will be released from "the burthen of the mystery," the "heavy and the weary weight of all this unintelligible world," and allowed to "see into the life of things." One way or another, a reader may be led to expect some resolution, and, indeed, his expectations are rewarded, although—and this too is characteristic of the sublime—not in quite the form he may have anticipated.

For the movement of these pages seems to issue in not one but three moments that qualify as "resolutions," partly because of their position in the text, partly because of the level of their diction and the nature of the metaphors of which they are composed. One of these, the last in the sequence, I have already described in some detail: it is the paragraph with which Chapter 21 concludes, the paragraph beginning "We are all of us born in moral stupidity." For if it is the "dream-like strangeness of her bridal life" that Dorothea is confronting in the opening pages of Chapter 20, the baffling disparity between her sense of whom she was marrying and the realities of living with Mr. Casaubon, then her acknowledging that she had "been under a wild illusion" can be thought of as one response to the shock she registered in the previous chapter, a response that is deferred chiefly for reasons of dramatic verisimilitude, because it takes time to adjust to such new awareness. Here the sequence of sublime checking followed by some resolution underlies the ethical scenario we noticed earlier, where a character is jolted out of moral stupidity into the recognition of something apart from the self.

But the intensity of Dorothea's feelings, as they are presented in those opening paragraphs, as well as the scope of George Eliot's rhetoric, are far in excess of anything that could be resolved dramatically: she has been shown attempting to come to terms not simply with her husband, but with the heterogeneous assault of Rome, with a collection of signs that may be "summed up" in a verbal formulation (e.g., "all this vast wreck of ambitious ideals") but which neither Dorothea nor the author is in a position to render as a totality. The resolution of *this* aspect of Dorothea's experience is to be found in the sentences immediately following those on the checking of the flow of emotion, and in one sense it is no resolution at all: it takes the form of a compulsively repeated set of images, fixed in Dorothea's memory for life and unexorcisable. The plurality of unmasterable fragments is converted into a repetitive series of painful tokens. This is a dark sublimity, beyond the pleasure principle for Dorothea, and sufficiently at odds with the values of Victorian humanism to be distressing to George Eliot as well. The later paragraph, in which Dorothea recognizes Casaubon, may be read as, quite literally, a domestication of the anxiety associated with this earlier moment.

If one wanted to demonstrate that *Middlemarch* offers a reader two incompatible systems of value, conflicting views of the interpretation of history, of the possibilities of knowledge, of the consistency of the self, few passages in the novel would provide better evidence. One could contrast the sublime of repetition with that of recognition, then read the first as an undermining of moral and metaphysical categories, the second as the recuperation of those same categories. But what, then, are we to make of still another moment in these pages that is bound to strike a reader as "sublime"? It is to be found in the paragraph immediately following the description of Rome, and it has been cited, admiringly, perhaps as much as any other passage in George Eliot's works:

> If we had a keen vision and a feeling for all ordinary human life, it would be like hearing the grass grow and the squirrel's heart beat, and we should die of that roar which lies on the other side of silence. As it is the quickest of us walk about well wadded in stupidity.

(144)

We might begin by noticing that these sentences, although they share with the other "resolutions" a sense of high-powered epistemological confrontation, are not about Dorothea's response either to Rome or to Mr. Casaubon; they are, rather, about how "we"—the reader and the narrator—might respond to Dorothea, and indeed they come at the end of a paragraph that had begun with a slightly awkward wavering of tone, as the narrator seemed to back off from the intensities of Dorothea's experience:

> Not that this inward amazement of Dorothea's was anything very excep-
> tional: many souls in their young nudity are tumbled out among incon-
> gruities and left to "find their feet" among them, while their elders go
> about their business. Nor can I suppose that when Mrs. Casaubon is
> discovered in a fit of weeping six weeks after her wedding the situation
> will be regarded as tragic.

One of George Eliot's most acute contemporary readers, Richard Holt
Hutton, was struck by the oddness of these lines, and bothered by what he
heard as a "bitter parenthetic laugh" at the expense of those souls tumbled
out "in their young nudity." I think it *is* an odd moment, but that the
tonal irony seems less directed at the "souls"—that is, at Dorothea—than
it does at some imagined insensitive reader: the "Nor can I suppose" is
somewhat heavy-handedly reminding the reader of the limits of his perception of the tragic, of the limits of those powers of sympathetic imagination which would enable him to discern the tragic in "the very fact of
frequency." Still more puzzling, however, is the combination of this
sardonic diction with the note of high assurance the narrator strikes in the
sentences about "the roar . . . on the other side of silence."

What is going on in this passage makes more sense once we learn
that it is dense with self-quotation, with allusions to George Eliot's earlier
fiction. Those "souls in their young nudity," for example, "tumbled out"
and left to "find their feet" would seem to be a rendering as a figure of
speech of what was once, in a story called "Janet's Repentance" (one of
the *Scenes of Clerical Life*), a piece of dramatic action: there the heroine is
literally thrown out of her house by her drunken husband, and her
situation is described in these terms:

> The stony street, the bitter north-east wind and darkness—and in the
> midst of them a tender woman thrust out from her husband's home in
> her thin night-dress, the harsh wind cutting her naked feet, and driving
> her long hair away from her half-clad bosom, where the poor heart is
> crushed with anguish and despair.

Also to be found in "Janet's Repentance" are lines which echo in the
squirrel's heartbeat:

> Yet surely, surely the only true knowledge of our fellow-man is that
> which enables us to feel with him—which gives us a fine ear for the
> heart-pulses that are beating under the mere clothes of circumstance and
> opinion. Our subtlest analysis of schools and sects must miss the essential
> truth, unless it be lit up by the love that sees in all forms of human
> thought and work the life and death struggles of separate human
> beings.

In still another story, "The Lifted Veil," the hero discovers in himself a power that torments him and which he describes as a "diseased participation in other people's consciousness": "It was like a preternaturally heightened sense of hearing," he relates, "making audible to one a roar of sound where others find perfect stillness."

The validity of the novelist's imagination of others, whether it is seen as a saving gift or as a curse, is what is at stake in this paragraph in *Middlemarch*. Placed between Dorothea's failure to reconstruct the fragments of history and her success in recognizing her husband as someone with an "equivalent centre of self," this passage seeks language adequate to a slightly different task, that of stabilizing the incommensurable relation between an author conceived of as somehow "outside" (but uncertainly outside) her creation and a privileged (but fictitious) consciousness within that imagined world. The allusions to earlier works of fiction, the reappearance of those evocations of pathos or of imaginative power, are accompanied by the reversal of their original meanings: what had seemed pathetic reality in "Janet's Repentance" has been transformed into a metaphor, and the "fine ear for heart-pulses," the ability to hear "a roar of sound where others find perfect stillness"—these are precisely the faculties that a reader is now told he does not possess. The wavering, then steadying of tone in which the narrator addresses the reader may be read as one way of readjusting to the felt instability of the author's relation to her character, to the unsettled sense that it was through an intense identification with Dorothea's experience in Rome that the magnificent previous paragraph had been written, but that the burden of that paragraph was the fictitiousness and the willfulnnes of such identifications. The sublimity of the image of the roar on the other side of silence emerges from this thoroughly negative insight.

Behind this language about the limits of perception is still another text, one with a long history in eighteenth- and nineteenth-century writing about the sublime: it is the passage in the *Essay Concerning Human Understanding* in which Locke is praising the aptness with which the human senses are scaled to man's position in the hierarchy of creatures:

> If our sense of hearing were but a thousand times quicker than it is, how would a perpetual noise distract us. And we should in the quietest retirement be less able to sleep or meditate than in the middle of a sea-fight. Nay, if that most instructive of our senses, seeing, were in any man a thousand, or a hundred thousand times more acute than it is by the best microscope, things several millions of times less than the smallest object of his sight now would then be visible to his naked eyes, and so he would come nearer to the discovery of the texture and motion of the

> minute parts of corporeal things; and in many of them, probably get ideas of their internal constitutions; but then he would be in a quite different world from other people: nothing would appear the same to him and others.

Locke's language converts a scaled continuum into an opposition between the ordinary world of sensation and sociability and the "quite different world" in which the man with microscopic vision would find himself. To allude to that language in *Middlemarch* is to stress that discontinuity at the moment when the incommensurability between an author and the creatures of her pen is under consideration. Suppose, to draw out the turns of this figure, one *were* to hear the roar which lies on the other side of silence. Possibly one might not die of it; instead—and this may not be the preferable alternative—one might become like Locke's man, moving nearer to the discovery of the texture and motion of things, but in a quite different world from other people. If, for example, one were to bring a drop of Mr. Casaubon's blood into focus, one might see nothing but semicolons and parentheses. That is the possibility that is written into *Middlemarch* in the idiom of the sublime; it is clearly not a possibility to be steadily contemplated by a working novelist—it must be repressed if books like *Middlemarch* are to be written at all. One sign of that repression is the recognition and exorcism of Casaubon.

BARBARA HARDY, J. HILLIS MILLER,
RICHARD POIRIER

"Middlemarch," Chapter 85: Three Commentaries

CHAPTER 85

"Then went the jury out, whose names were Mr. Blindman, Mr. No-good, Mr. Malice, Mr. Love-lust, Mr. Live-loose, Mr. Heady, Mr. High-mind, Mr. Enmity, Mr. Liar, Mr. Cruelty, Mr. Hate-light, Mr. Implacable, who every one gave in his private verdict against him among themselves, and afterwards unanimously concluded to bring him in guilty before the judge. And first among themselves, Mr. Blindman, the foreman, said, I see clearly that this man is a heretic. Then said Mr. No-good, Away with such a fellow from the earth! Ay, said Mr. Malice, for I hate the very look of him. Then said Mr. Love-lust, I could never endure him. Nor I, said Mr. Live-loose; for he would be always condemning my way. Hang him, hang him, said Mr. Heady. A sorry scrub, said Mr. High-mind. My heart riseth against him, said Mr. Enmity. He is a rogue, said Mr. Liar. Hanging is too good for him, said Mr. Cruelty. Let us despatch him out of the way, said Mr. Hate-light. Then said Mr. Implacable, Might I have all the world given me, I could not be reconciled to him; therefore let us forthwith bring him in guilty of death"

(*Pilgrim's Progress*)

When immortal Bunyan makes his picture of the persecuting passions bringing in their verdict of guilty, who pities Faithful? That is a rare and blessed lot which some greatest men have not attained, to know ourselves guiltless before a condemning crowd—to be sure that what we are

From *Nineteenth-Century Fiction* 3, vol. 35 (December 1980). Copyright © 1980 by The Regents of the University of California. The University of California Press.

denounced for is solely the good in us. The pitiable lot is that of the man who could not call himself a martyr even though he were to persuade himself that the men who stoned him were but ugly passions incarnate—who knows that he is stoned, not for professing the Right, but for not being the man he professed to be.

This was the consciousness that Bulstrode was withering under while he made his preparations for departing from Middlemarch, and going to end his stricken life in that sad refuge, the indifference of new faces. The duteous merciful constancy of his wife had delivered him from one dread, but it could not hinder her presence from being still a tribunal before which he shrank from confession and desired advocacy. His equivocations with himself about the death of Raffles had sustained the conception of an Omniscience whom he prayed to, yet he had a terror upon him which would not let him expose them to judgment by a full confession to his wife: the acts which he had washed and diluted with inward argument and motive, and for which it seemed comparatively easy to win invisible pardon—what name would she call them by? That she should ever silently call his acts Murder was what he could not bear. He felt shrouded by her doubt: he got strength to face her from the sense that she could not yet feel warranted in pronouncing that worst condemnation on him. Some time, perhaps—when he was dying—he would tell her all: in the deep shadow of that time, when she held his hand in the gathering darkness, she might listen without recoiling from his touch. Perhaps: but concealment had been the habit of his life, and the impulse to confession had no power against the dread of a deeper humiliation.

He was full of timid care for his wife, not only because he deprecated any harshness of judgment from her, but because he felt a deep distress at the sight of her suffering. She had sent her daughters away to board at a school on the coast, that this crisis might be hidden from them as far as possible. Set free by their absence from the intolerable necessity of accounting for her grief or of beholding their frightened wonder, she could live unconstrainedly with the sorrow that was every day streaking her hair with whiteness and making her eyelids languid.

"Tell me anything that you would like to have me do, Harriet," Bulstrode had said to her; "I mean with regard to arrangements of property. It is my intention not to sell the land I possess in this neighborhood, but to leave it to you as a safe provision. If you have any wish on such subjects, do not conceal it from me."

A few days afterwards, when she had returned from a visit to her brother's, she began to speak to her husband on a subject which had for some time been in her mind.

"I *should* like to do something for my brother's family, Nicholas; and I think we are bound to make some amends to Rosamond and her husband. Walter says Mr. Lydgate must leave the town, and his practice is almost good for nothing, and they have very little left to settle anywhere with. I would rather do without something for ourselves, to make some amends to my poor brother's family."

Mrs. Bulstrode did not wish to go nearer to the facts than in the phrase "make some amends"; knowing that her husband must understand her. He had a particular reason, which she was not aware of, for wincing under her suggestion. He hesitated before he said—

"It is not possible to carry out your wish in the way you propose, my dear. Mr. Lydgate has virtually rejected any further service from me. He has returned the thousand pounds which I lent him. Mrs. Casaubon advanced him the sum for that purpose. Here is his letter."

The letter seemed to cut Mrs. Bulstrode severely. The mention of Mrs. Casaubon's loan seemed a reflection of that public feeling which held it a matter of course that every one would avoid a connection with her husband. She was silent for some time; and the tears fell one after the other, her chin trembling as she wiped them away. Bulstrode, sitting opposite her, ached at the sight of that grief-worn face, which two months before had been bright and blooming. It had aged to keep sad company with his own withered features. Urged into some effort at comforting her, he said—

"There is another means, Harriet, by which I might do a service to your brother's family, if you like to act in it. And it would, I think, be beneficial to you: it would be an advantageous way of managing the land which I mean to be yours."

She looked attentive.

"Garth once thought of undertaking the management of Stone Court in order to place your nephew Fred there. The stock was to remain as it is, and they were to pay a certain share of the profits instead of an ordinary rent. That would be a desirable beginning for the young man, in conjunction with his employment under Garth. Would it be a satisfaction to you?"

"Yes, it would," said Mrs. Bulstrode, with some return of energy. "Poor Walter is so cast down; I would try anything in my power to do him some good before I go away. We have always been brother and sister."

"You must make the proposal to Garth yourself, Harriet," said Mr. Bulstrode, not liking what he had to say, but desiring the end he had in view, for other reasons besides the consolation of his wife. "You must state to him that the land is virtually yours, and that he need have no transactions with me. Communications can be made through Standish. I mention this, because Garth gave up being my agent. I can put into your hands a paper which he himself drew up, stating conditions; and you can propose his renewed acceptance of them. I think it is not unlikely that he will accept when you propose the thing for the sake of your nephew."

BARBARA HARDY

Like every chapter of *Middlemarch*, this one dilates and contracts. In its brief space (only chapter 79 is shorter), it shows George Eliot's powers of analysis, drama, form, language, and allusion. It is an organ to the whole, but has its own shape and growth.

It begins with the quotation from Bunyan's *The Pilgrim's Progress*, which shows the complexity of George Eliot's use of motto. The modulation is fluent: the account of Faithful's trial in the motto does not name the accused, so that his naming in the first sentence of the narrative bridges and completes. A further and economical link is the attribution to author; this is made in the opening sentence of the narrative, so not attached to the motto. As well as modulation, there is the making of narrative tension: if we do not immediately identify the anonymous personal pronoun in the motto, we find it in the narrative. (If we do, there may still be a slight pause of expectation.) George Eliot begins with another author's particularity, using it to edge her way toward her own particulars. (Her modes of generalization are many and varied.) The first paragraph is a daring dilation in such a short and condensed chapter. It is beautifully built. Bunyan bridges motto and text. The reference in the first sentence is made dynamic by one of the novelist's skillfully placed questions, addressed to the reader and to human nature: "who pities Faithful?" The question arrests us not simply by being a question, but by its surprise—we are likely to expect to pity the victim of such a jury, but by a subtle moral turn we are told why the pity is not appropriate. The turn takes us further into generalization as the commentator explains, with firm confidence, the nature of that "rare and blessed lot" which is the certainty that we are denounced only for the good in us. Then follows a further balancing generalization, through antithesis, about the pitiable lot of the man who suffers denunciation without any conscientious defense. Then the second paragraph takes us from this process of graduated generalization to the particular case of Bulstrode's consciousness.

The Bunyan extract, dwelt on in the motto and the narrative, has other functions too. It draws attention sharply to the moral clarity of the issues before us. It announces the ruling theme of the chapter—moral consciousness or conscience. It is a little matrix of imagery: the legal metaphors of "tribunal," "advocacy," "judgment," "warranted," "pronouncing," and "condemnation," which describe Mrs. Bulstrode's implicit rebuking presence spring from it, and use an allegorical and semiallegorical method which is one of George Eliot's many ways of dramatizing the life of mind and feeling. (We may notice it particularly in this chapter because of the motto, but it is present from the beginning of her work to the end and prominent elsewhere in *Middlemarch*.) The function of the motto which I want to stress is its duality: it is appropriate to the narrative tone and temper, in the fullest sense, and more narrowly and locally appropriate to Bulstrode. There is a sadly but strongly ironic point in having this phase in the life of a hypocrite (Faithful's opposite, and Bunyan's degenerate successor in faith) conducted under the aegis of *The Pilgrim's Progress*. George Eliot uses religious imagery in all her novels, very strongly in this one, but the local potency of imagery is usually notable. The imagery of Bunyan's vivaciously named jurors and Faithful's fate underline what is happening to Bulstrode. Some of his opponents may be seen, by him or by us, or by Lydgate, as "ugly passions"; George Eliot's display of passions in the scenes of public condemnation in the streets and the Town Hall (chap. 71) is a Victorian conversion of Bunyan's method. But it also allows George Eliot, or the narrator (if we wish to make this discrimination), to control our awareness of character with the sense of superior direction. This second paragraph is a masterpiece of the free indirect style, and the imagery belongs at once to the simplifying traditions of Bulstrode's puritanism as to the larger resonance of George Eliot's moral personifications.

The sense that the style colors the double point of view of character and narrative guidance is stable and subtle. Bulstrode's superficial and false assumptions of language shade into, or are covered by, the narrative's sobriety and solemnity. He "withers" under his own consciousness, and his life is "stricken." In the third sentence of this paragraph the narrator uses two metaphors which combine to make us move from one to the other with a slight jolt: "the acts which he had washed and diluted with inward argument and motive, and for which it seemed comparatively easy to win invisible pardon—what name would she call them by?" This glide into the free indirect style is another specimen of George Eliot's combination of dramatization and superior direction, as of her linking and bridging. The word "washed" may at first sight seem to belong only to the biblical imagery of Bulstrode's consciousness (the language of baptism and washing in the blood of the Lamb), but it is strongly qualified by "diluted" and so drawn into the orbit of the narrator's moral definiteness. To call the effect irony is too crude: it is as if an equivocal association is briefly offered and then withdrawn. Water washes, and washing is good. But the metaphorical action of dilution, since it is the dilution of acts, is not good. There is a tug or tension here between what seems to belong to Bulstrode's consciousness—its "equivocations," as they are clearly called at the beginning of this sentence—and that which is unequivocal and inescapable. It seems to belong to the stern language of George Eliot's old evangelicalism and the cant of Bulstrode. The narrative keeps moving us from cant to truth. There is another pull of tension in the metaphor "shrouded" in the next sentence but one: "He felt shrouded by her doubt: he got strength to face her from the sense that she could not yet feel warranted in pronouncing that worst condemnation on him." He is clearly engaged in the dubious activity of finding protection and cover in deadly garments; once more the application to him is in keeping with his stylistic register and suggests a level of linguistic application to which he is blind. The narrative direction makes us perceive his blinkered, dangerous, mistaken selection in imaging, and the larger implications to which he cannot reach. The last example comes in the last two sentences of this condensed paragraph:

> Some time, perhaps—when he was dying—he would tell her all: in the deep shadow of that time, when she held his hand in the gathering darkness, she might listen without recoiling from his touch. Perhaps: but concealment had been the habit of his life, and the impulse to confession had no power against the dread of a deeper humiliation.

Again, there is a reliance on the traditional imagery of deep shadow and gathering darkness, the language of Bible and hymn. And it makes a strong emotional appeal, an appeal which is transiently felt by the reader as it internalizes his own self-pity and indulgent fantasy. The narrative guidance is inexorable, and we are pulled back from the dramatizing images to a sense of their fiction. The first "perhaps" belongs to his equivocations, to his customary habit of deceptive procrastination, which contrasts here very strongly with his retreat from the act. The second "Perhaps," emphatically placed, and isolated solemnly behind the colon, leads us to the enlarged sense of the unreliability of the first "perhaps" and of the imagery and fantasy of a gentle deathbed and forgiveness. We already know, from much explicit commentary and from the moral action, how Bulstrode's mature deeds have been schooled by younger foredeeds.

What is emphasized by the imagery and diction of the free indirect style is also made plain by the internal narrative. Like all George Eliot's characters, Bulstrode is given his characteristic mode of narrative. It is a negative mode, a reticence which shrinks from painful narration of the past, both in memory and in confession. In chapter 61 we have seen how Bulstrode is made to endure a crisis in which he is oppressed and obsessed by memory, in a turning back of his wadded consciousness to those stories of the past which he has inhibited. The return of Raffles, with his threat to tell the secrets, makes Bulstrode's memories rise to haunt him. (At the point of revelation, they are disclosed to the reader.) We have also seen in chapter 74 how he does not need to confess to his wife: the town's gossip almost reaches her, but the story is eventually told to her, "very inartificially," by her brother Vincy. It is not until we get to chapter 85 that we feel the moral weakness of Bulstrode's continued refusal to tell: "The duteous merciful constancy of his wife had delivered him from one dread, but it could not hinder her presence from being still a tribunal before which he shrank from confession and desired advocacy."

The weakness of this fear and the procrastination are made crystal clear, but so too is Bulstrode's cause of fear. The free indirect style forces us to move from the personal whitewashing and dilution of his self-pity and self-deception to the verdict of the narrator. This verdict is that of a moral consensus that is silently or directly evoked, as in the chapter's first question. The style also makes an effective medium for revealing his feelings without too much interference from moral analysis and judgment. Just as we cannot stay within the narrow language and action of his dramatized consciousness, so we cannot wholly stay apart, distant and detached. The narrative cannot be described in the terminology of "distance": it moves to and fro; it dilates and contracts. Its contraction makes us feel the nature of the character's feelings. For instance, in the phrase, "that sad refuge, the indifference of new faces," the narrator expresses a pity which is authorial and in character. "Sad" contains no complexity, but belongs to either viewpoint. The quiet but shocking words, "the indifference of new faces," are hard to pinpoint. They concentrate the implications of this man's future, the "end" of his "stricken life," in the relentless plain statement, the reversal of what one usually expects from change and newness, but an exact forecast here. The other example of George Eliot's plain style comes in the following sentence, "The duteous merciful constancy of his wife. . . ." The style dares to make this three-fold pile of abstractions, "duteous," "merciful," and "constancy." Because they are so pressed together we cannot simply run along the sentence, but have to pause and weigh each word. The accumulation, plainness, and slow pace make us look at each abstraction and review it in the light of all we have seen of Harriet Bulstrode. Again, plain and simple language says something surprising. Like "who pities Faithful?" and "the indifference of new faces," the collocation of abstract moral qualities forces us to respond. The language is not transparent, and we ponder its opacity. One by one, almost as if they are personified qualities, like those of Bunyan, we look at Duty, Mercy, and Constancy, accepting each one and the hard fact of their combination. We had the sublime moment of acceptance when Harriet, appropriately attired in the austere costume of pity, showed her mercy and constancy. By the time we reach this chapter, it all seems less sublime, belonging to the hard psychological realities of this life, this contemplated exile, this silence, fear and fantasy of bad faith, this withering to death. The word "duteous" forces a new concept on Bulstrode and on us. The generalizations are animated, as so often in George Eliot. They are often a source of her vivacious portrayal of a consciousness which is fully shown. It is there in its moral action, in its feeling and passion, and in its internal narrations and analyses.

The most violent generalization in the whole chapter also fixes his fear: "That she should ever silently call his acts Murder was what he could not bear." His movement of mind is wonderfully evasive. The word "Murder" is almost personified by its capital letter, in this context of allegorical vitality. It is not presented as the word he can ever call his acts but as the word he could not bear her "ever" and "silently" to call them. The action of this shrouded, dying, but painfully still alive consciousness is a powerful example of George Eliot's portrayal of the inner life. She presents restriction, evasion, equivocation. We move into, within, and out of, a shrouded consciousness.

The emotional life of Harriet is done more simply, from the outside, since, unlike Bulstrode's, it is largely articulated. We should notice George Eliot's notation of time. Like most of the chapters in the novel, this one generalizes and summarizes the movement of time but also dwells on a particular time and place at some point. George Eliot has a fine capacity to generalize the time which passes, and to do it with psychological particularity, as in the second paragraph here.

In the third paragraph the very rapidity of the motion is both an image and an appeal: "she could live unconstrainedly with the sorrow that was every day streaking her hair with whiteness and making her eyelids languid." This is generalized and sensuous, both in its physical detail, especially significant in the case of this woman, and in its reminder of the speed of the body's responsive deterioration. But George Eliot does not show husband and wife as entirely separate. This is a marriage. He cannot confess, and in the dialogue which ends the chapter, and which brilliantly combines psychological drama with important plot-making, we proceed painfully through reluctance and silence to some few necessary moments of telling. Bulstrode has to disclose Lydgate's refusal to accept the money, and Dorothea's help, both bitter pills for him to swallow. The bitter taste is renewed by the telling and the silent listening of Mrs. Bulstrode. There is another instance of quiet, plain, but effective language. George Eliot uses the dead metaphor of "wincing": in the seventh paragraph he is seen "wincing under her suggestion." The ninth paragraph, in which Mrs. Bulstrode reads Lydgate's letter returning the loan, begins with the words,

"The letter seemed to cut Mrs Bulstrode severely." The continuity of imagery is locally felt, and here it joins two pains. It shows her suffering, in this moment, as stronger than his; but his sense of her suffering then exacerbates his. It is a small detail of style, but an example of the strength of language in the novel. The animation of image is here, as so often in George Eliot, felt not through startling novelty or originality but through feather movements. This sense of a revival of deadened language and deadened response demonstrates her activity of language. This is the language of fiction fully energized. It shows the human consciousness, from outside and inside, in isolation and in relationship.

J. HILLIS MILLER

Like more or less any passage or episode in *Middlemarch*, chapter 85 can be shown to exemplify most of the novel's themes and issues. It can stand by synecdoche for the whole. This, however, is not so much because it contains the whole novel in reduced similitude, like a little wave within a big wave, repeating the structure of the big one, to use one of George Eliot's own figures, but because it raises questions about the adequacy of similitude and synecdoche. As George Eliot says in the "Finale" of *Middlemarch*, employing once more one of the grand organizing metaphors of the novel, "the fragment of a life, however typical, is not the sample of an even web." How can a fragment be typical, when it is not a valid sample? The answer lies in George Eliot's technique of "parable," to use her word for it, and on this I shall concentrate here.

Chapter 85 might be taken as a typical example of George Eliot's realism, the exact recording of speech and social fact along with that grave compassionate inwardness mixed with ironical judgment which characterizes her use of indirect discourse: "Some time, perhaps—when he was dying—he would tell her all: in the deep shadow of that time, when she held his hand in the gathering darkness, she might listen without recoiling from his touch. Perhaps. . . ." The chapter just before this one ends with Dorothea's refusal to tell her sister Celia how it came about that she and Will Ladislaw are to marry: "No, dear, you would have to feel with me, else you would never know." George Eliot's realism operates on the principle that knowledge of other human beings is only possible through sympathy or "feeling with." Chapter 85 has a chief goal leading us to understand Bulstrode and his wife by making it possible for us to feel with them, even though sympathy, in Bulstrode's case, is combined with implacable judgment. Though Harriet Bulstrode does not know it, the man is a murderer as well as a thief.

Harriet Bulstrode's "duteous merciful constancy" is shown in this chapter, as well as earlier, in chapter 74, in the admirable episode in which she comes to her fallen husband and bids him, "Look up, Nicholas," to bring good out of evil. This happens despite that irrevocability of evil-doing on which George Eliot always insists. Good comes of evil in chapter 85 because Harriet's faithfulness to her husband leads him to do the one thing he can do to make amends to her and to her family. He enables Fred Vincy to find his vocation at last as the farmer-manager of Stone Court, which has of course become Bulstrode's property. To what degree does this depend on her ignorance of the right name by which her husband should be called? She renames his evil good, in part through her ignorance, and this enables him to do good. This question implicitly motivates the self-referential rhetoric of chapter 85. By "self-referential rhetoric" I mean the way the chapter accounts both for its own mode of narration and for the ethical judgments this mode supports. This occurs primarily in the epigraph and in the first two paragraphs. These set the stage for the narration proper of the conversation between Bulstrode and his wife.

It would seem that George Eliot builds the affirmations of chapter 85 on a straightforward deconstruction of both the narrative mode and the value judgments of The Pilgrim's Progress. George Eliot is among the most subtle of epigraph makers. Among the many ways in which she uses chapter epigraphs is as a demonstration of how not to do it. This makes an ironic clashing between epigraph and text. The juxtaposition of her chapter and a fragment from the trial of Faithful in the Vanity Fair section of The Pilgrim's Progress sets the abstractions of allegory against the minute psychological and social particulars of Victorian realism. These are two modes of faithfulness, faithfulness to spiritual realities as they were seen by Bunyan as against what George Eliot in Adam Bede calls "the faithful representing of commonplace things." Epigraph and text also oppose the basing of ethical judgments on God's all-seeing eye to the Feuerbachian basing of such judgments on interpersonal relations in society. In The Pilgrim's Progress the jury of what George Eliot calls "the persecuting passions," "Mr. No-good, Mr. Love-lust, Mr. Live-loose," and the rest, brings in its verdict of guilty, but God sees and judges Faithful as faithful. After his martyrdom he ascends to heaven: "Now, I saw that there stood behind the multitude a chariot and a couple of horses, waiting for Faithful, who (so soon as his adversaries had dispatched him) was taken up into it, and straightway was carried up through the clouds, with sound of trumpet, the nearest way to the Celestial Gate." "Now, I saw. . . .": the authority of *The Pilgrim's Progress* is that of the dream vision, or at any rate of what the title page calls "the similitude of a dream." This means, ultimately, the authority of God's clear-seeing and all-seeing eye, granted for the moment, in the dream, at least in similitude, to John Bunyan. What is the source of George Eliot's judicial authority? Presumably it is the human authority of sympathy or penetrating "feeling with." George Eliot as narrator exemplifies this in relation to her imaginary personages, and she exhorts her readers to share it if they are to understand and to judge correctly the imaginary characters of the novel or their own real neighbors.

In the first paragraph of the chapter proper George Eliot opposes her procedure to Bunyan's. This happens not, as the reader might expect, by distinguishing the mode of realistic fiction from that of religious allegory, but by opposing the pity we should feel for Bulstrode to the lack of pity we feel for the triumphant Faithful. Faithful, who is after all an allegorical "abstraction," is spoken of as if he were as much a real person as Nicholas Bulstrode: "When immortal Bunyan makes his picture of the persecuting passions bringing in their verdict of guilty, who pities Faithful?" Faithful knows he is denounced solely for the good in him, while Bulstrode is pitiable because he knows he is justifiably stoned for hypocrisy, "not for professing the Right, but for not being the man he professed to be." We feel admiration for Faithful but not pity, and in that sense *Middlemarch* is superior to *The Pilgrim's Progress*. The former enhances, as the latter does not, that sympathy for our erring and imperfect neighbors which is the basis of all right-doing and of all community cohesion.

The ground of the comparison between Faithful and Bulstrode, and the basic figure underlying the whole chapter, is the "real-life" situation of a man on trial, confronting a jury of his peers. This may occur either in an actual courtroom or in that more informal but no less implacably judicial situation of a man surrounded, as Bulstrode is, by his neighbors in a closed community. Chapter 85 opposes not just two but several different ways of being on trial. It seeks, on this basis, to identify the grounds of right ethical judgment or the right naming of human acts. Who has the right to judge and to name, and how would we know the correct judgment has been made? Correct judgment is defined as correct denomination, naming the person and his deeds correctly as what they are. To call a person or a deed by its right name is proper realism or faithfulness in narration. The question of ethical judgment is, it can be seen, intimately associated with the question of the proper narrative mode.

The condemnation of Faithful in the courtroom of Vanity Fair by Mr. No-good, Mr. Malice, Mr. Blindman, and the rest is parallel to the condemnation of Bulstrode by his neighbors. Faithful is named faithless, a heretic ("Mr. Blindman, the foreman, said, I see clearly that this man is a heretic"), while Bulstrode is named thief, liar, hypocrite, if not murderer. The difference is that Faithful is not what he is named by his neighbors. He is renamed Faithful by God and by the visionary narrator. He is therefore not by any means pitiable. Bulstrode is what he is named by his peers. Therefore he is pitiable. The double structure of *The Pilgrim's Progress* sets God's true judgment against the false judgment of sinful man or "the persecuting passions." This construction, however, is dismantled. It is "deconstructed" by what George Eliot says of Bulstrode's ability to exonerate himself before the imaginary bar of the God to whom he prays. For George Eliot, God does not exist except as an individual or collective projection. It is therefore possible, in a false imaginary transaction with this nonexistent deity, to rename any bad act a good one by a species of metaphor or metamorphosis, as stolen money is "laundered" in another country, the black made white. The tendency in religious belief to baseless self-justification and hypocritical false renaming is the basis of George Eliot's repudiation of Christianity throughout her work: for example, in her early reviews, "Evangelical Teaching: Dr. Cumming" and "Worldliness and Other-Worldliness: The Poet Young." Of this false renaming the religious hypocrite Bulstrode is the most celebrated incarnation in the novels. Bulstrode's wife, on the other hand, is a real person, not an imaginary deity. Before her potential condemnation of him, Bulstrode shrinks into his usual secrecy. He "takes the fifth," so to speak, refuses to incriminate himself, and cries out for a lawyer:

> The duteous merciful constancy of his wife had delivered him from one dread, but it could not hinder her presence from being still a tribunal before which he shrank from confession and desired advocacy. His equivocations with himself about the death of Raffles had sustained the conception of an Omniscience whom he prayed to, yet he had a terror upon him which would not let him expose them to judgment by a full confession to his wife: the acts which he had washed and diluted with inward argument and motive, and for which it seemed comparatively easy to win invisible pardon—what name would she call them by? That she should ever silently call his acts Murder was what he could not bear. He felt shrouded by her doubt: he got strength to face her from the sense that she could not yet feel warranted in pronouncing that worst condemnation on him.

This admirably eloquent passage is the core of chapter 85. It is implicitly a devastating rejection of Bunyan's religious allegory. Bunyan's naming of Faithful as faithful in the name of his imaginary deity must be as unreal as Bulstrode's naming of his evil as good in the name of *his* invisible Omniscience. When one goes by the detour of a nonentity, one can turn anything into anything else. At the same time, the passage replaces the unreal religious tribunal with the real one of those direct I-thou relations which are the basis of right action and of community solidarity in George Eliot's Feuerbachian view of man. Allegory is set against realism. A false mode of ethical judgment and a false mode of literature are opposed to the right ground of ethics and the right kind of literature.

A moment's reflection, however, will show that things are not so simple here. George Eliot undermines her own affirmations at the same time as she dismantles those of Bunyan. For one thing, Bunyan is as much a realistic novelist as George Eliot is. To put this another way, she is as much an allegorist as he is. To call the jury which condemns Faithful a list of "persecuting passions" is clearly reductive. The allegorical names ("Mr. Blindman, Mr. No-good, Mr. Malice, Mr. Love-lust, Mr. Live-loose, Mr. Heady, Mr. High-mind, Mr. Enmity, Mr. Liar, Mr. Cruelty, Mr. Hate-light, Mr. Implacable") are as much kinds of persons as they are denominations of faculties or passions. The list is heterogeneous. It cannot be subsumed under a single conceptual type. The names of the jury exceed abstract allegory, as *The Pilgrim's Progress* does throughout. The names verge on becoming a list of metaphorical proper names such as people in the real world or in a realistic novel might have. In the same way, the power of Faithful, as of *The Pilgrim's Progress* as a whole, lies in the way he ceases to be an abstraction and comes to be taken as a real person by the reader. "Who pities Faithful?" We forget that the truthfulness of *The Pilgrim's Progress* lies not in its novelistic realisms but in what these stand for, according to the law of language formulated in the epigraph from Hosea 12.10 on the title page: "I have used similitudes." Allegory as a mode is by no means incompatible with realism in the sense of psychological and social verisimilitude. Far from it. Allegory in fact is a name for literature in general in its uneasy combination of a referential dimension which supports and contradicts an abstract, conceptual, or linguistic dimension. The latter both is based on the referential dimension and denies it. Ethical judgment, which belongs simultaneously to the referential and to the conceptual dimension of literature, is caught between the two.

If *The Pilgrim's Progress* is both realistic and allegorical, the same thing may be said of *Middlemarch*. "Bulstrode," like the other names in *Middlemarch* or in any other realistic novel, or like the proper names of real people, shimmers with possible metaphorical meanings. Dorothea is not given her name for nothing, nor is Casaubon, nor Ladislaw, nor Lydgate. Bulstrode: strode like a bull? Bull-lode? Is Bulstrode not bulldung, according to a twentieth-century meaning of a more vulgar word signifying empty language, or is he not a "bull" in the good nineteenth-century sense of an Irish bull, a living contradiction or linguistic aporia? Bulstrode, heavy and lumpish, the Merdle of Middlemarch, blindly justifies his wrong exercise of power. If the jury in *The Pilgrim's Progress* incarnates "the ugly passions," Bulstrode, as I have said, "incarnates" George Eliot's theory of religious hypocrisy. He is an allegory or parable of that theory, just as George Eliot's scrupulously realistic description of a pier glass, in a famous passage at the opening of chapter 27 of *Middlemarch*, is a parable of the egoism of Rosamond or of all mankind. "These things are a parable. The scratches are events, and the candle is the egoism of any person now absent—of Miss Vincy, for example." *Middlemarch*, like *The Pilgrim's Progress*, is simultaneously realistic and parabolic throughout. The difference is in the mode of allegory. George Eliot does not replace allegory by realism but one kind of allegory by another.

However, George Eliot's condemnation of the false denominations of Bunyan's allegory also implicitly condemns her own procedure. Bunyan names Faithful Faithful on the basis of a nonexistent God. George Eliot names Bulstrode Pitiable. She makes that the basis of Harriet's sympathy for him, model of the sympathy we should all have for our erring neighbors. On the other hand, she shows us that his true name is Murderer. The chapter implies that if Harriet knew what we know of him she would be unable to maintain that sympathy for him which is the basis of her ability to draw good out of evil. The ethical and the epistemological dimensions of George Eliot's humanist allegory contradict one another. The ability to do good in George Eliot's novels always in one way or another depends on ignorance, while the novels themselves show over and over the terrible dangers of ignorance (for example, Dorothea's illusions about Casaubon in *Middlemarch*). The novels exhort the reader to clear-seeing knowledge and imperturbably provide him with the sort of knowledge which, if taken seriously, would inhibit or thwart the doing good she praises in her characters. How can we help taking it seriously? Once we know, we know. While persuading the reader to have sympathy, she gives that knowledge which shows the reader that the sympathy which finds one's neighbors pitiable is as epistemologically groundless as the religious naming which calls Faithful worthy of salvation. Ethical good for George Eliot is based not on sound judicial verdict but on a performative fiat. It is an act of arbitrary renaming which has no more solid base than the religious denominations it replaces. It therefore is precariously balanced in the air, vulnerable to the knowledge which would make it impossible. It is always endangered by just that insight her dismantling of religious naming gives.

The unreadability of chapter 85 of *Middlemarch*, as of the novel as a whole, lies in the way it simultaneously shows the reader he can and must know, and shows him he cannot and must not know. The "can" and "must" here are both an ethical and a linguistic imperative. We should know and not know, and we cannot help both knowing and not knowing, both reading and failing to read. It is indeed the case that parables should not be despised, since they have the power both to hurt and to do good. The problem is that we can never know, even on George Eliot's own terms, which of these is happening with a given parable. We cannot know whether it is better to read *The Pilgrim's Progress* or to read *Middlemarch*.

RICHARD POIRIER

What I notice first when I get to chapter 85 is the size of the quotation from Bunyan's *The Pilgrim's Progress*. This longest of the headnotes enumerates the verdicts of "guilty" brought against Faithful—with that special vehemence of those who are themselves culpable—by Mr. Malice, Mr. High-mind, Mr. Liar, Mr. Implacable, and others like them. By this time it has been borne in on us, perhaps more than once too often, that we are not to judge others too harshly in *Middlemarch*, Mr. Bulstrode being the case at hand. The injunction may have begun to lose some of its power. Too many people, too many incidents have been the occasion for its evocation, and by this late chapter I have already been made less rather than more patient with such prolongations as Dorothea's obtuse incapacity to see that Casaubon is jealous of Ladislaw or that Ladislaw is in love with her, and I have long since become exasperated with displays of tolerance on behalf of the despicable Casaubon. What we learn with respect to the latter is not, I submit, the virtues of compassion and forbearance but rather the virtues of brute intuition. Celia was right to begin with, regardless of the fact that the form of her objections includes the way the gentleman eats his soup. It is to George Eliot's purpose to load the dice by contriving that the early objections to Casaubon should be so trivial that we can do nothing but dismiss them immediately, in favor of the author's hortatory admonition against "too hasty judgment":

> If to Dorothea Mr. Casaubon had been the mere occasion which had set alight the fine inflammable material of her youthful illusions, does it follow that he was fairly represented in the minds of those less impas-

sioned personages who have hitherto delivered their judgments concerning him? I protest against any absolute conclusion, any prejudice derived
from Mrs. Cadwallader's contempt for a neighbouring clergyman's alleged
greatness of soul, or Sir James Chettam's poor opinion of his rival's
legs,—from Mr. Brooke's failure to elicit a companion's ideas, or from
Celia's criticism of a middle-aged scholar's personal appearance. I am not
sure that the greatest man of his age, if ever that solitary superlative
existed, could escape these unfavorable reflections of himself in various
small mirrors; and even Milton, looking for his portrait in a spoon, must
submit to have the facial angle of a bumpkin.

(Chap. 10)

George Eliot, novelist with a novel to write, will take *her* revenge on
Casaubon in her own good time, in the big "mirror" of her book.
Meanwhile, she needs him around, and she is not above question begging
to keep him there. Quite aside from the fact that no one is talking about
"the greatest man of his age" or John Milton, is it not to the point that,
except for literary snobbery, neither of these worthies would necessarily be
considered a fit candidate for the post in question: husband to a fresh,
eager, lovely girl of eighteen? Whatever moral urgency there may be in
the heavy sarcasm of such a passage is merely a cover, I suspect, for her
more necessary literary maneuvers. She needs the kind of toleration she is
asking because it is essential to the slow pace, the massive extent of a
novel that will require the simultaneous array, at some point, of interacting
and representative social forces. The only quick judgments she allows are
those of instantaneous compassion, and these are excused precisely on the
grounds that they are derived from prolonged intimacy, such as exists
between Bulstrode and his wife.

And yet, boorish as it may sound, there is reason to insist that for
all practical purposes—of getting married, of doing business, as distinct
from reading novels—the "hasty judgments" made of Bulstrode and of
Casaubon turn out to have been the right ones. We are brought to a
question to which, in my view, the later novels of James would have to be
even more rudely submitted. Of what practical good are the expenditures
of feeling and intelligence that are not "hasty"? What is the destiny of that
exercise of intelligence which follows from her "protest against any absolute conclusion"? Must we not wonder what is gained by all the demonstrations of caution and compassion—demonstrations on the part of the
heroine and of George Eliot—for a man who, in the progress of the novel,
reveals himself as even more wretched than anyone supposed him to be?
The book raises one of the central issues having to do with the so-
called educated heart—of what use is it? What are the benefits of mature

intelligence, in George Eliot's sense, which I take to be the sense also of most people who look into novels for exemplifications of intelligence?

Obviously, any answers I might have to these questions can only be hinted at in an essay so limited as this. They are questions, nonetheless, that I increasingly ask myself about certain high-minded authors like Henry James and George Eliot and E. M. Forster, for example, and by the time I have finished eighty-four chapters of *Middlemarch* and then hit the opening of chapter 85, the questions have become acute. One good way to deal with the problem is to remember that only second-rate writers are proud of their ideas. The great ones (and the cheap ones) are alike in that they exploit whatever is at hand for the purpose, not of the reader, but of the book. If, for the sake of the book, the reader must be persuaded that his or her soul is being saved, then George Eliot will set about to save it, even believe in saving it. But she will have done it all *for* the book. Let it be granted, for the sake of getting on with the argument, that George Eliot's moralizing and instructive rhetoric offers an education useful to the conduct of life outside as well as in her book. It is, nonetheless, a "trick" or device essential to the kind of novel she wants to write, a device meant to slow us up, allow her to slow up, slow the narrative, exonerate it for not providing certain pleasures, like Trollopean allegory, and all the while provide room for things to happen that would be impossible if a different kind of intelligence were being promoted along with a different structure for making judgments. Her "protest against any absolute conclusion" can be read, without her intending or wanting it to be, as a protest in favor of her own procedures and against those of earlier (and later) novelists. Judgments are delayed even when they become inevitable, and always by an appeal to our pity or understanding or by an induced appreciation of necessary complexity.

It is a measure of George Eliot's anxiety lest we rush past her toward a hasty and conclusive judgment of her people, that, for all its length, the passage from *The Pilgrim's Progress* is only very tangentially appropriate to the situation of Bulstrode. In the paragraph immediately following the passage from Bunyan, she in fact makes the point that Faithful is extraordinarily unique in literature or history, in that though condemned he is "guiltless." As in the cautionary passage about judgments of Casaubon, she here evokes the image of the "great" man who cannot measure up to simple expectations or moral absolutes: "That is a rare and blessed lot which some greatest men have not attained, to know ourselves guiltless before a condemning crowd—to be sure that what we are denounced for is solely the good in us." Again, it seems to me that while the subject here apparently has to do with "guilt" and judgment, it is simultaneously, and as importantly, about something else. It is in praise of the difficulties she has set for herself by creating in Bulstrode a character without a semblance of heroism or greatness and, at the same time, for creating for him a situation in which it is impossible to reach an "absolute conclusion"—narratively, as well as morally. Because he "knows that he is stoned, not for professing the Right, but for not being the man he professed to be," Bulstrode is in a position which he finds difficult to sustain. But this is hardly separable from the suggestion that his situation is more difficult to render novelistically than is the equivalent position of romantic heroes or "greatest men," whose roles, like the kings in Shakespeare, are always inherently schizophrenic anyway.

No one will be surprised at this kind of self-advertisement who recalls the characterization of Casaubon or, even more, of Lydgate, with his "spots of commonness":

> Some gentlemen have made an amazing figure in literature by general discontent with the universe as a trap of dullness into which their great souls have fallen by mistake; but the sense of a stupendous self and an insignificant world may have its consolations. Lydgate's discontent was much harder to bear: it was the sense that there was a grand existence in thought and effective action lying around him, while his self was being narrowed into the miserable isolation of egoistic fears, and vulgar anxieties for events that might allay such fears.
>
> (Chap. 64)

What George Eliot does to Lydgate here, with her fillip of sarcasm at the "amazing figure" of "gentlemen" with "their great souls," is what she elsewhere does to Casaubon and to Bulstrode—all men of considerable, if quite different, public aspiration. By her quite edgy rhetoric of compassion she makes them at last indistinguishable from "later-born Theresas," while at the same time she pities them for the presumption that they might have been otherwise. The eventual fate to which she dooms them is the initial fate of her heroic women. Her attack on the hyperbolic imagination of the self, so brilliantly executed in her essay on the poet Young, "Worldliness and Other Worldliness," is in effect a disparagement of the epic life. If it is to be denied to women by force of historical circumstance, she will deny it to men by novelistic arrangements. But the disparagement goes further than that. It also denies the value of those consolations, following on the failure of heroic enterprise, which have traditionally been the province of men in history and literature. She proposes, and quite rightly I think, that heroic failure, and the admirations that attend it, are far easier to bear than is "discontent." As the Prelude makes clear, "discontent" is the destiny of aspiring women, but George Eliot so contrives things that "discontent," rather than the glamour of heroic failure, gradually emerges as the destiny of all the men in the novel, except someone like Fred Vincy, who accepts his lot as a child-producing, beloved, and patronized husband.

By inference, she offers a radical critique of American epic fiction of the nineteenth century—hers is the "home epic"—and of modernist posturings of the self as against so large an abstraction as "the culture." It does not diminish her accomplishment as a critic of these, and also of English fiction acclaimed in her own time—a critic *in* her novel—to suppose that within the complex of her attitudes we hear also the accents of feminist revenge. It manifests itself not merely in the killing off, as noted by Sandra M. Gilbert and Susan Gubar in *The Madwoman in the Attic*, of the significant males in the book—Casaubon dies, Lydgate's death is reported, Bulstrode's in this chapter is rather theatrically imagined—but, more significantly, in those moments where we can see that her moral rhetoric is inextricable from a novelistic form designed slowly and relentlessly to impose the domestication of life on everyone. Both the rhetoric and the form protest against "absolute conclusions" as if nature itself will not permit them, especially the nature of family life. All the failures of male ambition are transformed by women—think of the peripatetic psychiatric social work of Dorothea after Casaubon is out of the way—into modest forms of social reality, social accommodation. At the end Bulstrode finds it easier to imagine the "invisible pardon" of God than to settle things with his remarkable wife by telling her the whole story, so far as he himself understands it. He will apparently pay for her complete forgiveness only with his life: "some time, perhaps—when he was dying—he would tell her all." Meanwhile, it is also suggested that because, like Dorothea, she cannot or refuses to know certain things, refuses any "absolute conclusion," she is able still to nourish certain fragile webs of connection with her family and thus with the Middlemarch community, into which she had introduced her husband in the first place. She so arranges it that Bulstrode sets up Fred Vincy as manager of Stone Court. The very scene of Bulstrode's crime and hence of his disgrace thus becomes the homestead of a happy marriage, clearly dominated by a wife whose many children will carry the benefit of Bulstrode's penance into an "inconclusive" future.

GEORGE LEVINE

The Scientific Texture
of "Middlemarch"

The scientific texture of *Middlemarch* is even denser than the usual recognition of its many scientific metaphors might suggest. Henry James's general objection to Eliot that she worked too consistently from an idea to dramatic embodiment might seem, on the basis of *Middlemarch*, quite reasonable. The novel's most intense dramatic moments are recognizable as articulations of the same scientific vision that impelled G. H. Lewes's astonishingly ambitious, and uneven, *Problems of Life and Mind*, the first two volumes of which were being written at the same time. Yet to criticize George Eliot for such sweepingly intellectual structure is to miss the point of *Middlemarch*, almost to fail to read its subtexts. For among other things, that book, with *Daniel Deronda* after it, is a demonstration of the human and moral necessity of the scientific vision. Dorothea's recognition of her participation in the "involuntary, palpitating life" of mankind is dramatically powerful; but it is comprehensible in terms of the Victorian debate over evolution and the place of consciousness in nature. The ideas are dramatically central to Eliot's imagined universe, for her novels participate in a program like that of many writers on science: by virtue of rigorous secularity they attempt, in a way comparable to that of Feuerbach, to resacralize a world from which God has been dismissed.

Science stands to the text of *Middlemarch* as religion stands to that of *Paradise Lost*. It makes sense of an experience that threatens, to the

From *The Realistic Imagination: English Fiction from Frankenstein to Lady Chatterley*. Copyright © 1981 by The University of Chicago. The University of Chicago Press.

perceptions of common sense, to disintegrate into meaninglessness. In his remarkable review of *Middlemarch* in 1873, Sidney Colvin sensitively noted the great ambition of the book and the integral part played in it by science. But he did not find the book "harmonious." The massive attempt to encompass everything was a grand failure. "Is it," he asks, "that a literature, which confronts all the problems of life and the world, and recognises all the springs of action, and all that clogs the springs, and all that comes from their smooth or impeded working, and all the importance of one life for the mass,—is it that such a literature must be like life itself, to leave us sad and hungry?" Colvin finds the consolation of mere meaning, as opposed to more direct satisfaction, inadequate. The tough-minded disenchantment implicit in much of the narrative, corresponding, of course, to George Eliot's belief in the "externality of fact," and as Lewes was to call it, the "physical basis of mind," provides the wrong *kind* of meaning.

By detecting so well the way science works in the book, Colvin demonstrates, however, that there is an "ideal" shape to the narrative of *Middlemarch*. We are now perfectly comfortable with criticism that shows us how intricately and minutely Eliot makes everything connect (as everything in science was believed to connect). It is worth briefly noting here the unprovable assumptions Huxley says underlie Victorian science: the "objective existence of a material world," the "universality of the law of causation," and the truth "for all time" of "any of the rules or so-called 'laws of Nature,' by which the relation of phenomena is truly defined." *Middlemarch*, through many devices that imply the coherence "assumed" by science, makes sense. But even these assumptions were under attack, and it was part of the enterprise of Lewes's intended magnum opus to provide a metaphysical ground for the assumptions of coherence on which science is based. In any case, Eliot gives us, in Dorothea's central act, the experience writ large of every human being. Dorothea chooses to do what is required of us all—not by God but by the evolution of our species. In the abstract, her absorption into an "involuntary, palpitating" life is grim and without warmth; in the dramatic experience, its incarnation, it is a remarkable and bracing moment.

Huxleyan science becomes a fully human, not merely an intellectual, possibility, and the novel here, the "nearest thing to life," or Lawrence's "one bright book of life," resists the abstraction for the incarnation. And the incarnation confirms the idea. Without the idea, ironically, the flesh would disintegrate, the real would become that corrupting horror that, as we shall see, Lewes observed in the world available to common sense, that Newman saw in the world without God, that Conrad's Kurtz was to see lurking in the mystery beyond the idea, beyond the Victorian faith that the mystery might be benign.

Of course it is not merely contemporary science that informs *Middlemarch.* That novel seems, encyclopedically, to participate in a vast range of intellectual activity. But George Eliot does attempt to make that activity ultimately consonant with the scientific vision. Her preoccupation throughout the novel with the problem of perception, for example, belongs in the whole tradition of Victorian concern with what it means to "see," and, once again, reminds us of the connection between Victorian realism and Ruskin. Ruskin may have sought the "innocent eye," but he knew that we had to be taught how to see. His recognition that one must "learn" to see as Turner saw, his attempt to see the noble and the grand in life and art—all make impossible for him the notion that the great artist simply records what is there. Among the earliest passages in *Modern Painters* are discussions of what it is possible to "see" and how what is seen may be "represented": "Thus nature is never distinct and never vacant, she is always mysterious, but always abundant; you always see something, but you never see all."

Although the argument is offered only as an early step in an extensive justification of Turner's later style, and although the language echoes a more traditional sense of the world as an ordered plenum, the direction here is toward the position of scientific empiricists of the second half of the century. Like Ruskin, they were forced to explore certain crucial epistemological problems involved in the attempt to represent reality truthfully. Since all empirical data come through our senses, how do we know what is really out there? Do we not have evidence for the existence of physical phenomena not detectable by the senses? How do we know whether the sensations of phenomena we receive are not "supplied by ourselves"? In a brilliant essay, "The Unseen Universe," William K. Clifford demonstrated as a starting point that "innocent" perception is no part of experience: "However we express it, the fact to be remembered is that not the whole of a sensation is immediate experience . . .; but that this experience is supplemented by something else that is not in it."

George Eliot was aware of such complication while she tried to sustain the ideal of realistic representation by supplying multiple perceptions and helping to make us understand what is "not in" the immediate experience. While modifying her actual practice and leaning toward the relativism that was shortly to dominate scientific thought itself, and toward the idea of complementarity already implied by her friend Clifford, she was attempting to avoid implication in the whole cultural movement to blur the distinction between the inner and the outer. That movement was incipient in Ruskin, who dogmatically denied it, but was developed self-consciously by Walter Pater, whose sensitivity to the new knowledge of science was profoundly informing his aestheticism. If Ruskin talked, as Arnold wished to talk, of the object as in itself it really is, Pater could talk of *that*, through a method consistent with developments in science, only by registering the object as it seemed to him to be. Ironically, that is, empiricism was making objectivity impossible. Matter comes to us only through sensation. If we are honest and "realistic," we must talk not of matter but of our own sensations.

While during the late century the intellectual avant-garde was moving toward an ultimate confrontation with subjectivism, or pluralism, in the years before *The Origin of Species* George Eliot could be an unambiguously enthusiastic "realist." It was, indeed, only in those years just before Darwin that the word "realism" began to come into common usage in England. And in 1856, Eliot could say in her review of volume 3 of *Modern Painters:* "The truth of infinite value that he teaches is *realism*, the doctrine that all truth and beauty are to be attained by a humble and faithful study of nature, and not by substituting vague forms, bred by imagination on the mists of feeling, in place of definite, substantial reality." Even then, Marian Evans knew that the reality of "substance" was not so easily attainable, but on the whole she seemed to believe that by strenuous effort she could establish the distinction between "vague forms" produced by one's own desires, and "definite" reality.

Yet, of course, almost every term in this passage would require alteration in the progress of realism through the century and in her art. Imagination, disentangled, one would hope, from the "mists of feeling" was important to science as well as to poetry. Lewes argued that imagination was essential to valid scientific exploration. So too did Tyndall, Huxley, and all serious propagandists for science. In his well-known essay "The Use and Limit of the Imagination," for example, Tyndall almost echoes Lydgate: "Philosophers may be right in affirming that we can not transcend experience. But we can, at all events, carry it a long way from its origins. . . . We are gifted with the power of Imagination. . . . and by this power we can lighten the darkness which surrounds the world of the senses." Lewes put the point more extravagantly in *Problems of Life and Mind:* "No speculation, however wide of actual experience, can be valueless, if, in any way, it enlarge our vision of the Real." "Doubtless," says the narrator of *Middlemarch*, "a vigorous error vigorously pursued has kept the embryo of truth a-breathing." The "definite substantial reality" George Eliot sought was becoming anything but substantial. Rather, by the time of *Middlemarch*, it had become microscopically attenuated, or so densely implicated in process and relationship that it seemed at times indistinguishable from the ideal.

Some of the latent problems might be inferred from another of Marian Evan's early statements about the necessity for precise study of nature. In her 1851 review of R. W. Mackay's *The Progress of the Intellect*, she wrote:

> The master key of this revelation [the "divine revelation" that is coextensive with the history of human development], is the recognition of the presence of undeviating law in the material and moral world—of that invariability of sequence which is acknowledged to be the basis of physical science, but which is still perversely ignored in our social organization, our ethics and our religion. It is this invariability of sequence which can alone give value to experience and render education in the true sense possible. The divine yea and nay, the seal of prohibition and of sanction, are effectually impressed on human deeds and aspirations, not by means of Greek and Hebrew, but by that inexorable law of consequences, whose evidence is confirmed instead of weakened as the ages advance; and human duty is comprised in the earnest study of this law and patient obedience to its teaching.

Marian Evans was here putting her faith in the assumption that T. H. Huxley would be describing thirty-five years later, and that led him to argue that a "rational order . . . pervades the universe." That rational order, for George Eliot, was not Providential, but scientific, explicable in terms of the mechanics that govern the relations of matter, and essential in the arguments of scientists defending their mechanical explanations of inorganic and organic nature. For Tyndall, the insistence on miracles, on discontinuities in the order of nature, releases the monster of irrationality in society. W. K. Clifford makes a similar point, seeing the idea of "discontinuity" as monstrous and immoral, undermining our acceptance of responsibility for our actions, and introducing a deadly fatalism for the manipulation of "the fanatic or the adventurer . . . conspiring against society." All of this, however, effectually turns traditional notions on their head, for it associated determinism not with moral bondage and fatalism but with freedom, education, and responsibility. Eliot could reconcile her early epistemology with this scientific insistence on "law and order."

The law and order revealed by science were not, however, easily available to the consciousness of the ordinary person (nor, as Lewes was discovering, could the laws be rationally explained). In the close range of personal relations, scientific law must have seemed as much like "faith" as religion itself, as much to be learned as Turner's "nature." The consolation of law and order was, moreover, very different from the consolation of immortality. For though both consoled by making sense of the world, explanation is *all* that scientific law offers. George Eliot, like Tyndall and Clifford, rejected the religious insistence on immortality as mere selfishness, a bribe of ultimate satisfaction in a world whose moral being depends on human ability to renounce personal satisfaction and thus the immediate link with ape and tiger. "Invariability of sequence" makes learning possible, but what one must learn—in keeping with the dominant traditions of realistic fiction through the century—is the necessity to accommodate personal need and desire to the requirements of the "material and moral world."

The adjustment of desire to external fact requires, in George Eliot's fiction, and in Victorian moral thought, the finest discernment, and is further complicated by the possibility that "external fact" does not deserve accommodation—as seems true in *Daniel Deronda*. One's own sensations complicated the "earnest study" Marian Evans sought, for disentangling objective reality from individual perception required nothing less than scientific rigor and seemed increasingly difficult the more science revealed about nature. Victorian astronomers, for example, had taken account of the fact that the reaction time of different observers varied by fractions of seconds, but sufficiently to throw off astronomical calculations vastly. There was introduced then into the earnest study of the heavens what was called the "personal equation," which would help correct for human differences. George Eliot's famous statement in *Adam Bede* already notes how the narrator will attempt to "give a faithful account of men and things as they have mirrored themselves in my mind." But the narrator knows that the mirror is "defective" and that "the outlines will sometimes be disturbed, the reflection faint or confused."

The deficiency of the mirror, the growing awareness of the possibility of pluralism, increasing dissatisfaction with any modes of dogmatism, lead directly to the preoccupation with perspective in *Middlemarch*, and to the possibility of reading that book either as a subtle deconstruction of objectivist narratives or as an inadequately self-conscious assertion of objectivity in the face of its own awareness of the inadequacy of any single perspective. The problem of Eliot's epistemology in *Middlemarch* is treated exhaustively by K. K. Collins, but here it is important to insist that Eliot's enterprise was that of reconstruction. *Middlemarch* begins with a sense of the world in fragments; it demonstrates the way conventional modes of narration and perception lead inevitably to fragmentation and division. And its story focuses on the attempt to find a new kind of order by discovering the true—and scientifically imaginable—orders of reality that lie beyond the reach of simple common sense, of simple chronological

progress, of single structures of language and statement. The subtle adjustment of perspectives in the book is a movement toward a new reality not
quite available even to the narrator, whose wisdom can mislead us into
thinking she knows all the answers. The structure of language does not
correspond to the structure of nature. By honoring the complexities of the
new reality and the new epistemology, George Eliot breaks out of the
literary modes to which she was committed at the start of her career and
evolves from them new forms, which changed from *Middlemarch* to *Daniel
Deronda*, and obviously would have kept on changing had she lived
longer.

The trustworthy narrator of *Adam Bede* describes a culture whose
stable values provide a defining frame for each of the characters; expulsion
is a kind of death. But by *Daniel Deronda*, Eliot was writing novels in
which the stable values were merely ossified and inorganic conventions,
and in which expulsion was a kind of life. It is not only that the "stable
society" George Eliot describes in *Adam Bede* was a retrospective creation,
but that the "earnest study" entailed in Eliot's moral-realist program
required a pervasive skepticism, an openness to alternative possibilities,
and an experimental freedom that would reveal as it enacted the evolving
nature of reality.

"The improver of natural knowledge," wrote T. H. Huxley, "refuses to acknowledge authority, as such. For him scepticism is the highest
of duties." Skepticism, with all of its negative implications, would never,
it seems, have been a very powerful virtue for George Eliot. Yet skepticism
before the unverifiable—"the man of science," continues Huxley, "has
learned to believe in justification, not by faith, but by verification"—was
essential. "The men of maxims," the unreflecting dogmatics of our culture, fail to understand "that the mysterious complexity of our life is not
to be embraced by maxims, and that to lace ourselves up in formulas of
that sort is to repress all the divine promptings and inspirations that spring
from growing insight and sympathy." It is the mysterious complexity with
which Eliot grapples, and which is the condition for her fictions as it is for
life itself as she imagines it. Skepticism and a more sensitively registered
morality are aspects of the scientific-empiricist world view she struggles to
sustain. From Mill to Bertrand Russell skepticism is indeed both an
intellectual and a moral virtue. As Russell was to put it in 1928: "I wish to
propose for the reader's favorable consideration a doctrine which may, I
fear, appear widely paradoxical and subversive. The doctrine in question is
this: that it is undesirable to believe a proposition when there is no ground
whatever for supposing it true. I must of course admit that if such an

opinion became common it would completely transform our social life and our political system."

The association of a higher morality and a greater sensitivity with a world view condemned by contemporary clergymen as atheistic and materialistic was, in fact, fairly common. Note for example the uplifting tone with which Tyndall confronts the limits of human knowledge: "Meanwhile the mystery is not without its uses. It certainly may be made a power in the human soul; but it is a power which has feelings, not knowledge, for its base. It may be, and will be, and we hope is turned to account, both in steadying and strengthening the intellect and in rescuing man from that littleness to which, in the struggle for existence, or for precedence in the world, he is continually prone." From the displaced religion, the new voices for science obviously appropriated the highest moral ideals, and a spirituality differing from the religious only in that its source was not God but Matter. The opening of Walter Pater's essay "Coleridge," for example, echoes in almost all its details the ideals of George Eliot:

> The moral world is ever in contact with the physical, and the relative spirit has invaded moral philosophy from the ground of the inductive sciences. There it has started a new analysis of the relations of body and mind, good and evil, freedom and necessity. Hard and abstract moralities are yielding to a more exact estimate of the subtlety and complexity of our life. Always, as an organism increases in perfection, the conditions of its life become more complex. Man is the most complex of the products of nature.

Pater, we know, takes an altogether different direction from that of Eliot, yet his starting point is strikingly similar, and the connections among the matter, complexity, and morality are the same. The sense that dogmas are obsolete and that a new and universal quest for a fully coherent vision, in which body and soul, matter and morality, coalesce predominates here.

That quest for unity (and the belief that empiricism can provide it) is central to Eliot's work. Her narrators labor—with the same commitment to truth as if they "were in the witness box narrating [their] experience on oath"—to speak the truth of what they see. They labor equally to present a world ultimately explicable, coherent, pushed as little askew as possible by the personal equation, and finally consistent with the framework of the empiricist and positivist philosophy she shared with G. H. Lewes (though in her integrity as a "witness" she risked violating the frame).

II

In the course of the Victorian debates on science and religion, a great many distinctions were blurred. Huxley, for example, claimed to be neither atheist nor materialist, while John Tyndall claimed to be both, although it would be difficult to distinguish their actual positions. John Stuart Mill attempted to reconcile empiricism to rationalism and ended his career inching toward belief in a deity. And Darwin, of course, tried assiduously to withdraw from the field of combat. Even the positivists were divided among themselves on key issues. The blurring, however, was the condition of developing both a new language and a new reality, and it was characteristic of a movement that was turning the world upside down, making matter ideal and the ideal material, and implying a secular world as mysterious as the religious.

For the sake of convenience, in spite of important subtleties, it is reasonable to talk of George Eliot and G. H. Lewes as empiricists and materialists, although they would have rejected the latter label. Lewes specifically rejected materialism as a full explanation of life, as completely as he did spiritualism. . . . But both of them believed in the "physical basis of mind," and both of them demanded "positive" knowledge, assertions that might be verified experimentally. Neither of them, however, was an enthusiastic propagandist for science, although Lewes had propagandized for Comtism for a while. Rather they were among the skeptics R. H. Hutton described as possessing "those many fine chords of sympathy with [their] fellow-men which . . . securing for them a certain community of sentiment with their fellows, long after the sympathy of conviction necessary originally to agitate them to their full extent, has vanished."

It was not, however, only George Eliot's famous commitment to the truth of feeling that gave to her empiricist commitments a push toward the values of religion. Feeling, in empiricist thought, is unquestionable fact; it is, indeed, knowledge itself. The question running from Hume through Newman and George Eliot herself is about the nature of that knowledge, the kinds of inferences to be built on. Moreover, empiricism, while seeming to imply a commitment to the primacy of direct experience in the quest for knowledge, has invariably led to confrontation with the mysterious and unknowable. . . . To penetrate the mysteries of the unknown without surrendering faith in the reality and validity of the material world and the empirical method was the object of both Lewes and George Eliot.

The closest approximation to the sort of intuition necessary for penetrating the mysteries comes, in George Eliot's later novels, in the voice of the narrator which . . . raises important problems about reliability. But within the novels proper, George Eliot's vision required that she move beyond the world of the "dull grey eyes," since the fullest moral action, dependent on the fullest knowledge, which is itself dependent on the deepest feeling, is available only to the exceptional people in her provincial settings. The moral superiority of the untutored Dorothea Brooke, even over the sensible and educated Mr. Farebrother (who, it turns out, is a bad scientist), derives, for example, from her response to her own deep feelings, her intuitive recognition of "unapparent relations." It is this that leads her to support Lydgate. But Dorothea's moral imagination reflects the other truth—that she is an alien in a world that does not offer itself to common sense, either to Mrs. Cadwallader's or to Celia's. Such people, impelled by feelings issuing only from the experience of "direct relations," act and judge hastily. "There is nothing petty," George Eliot wrote as early as *The Mill on the Floss*, "to a mind that has a large vision of relations." But the question is, how does one achieve such a vision?

The answer, in Dorothea's case and in Lewes's theory, is at least partially clear: one must be capable of standing outside of oneself (of what might, indeed, be called an ecstasy, so rare and religious in tone does it become). It is to such an ecstasy Dorothea forces herself in the remarkable eightieth chapter of *Middlemarch*. Her immediate feeling of "direct relations" —particularly with Will Ladislaw, whom she has found in a compromised position with Rosamond—has led her for a moment to give up her generous mission to help Rosamond understand Lydgate and to soften the pain of that painful marriage. "How should I act now," she cries almost in prayer near the end of her night's vigil, "if I could clutch my own pain, and compel it to silence, and think of those three?" This familiar and moving sequence in Dorothea's history has its precise analogue in Lewes's evolving theory. It is also coherent with George Eliot's belief in the connection of feeling to knowledge, of knowledge to moral action. In her early review of Mackay's *Progress of the Intellect*, she noted that "we have long experienced that knowledge is profitable; we are beginning to find out that it is moral, and shall at last discover it to be religious."

Dorothea struggles, beyond the limits of self by virtue of the power of "feeling," the source, in Lewes's epistemology according to *Problems of Life and Mind*, of all knowledge ("by the Real is meant whatever is given in Feeling"). The power of her own feeling allows her to imagine the reality of other people's feeling (Lewes: "by the ideal is meant what is virtually given, when the process of Inference anticipates and intuites [sic] what *will* be or *would* be feeling under the immediate stimulus of the object"). We are in the presence here of what we have long recognized as George Eliot's "moral aesthetic," articulated frequently and less "scientifically" in the novels themselves. Obviously, in Lewes's theory and in George Eliot's fiction, the ideal, the making present to self of feelings literally present only to others, is achieved by virtue of the imagination, or, one might say, the power to create workable hypotheses. Only the facts given us by the narrator allow us to verify Dorothea's belief in Lydgate; for Dorothea herself, Lydgate's own explanation is the only evidence. But her hypothesis that Lydgate would not do what the town assumes he has done is a condition for useful action. Imagination seems, in the details of novelistic life, to *create* reality as much as it "penetrates" it.

But the imagination, in this view, is potentially more real than the observable external fact, the apparent relations; for the imagination can fuse together what the analytic mind has necessarily but arbitrarily separated. For both Lewes and George Eliot, organism was not a metaphor but a fact. Psychology was comprehensible only by bringing together the study of biology, of the organism in which mind is located, and of society, that larger organism—the "medium"—in which the smaller organism of the self exists by virtue of its myriad and complex relations. These conceptions were ultimately verifiable; indeed, the novels test their validity, and (putting aesthetic questions aside) justify themselves as hypotheses are justified—as imaginative constructs essential to the progress of knowledge (hence, of morality), but still only provisionally true. In Lewes's philosophy we find an attempt to construct a large unity of psychology (a discipline avoided by Comte because too focused on the individual) and sociology (the locus of "humanity"). In this construct the self and the other are not two things but one; the objective and subjective are indispensable to each other, are indeed merely different aspects of the same thing. There is no existence without relationship: "Nothing," writes Lewes in *Problems of Life and Mind,*

> exists in itself and for itself; everything in others and for others: *ex-ist-ens*—a standing out relation. Hence the search after *the thing in itself* is chimerical: the thing being a group of relations, it *is* what these are. Hence the highest form of existence is Altruism, or that moral and intellectual condition which is determined by the fullest consciousness—emotional and cognitive—of relations.

George Eliot herself, writing in 1868 her "Notes on Form in Art," reiterates this organicist view: "Forms of art can be called higher or lower only on the same principle as that on which we apply these words to organisms; viz. in proportion to the complexity of the parts bound up into one indissoluble whole." Complex unity is the ideal, both in art and life.

To sustain their tough willingness to acquiesce in the very changes that were fragmenting and desacralizing their worlds, Lewes and George Eliot had to incorporate as richly as possible the complexities which—to common sense—seemed to be shattering the unified vision of an earlier age, and which to Victorian culture as a whole challenged dangerously all the inherited traditions of religion and morality.

But we can see here that for Lewes and George Eliot, unity is transferred from God to organism, an entity that implies continuity and growth, through evolution, interdependence, and therefore self-denial, love, morality, complexity, and mystery. Altruism, a positivist ideal, becomes both a Christian moral imperative and a scientific one.

But here, the impulsion to unity—echoing in the traditional Victorian insistence on self-denial—has the further complication of threatening the very conception of selfhood. The self, in Lewes's view, cannot be understood as a thing in itself, but only as a set of relations. He speaks moreover, elsewhere in *Problems of Life and Mind*, of "mind" as an abstraction that names a process and a set of relationships, not as a stable thing that can explain anything. The self is both "the generalised abstraction of continuous feeling," and a series of "concrete discontinuous states." The self, then, is a sum of qualities forever in process. "Character too," says the narrator of *Middlemarch*, "is a process and an unfolding." The notion is put yet more strongly by Clifford. "The universe," he says, "consists of feelings. A certain cable of feelings, linked together in a particular manner, constitutes me. Similar cables constitute you. That is all there is."

As a mere part of an "involuntary, palpitating life," Dorothea's self is almost an illusion and has its value in the larger fate of the species. Although, in accordance with George Eliot's realist aesthetic and her refusal to sacrifice immediate feeling and particularities to ideas, the image that Dorothea sees at the window is particularized, her vision is rapidly assimilated to larger significances. Her moral triumph entails the disappearance of the self and slips back from science to Carlylean self-annihilation. Similarly, the character of the "highest" (i.e., most "altruistic") beings in Eliot's novels is increasingly defined by the absence of what we traditionally think of as character. Where Hardy gives us a "man of character" in Henchard, Eliot gives us Daniel Deronda. That special self-identifying eccentricity, whether Micawber's lamentations or Casaubon's austere defensiveness, is a sign of a demanding self incapable of the necessary absorption in the Lewesian organism.

The austerely theoretic force that lies behind Dorothea's vision is more immediately recognizable in Eliot's poetry, where, as R. H. Hutton early remarked, "the rhythm and music drop a soft cloud over the moral detail of life, and fill her soul with the principles she has generalised from its study, rather than with the minutiae of its scenery." There are no such minutiae at the end of *Jubal*, when the angel comes to console Jubal after his people have failed to recognize him as the godlike founder of music whom they celebrate:

> This was thy lot, to feel, create, bestow.
> And that immeasurable life to know
> From which the fleshy self falls shrivelled, dead,
> A seed primeval that has forests bred.

The grim affirmation here and in *Middlemarch* is too reminiscent of the near despair of Tennyson's famous complaint of Nature: "So careful of the type she seems, so careless of the single life." But in the positivist context, what drives Tennyson to despair constitutes the highest moral affirmation. As Lewes sees the problem in *Problems of Life and Mind*, it is only when one gets beyond the sense of reality available to ordinary perceptions (and thus, also, beyond the conventional sense of character) that one can begin to find the possibility of affirmation.

> It is true that our visible Cosmos, our real world of perceptions, is one of various and isolated phenomena; most of them seeming to exist in themselves and for themselves, rising and disappearing under changing conditions. . . . But opposed to the discontinuous Cosmos perceived, there is the invisible continuous Cosmos, which is conceived of as uniform Existence, all modes of which are interdependent, none permanent. The contradiction is palpable. On the one side there is ceaseless change and destruction, birth and death, on the other side destruction is only transformation, and the flux of change is the continuous manifestation of an indestructible, perdurable Existence.

"The discontinuous Cosmos perceived" is the Victorian world without God, Newman's living busy world that shows "no trace of my creator." The wider the vision of relations, however, and the more broad the range of imagination, the more beautiful the world becomes. What Rosamond, with her narrow Middlemarchian mind, finds hideous and monstrous, her husband finds beautiful. "The invisible continuous Cosmos" offers not, of course, a "trace of my creator," but another object of verifiable empirical study—the organism. And organism, in late-century thought, almost displaces God, for its vital complexity can help explain phenomena that seem merely irrational and fortuitous. The organism offers an ultimately intelligible universe, and it banishes monsters. What appears as "destruction" becomes only "transformation," and what appears as the "flux of change" turns out to be "the continuous manifestation of an indestructible, perdurable Existence." Thus, within the same empiricist tradition by which Newman learned to make the leap from the limitation of sense experience to God, Lewes makes the leap from that limitation to science, and scientific method. Progress, the diminution of evil, follows directly from the expansion of science beyond simple empiricism to an exploration of the "unapparent" by means of the refined instruments of hypothesis, imagination, and sheer intellectual energy.

In *Middlemarch*, Lydgate is on the verge of the imaginative genius required for true application of scientific method, and he is most directly engaged in the attempt to see "unapparent relations." In that brilliant passage, so easily read as a description of the novelist's art, in which Lydgate's investigative ambitions are described, we learn that he values

> the imagination that reveals subtle actions inaccessible by any sort of lens, but tracked in that outer darkness through long pathways of necessary sequence by the inward light which is the last refinement of Energy, capable of bathing even the ethereal atoms in its ideally illuminated space.

Every word here is alive with scientific or Lewesian implication. This is no mere vague celebration of scientific hopes and tenacity, but a precise articulation of the dream of meaning, of the melding together of object and subject, self and other, thought (or spirit) and matter. It is where Lewesian empiricism, in its later phases, desired to go. It may be, as the narrator remarks, that Lydgate has asked the wrong questions in his investigations, but he is not far askew; and in this passage George Eliot implies Huxley's world governed according to rational laws and uniform principles. In it, all phenomena will be made comprehensible by a unifying theory.

Lewes's empiricism is almost Berkeleyan in its insistence on the perceiver or "feeler" of experience. "The universe to us is," he says in *Problems of Life and Mind*, "the universe of Feeling, and all its varieties are but varieties of Feeling. We separate them into object and subject because we are forced to do so by the law of Relativity." The best scientist would be the most "sensitive," the most capable of the widest range and most intense registration of feeling. Such a scientist, we might say, would burn with a hard gemlike flame. Science depends on intensity for precision, and "precision is the one quality which impotent minds least appreciate." Thus Lydgate's "inward light" is the intense but disciplined feeling that allows imagination. "Light," contemporary science had shown, was, with heat, a product of energy, though more intense and more refined, moving its impulses through a matter so refined scientists named it "ether." But the light is also human consciousness, another even more refined product of material energy, though so subtle that no philosopher had been able to show its materiality. It is an energy that has no mass of its own. Thus it is also a subjectivity that allows for the construction of the ideal (hence "ideally illuminated space"), the process of inference that anticipates "what will or should be feeling under the immediate stimulus of the object." This light of scientific imagination thus follows "necessary sequence," the continuing impact of cause and effect through the material world. The scientific imagination does not extend to vague guesses, extravagant as it may seem to become, but works within the limits of the real and is controlled by the "law and order" that become evident in all of nature.

The full explication of this passage in Lewesian terms would take the five volumes he required—nor could he really finish before his death. But its references are as precise and specific as in the word "ethereal," where we have not a vague Miltonic reference to the unearthly but a precise allusion to the then accepted hypothesis that ether was the medium in which electromagnetic waves propagated, the very space in which illumination was possible. It was "unapparent" but "real."

Ethereal, of course, carries with it its prescientific connotations, as well, and further implies that union between spirit and matter that is the object of Lydgate's search, and Lewes's. Both fictional and real scientist seemed to feel that the spiritual would be explicable in terms of matter, and Lydgate is, like Lewes, attempting to to discover the "Physical Basis of Mind," is trying to "pierce the obscurity of those minute processes which prepare human misery and joy, those invisible thoroughfares which are the first lurking places of anguish, mania, and crime, the delicate poise and transition which determine the growth of happy or unhappy consciousness." Sadness, like madness, is a disease. The large vision of relations is perhaps the way to the cure.

But Lydgate fails, ironically, because he is not adequately "selfless." His attempt to banish the monstrousness of the "discontinuous Cosmos" for the impersonal immortality of the "continuous" one is flawed by the "spots of commonness" on his character. His uncommon, his Arnoldian "best self," which is properly distanced in his scientific work, is inadequately disciplined in his life. While the narrator watches his implication in the organism of Middlemarch, Lydgate fails to see beyond his immediate experience. He does not, in society, aspire to Dorothea-like selflessness that would allow him a full imagination of the paths of necessary sequence, nor does he understand, what George Eliot knew, that every biological issue has sociological implications.

Ironically, then, Dorothea is the better scientist, and the contrast between her success and Lydgate's failure raises directly a central aesthetic problem that arises from the aspiration to selflessness. The Victorian realist, we have seen, puts primary emphasis on character; and the shift of emphasis from character is part of the whole transformation away from realism. The beginning of the breakdown of the idea of the self is already visible in George Eliot, as traditional moral-religious concerns flow into scientific thought.

BARRY V. QUALLS

Speaking through Parable: "Daniel Deronda"

Perhaps *Daniel Deronda* is so disturbing because it seems, *ab initio*, like none of George Eliot's earlier works. There is no Wordsworthian glow of memory to displace the fragmented present with a Hayslope, no invocation of a St. Theresa to cushion the reader by framing and elevating the often confused and blind doings of a woman and a rural community living in an England with no certain notion of what the signs of the time might portend. Instead, we are placed "*in medias res*," in the readers' present. And the spiritual values of St. Ogg's, Stoniton, Lantern Yard, and Transome Court are combined and become horribly, because unmediatedly, present. A "scene of dull, gas-poisoned absorption," featuring men and women as drugged as any of the Veneering crowd, begins the novel; the Land of Goshen has become a casino. Yet it all ends with Manoa's elegy from the conclusion of *Samson Agonistes*—as if these Philistines had been destroyed and the children of light were quite triumphant in their cleansed Promised Land.

Which they in no way are. Yet we, as readers, have *seen* that land, and seen it in the most clearsighted way because George Eliot, after so many fictions alluding to the Judaic-Christian myth and Bunyan's use of it, constructs this final novel overtly around the chief situations and landscapes that had provided the texture of Puritan and evangelical biography and autobiography, and of Dinah Morris' sermons. The "children of light" are in bondage, to their own psychic heritage of slavery and

From *The Secular Pilgrims of Victorian Fiction: The Novel as a Book of Life.* Copyright © 1982 by Cambridge University Press.

to heathens "doing as they like" with more fervor than even Arnold's
Philistines. And lest any casual reader miss the analogies—the Morality
Play beneath the surface—the "children of light" in *Deronda* are not
sensitive "Christians" like Maggie and Dorothea, but actual Jews. One is
even a Moses as well ("an accomplished Egyptian"). The novel's formal
construction insists on our recognition of its epic historical foundation: a
beginning *in medias res*, constant allusions to Tasso's *Gerusalemme liberata*,
to Handel's *Rinaldo* (itself based on a scene in the Tasso), to Dante's
Commedia, and to the story of the Exodus and the Dispersion. Further-
more, the titular hero is himself identified as a savior-knight, as Moses
and Prince Camaralzaman, at once the leader of history and a hero of
romance. As in all romance, this hero does go off to found a newer world;
as in the history, on the final page he stands like Moses glimpsing the
promised land—although his sight is the vision and not Moses' reality.

In all of this tale-spinning, as readers since 1876 have been an-
nouncing, there is one flaw: the hero leaves the real—because palpably living—heroine behind him in the City of Destruction with no promise of a
Greatheart to bring her away towards some happy-ever-after. But in
making this complaint we respond more to the hero's failure to satisfy *our*
"dreams" than we do to the guideposts George Eliot gives us. The stories
of Dorothea and Esther also end with a sense of dissatisfaction, but in
each case the narrator shares the readers' letdown, even as together they
share Dorothea's or Lydgate's. The narrator of *Daniel Deronda*, on the
other hand, feels no melancholy sadness at the failure of youthful hope;
indeed, there is wellnigh euphoria. *Deronda*'s narrator is not *Middlemarch*'s
historian, nor *The Mill*'s remembrancer. Those narrators had told of the
necessity of giving up our fictions if we were ever to live adequately—albeit
never heroically—in the "real." But that forsaking of romance—whether
Maggie's, Esther's, or Dorothea's—had left the lives of these "substantive
and rare" human beings "absorbed" in the lives of others, or in death. All
vision narrows to domestic dimensions.

George Eliot's last "experiment in life" is her meditation on this
sense of loss when so much of romance is given up. *Daniel Deronda* asks,
more fearlessly than any Victorian novel, what is the place of art in our
lives, of the fictions we read and the paintings we see and the music we
hear? And it avows that all art, whether of words or colors or sounds,
distances and distorts reality: all becomes romantic to some degree.

> Perspective, as its inventor remarked, is a beautiful thing. What horrors
> of damp huts, where human beings languish, may not become pictur-
> esque through aerial distance! What hymning of cancerous vices may
> we not languish over as sublimest art in the safe remoteness of a

strange language and artificial phrase! Yet we keep a repugnance to rheumatism and other painful effects when presented in our personal experience.

Within this contrast—between the artificial and the severely real—how is art to function? How are mere words to tell morally? How are they to become a perhaps painful part of our personal experience in the way they burnt into Bunyan? The answer that *Daniel Deronda* implicitly offers is that art must find its sources in the religious myths that form part of man's consciousness, in the archetypal experiences that are innate. Bunyan's way is the only way. Otherwise art is, as Klesmer suggests, sheer idolatry.

George Eliot is not suddenly urging some creed on her readers. Her attitude is the same as Arnold's, and Carlyle's earlier. In 1875 Arnold had noted that "two things about the Christian religion must surely be clear to anybody with eyes in his head. One is, that men cannot do without it; the other, that they cannot do with it as it is." Carlyle had said the same thing in *Sartor Resartus* and thereafter, and had said it through structures and language that formed the central literary and religious heritage of his readers. Yet by the time of the *Pamphlets* he had become so frightened by the "aerial distance" that language seemed to confer on truth that he shrilly defended the *Iliad* and the Hebrew Bible against the "Fine Arts." These epics are not "Fiction" but "histories," he proclaimed, "burning with . . . *belief*," "before all things, *true*" because grounded "on the Interpreting of Fact." Obviously, he wants—has always wanted—another language to tell those eternal truths, but there was none available. "My friend, I have to speak in crude language, the wretched times being dumb and deaf: and if thou find no truth under this but the phantom of an extinct Hebrew one, I at present cannot help it."

By the time of *Daniel Deronda*, George Eliot has come to this same conclusion. Confronting the "wretched times" of the deaf and dumb men and women of the present day, she turns to the one ground of associations she hopes is still "deeply rooted in [her] readers' minds." Every major character in *Daniel Deronda* except Grandcourt thinks in terms of "genteel romance," fairy tales, or the Bible; and only those who use the latter survive spiritually. Every one of these people looks at the chaotic world around them in terms of old patterns that sort out the confusions of the present by showing their ordering, their beginning and end. George Eliot's men and women seek, or are forced to seek—if they would be alive—that symbolic situation in the past ("where peace and permanence seemed to find a home away from the busy change that sent the railway train flying in the distance") that will give meaning and understanding to their own lives; they look for some "accustomed pattern" for ordering the "un-mapped country within us" and without.

The only past that can provide such a "key" is, finally, the old Hebrew one. It is a memory based in fact. And to insure that no reader misses this idea, George Eliot uses an epic paradigm founded on the histories of the effort to retake Jerusalem from the "heathens." She bases the novel's structure—*its two plots*—on an episode in Tasso's *Gerusalemme liberata* and, very likely, on an adaptation of the episode by Giacomo Rossi for Handel's *Rinaldo*. The opera tells of a Christian knight in love with Almirena, daughter of Godfrey, the Christian leader of forces which will liberate Jerusalem. The opposition to the Christians—and to the heroine's love—is Armida, an enchantress who commands dragons and who loves Rinaldo. Her reward is conversion; his, Almirena; Godfrey's, Jerusalem. The chief difference between the opera and the Tasso episode is the absence of Almirena in the Tasso; there the enchantress takes both forms—helpless maiden in the water and queen of the heathen forces.

George Eliot makes one signal change in this old plot, an exact reversal: her Christians need the Jews for liberation. Otherwise, she exploits all of its romance possibilities. In *Daniel Deronda* she simply becomes, without apology, the sacred romancer—this even as she keeps a firm grip on the narrator's mirror-observer function. What she does is to juxtapose—*not* fuse—the dream worlds of Maggie and Dorothea to the quotidian world of the Poysers and Dodsons and Middlemarchers. In Deronda and Mordecai she gives scenes which seem remote and "romantic" because they center on "visions," on what Mordecai defines as "the creators and feeders of the world." In Gwendolen and Philistia we have Dodson Protestantism hardened and seen in a harsher light. The structures and language that express the teleological ideals of religious experience stand boldly beside language depicting the "puzzlin' " world that Mr. Tulliver experienced and Mary Garth accepts, the world of chance and no pattern that Godfrey Cass so easily thought himself born into. A world devoted to visionary experience confronts and affronts a world centered on satisfying its own immediate "natural" desires. And after George Eliot has given us the histories of her two protagonists, she makes the relationship of their lives quite clear. Within Deronda, she notes, "there was a fervour which made him easily find poetry and romance among the events of everyday life."

> And perhaps poetry and romance are as plentiful as ever in the world except for those phlegmatic natures who I suspect would in any age have regarded them as a dull form of erroneous thinking. They exist very easily in the same room with the microscope and even in railway

carriages: what banishes them is the vacuum in gentlemen and lady passengers. How should all the apparatus of heaven and earth, from the farthest firmament to the tender bosom of the mother who nourished us, make poetry for a mind that had no movements of awe and tenderness, no sense of fellowship which thrills from the near to the distant, and back again from the distant to the near?

It is the question the novel explores, and explores with "the apparatus of heaven and earth"—with the story of the Hebrews and Jerusalem which was first history and then the stuff of epic and romance.

None of this is apparent at the novel's beginning, any more than is its traditional *Bildungsroman* structure. George Eliot's manipulation of narrative time does not allow readers to see, until two hundred pages have passed, that her recountings of Gwendolen Harleth's and Daniel Deronda's histories begin at that moment in each of their lives which initiates all pilgrims' progresses: when the question "What shall I do?" forces itself on the consciouness. Gwendolen and Deronda, seeing each other for the first time, significantly in a casino, are trying to find a "pathway" (*passim*) towards freedom amidst the pressures of what seem intractable circumstances. Daniel "felt himself in no sense free." Gwendolen views "the life before her as an entrance into a penitentiary." Yet all this remains hidden from the readers for fifteen chapters.

George Eliot instead begins her "story" as Bunyan did his dream and Dante his journey: *in medias res*. But that itself is ambiguous. It means at once Gwendolen at the roulette table and Gwendolen "in Daniel Deronda's mind," which is the locus of the novel's opening paragraph. Yet instead of immediately exploring that mind, we enter Gwendolen's case history. Only when we know how and why she got to that casino do we return to Deronda; and then we immediately begin his history, one which seems to have about as much to do with Gwendolen in Philistia as Teufelsdröckh's story has to do with a drawing-room in *Pelham*. Whatever "romance" there is in the story of "the princess in exile" is, her uncle, Reverend Gascoigne, tells her, something quite inferior to the "higher" considerations of money, rank and marriage.

On the other hand, everyone (including himself) perceives Daniel's story as "romance"; and *it* centers on "higher" considerations which quite damn the parish minister. In outline it differs no whit from Teufelsdröckh's youthful history: though his childhood is happy, it is also marked by "the first arrival of care" at the age of thirteen, when the question "Who am I?" forces itself on the young boy. The need to know his parents, the shock of questioning his heritage and finding no answer, will mark an epoch for him:

he was romantic. That young energy and spirit of adventure which have helped to create the worldwide legends of youthful heroes going to seek the hidden tokens of their birth and its inheritance of tasks, gave him a certain quivering interest in the bare possibility that he was entering on a like track—all the more because the track was one of thought as well as action.

He sets out to involve himself in a significant action, to know the past—his and others—and to see its connection with the present. He "had a passion for history, eager to know how time had been filled up since the Flood, and how things were carried on in the dull periods."

But that passion cannot be satisfied until he knows his own heritage. Like Teufelsdröckh he feels himself an "Ishmaelite"; and his "inexpressible sorrow" over his unknown parentage similarly leads not to self-centeredness, but "takes the form of fellowship and makes the imagination tender." He yearns towards rescuing others, towards "telling upon their lives with some sort of redeeming influence," towards saintliness. This very yearning and his constant meditations paralyze his "Active Power (*Thatkraft*)."

> His imagination had so wrought itself to the habit of seeing things as they probably appeared to others, that a strong partisanship, unless it were against an immediate oppression, had become an insincerity for him . . . Few men were able to keep themselves clearer of vices than he; yet he hated vices mildly . . .

The yearning towards rescue and the love it brings has been for Deronda a way of escaping that isolated because unrooted self which has been his birthright.

> His own face in the glass had during many years been associated for him with thoughts of some one whom he must be like . . . He was forgetting everything else in a half-speculative, half-involuntary identification of himself with the objects he was looking at, thinking how far it might be possible habitually to shift his centre till his own personality would be no less outside him than the landscape . . .

It is at one of those moments of gazing on the blank which is himself that he finds Mirah beside the river. And his subsequent reference to himself as "Orestes or Rinaldo" is doubly telling. Through these namings, even as they are one more way of dealing with his sense of having no identity, he makes his own actions a part of that flow of time from past to present; the allusions insert him into the heroic frame of significant actions which he constantly seeks.

George Eliot keeps the romance analogies close to Deronda because he does indeed, and consciously, have "something of the knight-errant in his disposition"; and because, after Mirah's rescue, she wants the readers to share the experience with those who know Daniel. She wants us to feel ourselves like Mab and the others, "in the first volume of a delightful romance." By involving us so determinedly and allusively in romance, George Eliot for the last time examines the myths that sensitive men and women must have if the dead weight of present-day life is not to crush them. Teufelsdröckh falls into the abyss. Deronda avoids it by ascending consciously into heroic romance (and he significantly lacks the rational education that was part of Teufelsdröckh's undoing). His romance we may not find so interesting, but it tells why we miss the "shadow" in his life which we find in most romances—and in Gwendolen's story. Deronda deals with those demons of the self by distancing them; he understands their mythic analogues and thus retains his sanity.

If "demons" do not invade his own psyche, they abound in the lives of the women he would rescue. The story of Mirah has all the characteristic images we have come to see in the Victorian spiritual biography: the child who feels an orphan because she is so ill-used by her father (who would sell her into bondage if he could) leaves him only to find the world still a "hell," and herself a "poor wanderer" in it. Though she, a young Jewess, remembers her "People . . . driven from land to land and . . . afflicted," she finds hope gone and her mind "into war with itself." And then: "Faith came to me again: I was not forsaken"—Deronda saves her. The last song we hear her sing summarizes her history:

> Lascia chi'o pianga   [Let me lament
> mia cruda sorte,   My cruel destiny,
> e che sospiri   Let me sigh
> la libertà.   For freedom;
> Il duolo infranga   Let grief sunder
> queste ritorte   The chains that bind me,
> de' miei martiri   If only out of pity
> sol per pietà.   For my anguish.]

It is Almirena's aria from *Rinaldo*, sung when the heroine is imprisoned in the fortress of the sorceress Armida. The song tells the reader something of Mirah's feelings, of course; she sings just after Hans Meyrick has given his "romance" of "the Vandyke Duchess," complete with the baritone's death and her marriage to Deronda, "with [his] fine head of hair, and glances that will melt instead of freezing her" (Hans is borrowing Tasso's words for his description of the glance: *Gerusalemme liberata*, XVI: lxvii— Armida seducing Rinaldo). Mirah, not knowing Gwendolen's case, as the readers do, quite naturally and jealously sees her as some sorceress-queen enchanting Daniel.

But her song underlines what the reader has been experiencing from the novel's opening paragraph—albeit only consciously when Deronda's history has been juxtaposed to Gwendolen's. The readers know that Gwendolen's story is also summarized by "Lascia ch'io pianga":

> Il duolo infranga
> queste ritorte . . .

Gwendolen herself has announced early-on that she has "read and learned by heart at school" the *Gerusalemme liberata.* But not until she meets Deronda does her real education begin. And it will indeed involve her getting the Tasso "by heart." Only grief will, finally, sever the chains binding her.

The novel begins, literally, when Deronda discovers in the gambling Gwendolen "something of the demon":

> Was the good or the evil genius dominant in those beams? Probably the evil; else why was the effect that of unrest rather than of undisturbed charm?

Though he will come to see in her not some "vulgar" enchantress "setting snares" for him but rather one more of "the Hagars and Ishmaels" for whom he has such pity, he will discover that in her case a Rinaldo's rescue is not so easily effected. And in that, as George Eliot tells us, "some education was being prepared for Deronda." It is an education which will show the limits of romantic action.

George Eliot introduces Gwendolen at the first point in her life when she becomes aware, however glibly, that the world does not necessarily order itself to her desires. It is indeed a "break in consciousness" (as Frye calls the beginning of romance), for it is the point where Gwendolen is asking "What can I do?"

> And even in this beginning of troubles, while for lack of anything else to do she sat gazing at her image in the growing light, her face gathered a complacency gradual as the cheerfulness of the morning. Her beautiful lips curled into a more and more decided smile, till at last she took off her hat, leaned forward and kissed the cold glass which had looked so warm. How could she believe in sorrow? If it attacked her, she felt the force to crush it, to defy it, or run away from it, as she had done already. Anything seemed more possible than that she could go on bearing miseries, great or small.

But the burden on her will only increase.

Gwendolen's kissing of her mirrored image is a gesture perfectly appropriate to this "princess in exile" who has never had roots anywhere ("A human life," George Eliot writes of Gwendolen, "should be well rooted in some spot of a native land")—and whose roots will be in "romance" in its most demonic sense (the mirror-kiss reminds us that Tasso's Armida has a mirror about her when she seduces Rinaldo). George Eliot throughout her fiction has used the mirror as the emblem of self-absorption: Hetty Sorrel, Rosamond Vincy, Mrs. Transome, Gwendolen—all these women define themselves iconographically by their adoration of their mirrored images, a self-worship which places them amongst the Romantic egoists whose lives comprise, finally, a "Satanic masquerade, . . . entered on with an intoxicated belief in its disguises." Except for one moment Rosamond certainly never loses the intoxication. Hetty does so only when confronted with death. Gwendolen Harleth alone successfully goes through a fire-baptism. Her story, at its beginning a conventional "Sorrows of Gwendolen" tale, full of wanderings and ennui, becomes by its end a *Sartor Resartus*: very unRomantic and very full of romance. It introduces Gwendolen to a world of "fellowship" and "movements of awe and tenderness" undreamt of in her experience—even if they are in that *Gerusalemme liberata* she has "by heart."

Like Charlotte Brontë, George Eliot will find the vanity-mirror emblem the perfect embodiment of the kind of egoism that controls her men and women. It is an emblem for her, as for Quarles and Bunyan and for the Romantics, of being bound to and within the surface of self:

> Believe her not, her glass diffuses
> False portraitures: . . . she abuses
> Her misinform'd beholder's eye . . .

> In vain he lifteth up the eye of his heart to behold his God, who is not first rightly advised to behold himself: . . . for if thou canst not apprehend the things within thee, thou canst not comprehend the things above thee; the best looking-glass, wherein to see thy God, is perfectly to see thyself.

Know "the things within thee" first. But any world within hardly interests Hetty, or Rosamond, or Gwendolen as they gaze into their mirrors. They see nothing beyond their surfaces; they feel nothing beyond their desires. They are actresses, "representing" themselves according to Mrs. Lemon or "genteel romance," imagining themselves in dramas or romantic ballads, avoiding—if it threatens at all—any hint of demon-empires within the self. "I am not talking about reality, mamma," Gwendolen says when Mrs. Davilow reminds her that she is afraid of the dark. These egoists are what René Girard calls "romantic *vaniteux*"; living completely on their surfaces, they are perfect solipsists and have no sense of anything transcending themselves. To the narrator's constant urging that each see "que la terre tourne autour du soleil," the reply is "Je vous jure que je ne m'en estime pas moins." Convinced that they are utterly original and determined to be no one's disciples they intend to follow what Gwendolen calls "her favourite key of life—doing as she liked." Nothing, not religion, not romance, displaces them from their own self-esteem:

> the religious nomenclature belonging to this world was no more identi-fied for [Gwendolen] with those uneasy impressions of awe than her uncle's surplices seen out of use at the rectory . . . Church was not markedly distinguished in her mind from other forms of self-presentation, for marriage had included no instruction that enabled her to connect liturgy and sermon with any larger order of the world than that of unexplained and perhaps inexplicable social fashions.

Gwendolen may avow she has Tasso "by heart," but her fear of solitude and the dark and "the vastness in which she seemed an exile" tells us how little she understands his words. She thinks herself completely immune to Christian's need for journeying or to the quests in Tasso (reduced by her to "genteel romance"). And yet, as much as she would ignore the "unmapped country within," her unease upon first seeing Deronda and her fear of the picture of the dead head tell us that she is not—like Hetty—dead to any world above or below; the very fears show us that she is not a solipsist like Grandcourt. Gwendolen's increasingly terrifying isolation, always imaged by the mirror and finally climaxed by her mirrored entrapment on Grandcourt's boat, is the result of that impulse to exalt the self and obliterate all sense of anything beyond it. Her sighting of the novel's Rinaldo forces on her the encounter with, and conquest of, her own "Demon-Empire" (as it begins Armida's salvation process in Tasso). "You began it, you know, when you rebuked me," she tells Deronda, referring to her trouble. And he defines for her the "refuge" that will save:

> We should have a poor life of it if we were reduced for all our pleasure to our own performances. A little private imitation of what is good is a sort of private devotion to it . . . The refuge you are needing from personal trouble is the higher, the religious life, which holds an enthusiasm for something more than our own appetites and vanities.

It is indeed an answer to her question, repeated more and more as the glass's image becomes less fetching, "Why shouldn't I do as I like, and not mind?"

The language George Eliot employs as Gwendolen faces the "uncertain shadow [which] dogged her" and seeks help from her "priest" is baldly the language of religious romance, the language of an Armida losing control over her demon servants. The drugged air of the gambling halls that Gwendolen had chosen for "escape" follows her into marriage with Grandcourt, whose "sort of lotos-eater's stupor . . . was taking possession of her." She tries desperately for "new excitements that would make life go by without much thinking." Thus, the "demonic force" that Deronda witnessed at the gaming table seems to him even more at work within her after the marriage. And, as the readers know, "Furies" have entered her life because she violated that "question of right or wrong" which Lydia Glasher's existence forced her to see, and which "rouse[d] her terror." Thereafter life has become the "labyrinth" she had feared, and those mirrors she had worshipped become part of her "painted gilded prison." The "many shadowy powers" that haunt her force her to *see* what she will call the "two creatures" of her self, two creatures she sees objectified by Deronda and Grandcourt. The husband is the "monster," the total egoist who is the "immovable obstruction to her life, like the nightmare of beholding a single form that serves to arrest all passage though the wide country lies open"; he is her "worst self" personified, and the more terrible because he is connected in Gwendolen's mind with Lydia Glasher, a woman "who had the poisoning skill of a sorceress." Standing quite opposite to and above all of this, as in Tasso or any epic romance, is the savior, Deronda. Like Rinaldo, he is there to bring "that change of mental poise which has been fitly named conversion"; his "peculiar influence" will make of "heaven and earth" a "revelation" for Gwendolen, will arouse the godborn within her. He is her "recovered faith," kept "with a more anxious tenacity, as a Protestant of old kept his Bible hidden or a Catholic his crucifix." In the course of her story he becomes "a part of her conscience," precisely as Rinaldo becomes part of Armida's in the Tasso:

> My dear (she said), that blesseth with thy sight
> Even blessed angels, turn thine eyes to me,
> For painted in my heart and portray'd right,
> Thy worth, thy beauties, and perfections be;
> Of which the form, the shape, and fashion best,
> Not in this glass is seen, but in my breast. . . .
>
> O let the skies thy worthy mirror be.
> (*Gerusalemme liberata*, XVI: xxi)

The religious language that begins to accompany and color this demon-world in which the "princess" lives tells us what George Eliot is doing: Gwendolen is being dragged against her will into a life where "vision"—the word appears even more than in *Felix Holt*—either feeds life, or else destroys it. Such vision shows us the difference between heaven and earth, and gives us the possibility of escaping the hells of our own making. And it demands recognition of the demons of the inner self: "for if thou canst not apprehend the things within thee, thou canst not comprehend the things above thee," noted Quarles; "the best looking-glass, wherein to see thy God, is perfectly to see thyself." Standing between Grandcourt and Deronda, Gwendolen is poised between a hell of her own choice (she put the ring on too!) and a world of possible rescue if she can "escape from herself" and "the evil within." She learns "to see all her acts through the impression they would make on Deronda," and learns too (in his words) "more of the way in which your life presses on others, and their life on yours." And then: not healing, but its beginning—"the process of purgatory . . . on the green earth," "the awakening of a new life within her."

> Deronda could not utter one word to diminish that sacred aversion to her worst self—that thorn-pressure which must come with the crowning of the sorrowful Better, suffering because of the Worse.

This returns us to Mirah's aria: "Il duolo infranga queste ritorte." For Gwendolen, as for Teufelsdröckh, the " '*Divine Depth of Sorrow*' lies disclosed," and with it renunciation, where "Life, properly speaking, can be said to begin." "You have had a vision of injurious, selfish action—a vision of possible degradation," Daniel tells Gwendolen; "think that a severe angel, seeing you along the road of error, grasped you by the wrist, and showed you the horror of the life you must avoid . . . Think of it as a preparation." Gwendolen's regeneration is not cast in Carlyle's triumphantly apocalyptic tones, but the *fact* is there, in her appreciation of going home:

> All that brief experience of a quiet home which had once seemed a dulness to be fled from, now came back to her as a restful escape, a station where she found the breath of morning and the unreproaching voice of birds, after following a lure through a long Satanic masquerade, which she . . . had seen the end of in shrieking fear lest she herself become one of the evil spirits who were dropping their human mummery and hissing around her with serpent tongues.

She has been to the center of her own inferno. Emerging, she can see the world with new eyes, see its specialness apart from herself, see its "natural supernaturalism." And she will see what "a Minnow is man."

The world seemed getting larger round poor Gwendolen, and she more solitary and helpless in the midst . . . she felt herself reduced to a mere speck . . . she was for the first time feeling the pressure of a vast mysterious movement, for the first time being dislodged from her supremacy in her own world, and getting a sense that her horizon was but a dipping onward of an existence with which her own was revolving.

George Eliot, then, in the harsh light of her portrayal of Philistia, gives us as much of the language and situations of romance *within* Gwendolen's "unmapped" self as she does on the surface of Deronda's history. And yet this Rinaldo can not finally liberate the woman who will teach him so much. Like Tasso's Rinaldo, he can feel pity but cannot offer the love she craves (see *Gerusalemme liberata*, XVI: li; XX: cxxxiv–cxxxvi). The man whose "rescue" impulses have been so constantly rewarded must be separated from this "sorceress" whose demons have entered his life. It is a separation that *shows* the reader the limits of romantic action—*except*, as Deronda says to Gwendolen, *in the mind*: "Now we can perhaps never see each other again. But our minds may get nearer." Daniel's mind was the locus of the novel's opening; his statement at its end recalls us to his titular position. As in Bunyan's dream, the mind has been the place of Deronda's spiritual education through the agency of Gwendolen's sufferings. His historical yearnings, his need to participate in a significant action, both would be naive if he had only Mordecai's "visions"; Gwendolen's "visions" show the other—and more real—kind of visions in this world. Her case is as necessary for Deronda as his "romance" is for her: each exposes the other to worlds never before encountered, each gives leaven and needed pattern to the other's experience. Each redefines for the other—and for us—what "romance" is. "We *are* such stuff as dreams are made of." And Gwendolen's nightmare world of demons is *real* in a way that even Mirah's history can not be. It takes the two histories together to make the emphasis (and how alike Gwendolen and Mirah are is emphasized by Gwendolen's appropriating for herself a term Mirah applied to herself during their one interview: Gwendolen too will see herself as a "beggar by the wayside" when Deronda saves her, and both women have been seeking "deliverance" from their oppression). But Mirah, though once near to suicide, has had the sustaining thought of her people, and she has never seen herself as the center of all life.

Compared to her, Gwendolen's case is so strong because it forces Deronda into a life where sympathy is not so easily extended (we remember his early repugnance to the demon-filled gambler); her case and Grandcourt's will not allow him to "hate vices mildly." George Eliot tells us that what Deronda "most longed for was either some external event, or some inward light, that would urge him into a definite line of action, and compress his wandering energy." Gwendolen supplies both, as surely as Mordecai and Mirah, and she provides Deronda's *real* "education"; she makes him an "organic part of social life" rather than some "yearning disembodied spirit." His rescue of Gwendolen is not easy, is not even certain. But it keeps Deronda *alive* to the terrors of that unrooted self (he too is rootless) which has neither myths nor visions to keep hold of. It gives this man who "had never had a confidant" a vision of a world of inner darkness and isolation which he must acknowledge his if he is to *see* the "skies" of Mordecai's world. Daniel has in Gwendolen's experience an answer to his implicit question, that one which Bunyan asked himself: "whether we were of the Israelites, or no?" Gwendolen's suffering gives the triumphant answer; it is the "inward light" to the life Mordecai has envisioned. Their tears at the end signify this *shared* vision:

> At last she succeeded in saying brokenly—
> "I said . . . I said . . . it should be better . . . better with me . . .
> for having known you."
> His eyes too were larger with tears.

It is also the final vision of Rinaldo in Tasso: "From his pure fount ran two streams likewise,/Wherein chaste pity and mild ruth appears" (*Gerusalemme liberata*, XX: cxxxiv).

Lest we miss the way in which Gwendolen gives *life* to the Zionist visions of Mordecai, George Eliot parallels Daniel's efforts to help her at Grandcourt's death with his meeting of his mother. This woman, a princess who had been a great singer, is a Jew. Her suffering counterpoints Gwendolen's in extraordinary ways. Indeed, in this most operatic of novels, Alcharisi's words are yet one more capitulation—*da capo*—of Mirah's "Lascia ch'io pianga," a lament of her cruel destiny. And Daniel, whose "own face in the glass had during many years been associated for him with thoughts of some one whom he must be like," finds that likeness "amidst more striking differences": his mother seems part demon, "a Melusina, who had ties with some world which is independent of ours," a "sorceress," "like a dreamed visitant from some region of departed mortals." He finds one of the sources of himself a woman who loathes everything he believes in, who finds such visionary Jews as Mordecai jailers, and who sees in the myth of the Hebrews the way towards imprisonment. And as she tells her story, she recapitulates Gwendolen's life history: she has no "talent to love" (Gwendolen [claims earlier in the novel], "I can't love people") she feels that marriage stifles, she has never wanted to be "hampered with other lives" but to enjoy the "freedom to do what everyone else did, and be carried along in a great current, and not obliged to care." Unlike the young Englishwoman, Alcharisi has never been afraid of "the wide world"; it has been her passage to living a "large life." But her vision of being an artist has been smashed by her origins:

> "You may try—but you can never imagine what it is to have a man's force of genius in you, and yet to suffer the slavery of being a girl. To have *a pattern cut out*—'this is the Jewish woman, this is what you must be . . .' That was what my father wanted . . . He hated that Jewish woman should be thought of by the Christian world as a sort of ware to make public singers and actresses of. As if we were not the more enviable for that! That is a chance of escaping from bondage."

To her the "great current" was a life of choice. The Judaism of her father patterned everything to bondage. To free her unwanted son from the "bondage" of that heritage was for her the only act of "love" she was capable of: "I delivered you from the pelting contempt that pursues Jewish separateness." For her the deliverance is a triumph—even if the result has been her "poor, solitary, forsaken remains of self" and "ghosts upon the daylight."

In this we see Gwendolen's story without its end: Alcharisi's immense physical pain leaves her "alone in spots of memory" ("and I can't get away")—not the memory of the opera diva but of the daughter who denied her heritage and of the mother who denied the heritage of her son. Like Gwendolen, Alcharisi feels a kind of "retributive calamity [hanging] about her life"—and thus she makes her revelation to Deronda. Yet hers is a suffering no one—and certainly not her son—can comfort. His words to this determined woman—who demands that he "acknowledge" her right to be an artist, to be free of her father's "pattern"—are inadequate; they ring hollow in the face of her will. Although she "would bend . . . all to the satisfaction of self," we cannot help sympathizing with her need. Deronda's words will sustain Gwendolen, but he can not see round his mother. There is a Brontëan intensity in her anger and bitterness, in her sense that her history off the stage has been one long death-in-life, in her hatred of being a woman and a Jew, and it is an intensity that makes her case one which utterly negates Daniel's usual formulas. He has only the language that Gwendolen's life has been educating him to feel—and it is not enough. He is affronted by the fact that this "symbol of sacredness" does not conform to his imagined image, will not be comforted, can not be rescued and cared for. There is a force in her speech—in those "chest tones"—that wellnigh shatters the novel.

George Eliot makes no comment. The dangers of the very myths that animate *her* vision are exposed by Alcharisi, for whom they have been binding chains on her very nature. The "great current" the novel celebrates has been for her a drowning. And the paradox is not resolved by the "Judaism with a difference" that will be Deronda's messianic theme. It is the paradox involved in the very need of myths. (George Eliot's women constantly feel the entrapment of being female: Maggie notes how it hinders significant action for her, Mrs Transome curses it, even Gwendolen early on jokes about it: "We women can't go in search of adventures . . . We must stay where we grow, or where the gardeners like to transplant us." Perhaps one of the problems in *Deronda* is that Daniel never seems to register significantly Alcharisi's indictment.)

Deronda would be a modern Moses—in the middle of his mother's monologue Mordecai is heard telling Mirah that Daniel is "an accomplished Egyptian"—but he cannot be that for his mother. The Moses reference calls our attention to the "Egyptian's" efforts to free the Jews from two kinds of bondage—to the Egyptians, and to their own slave mentality (that mentality which for Mordecai is a "darkness" blocking "vision"). Daniel will be able to help Gwendolen get free of such bondage, but for his mother nothing is possible. She remains the unrescued and unredeemed soul. She remains that part of vision which is ghastly, and which opposes Mordecai's "vision" of "action, choice, resolved memory" with its ugly demonic side. More importantly, she remains that part of Deronda—that likeness of him, that source of him—that can not be altered, that will not fit into Mordecai's vision unless its historical basis, the suffering Jews, serves to animate it. In Daniel's interview with her, he sees that part of himself that no "romance" has ever suggested to him. It prepares for him for his coming meeting with Gwendolen; it indeed makes their final encounters the keystone of the "education" his experience of her has been. Alcharisi's case highlights Gwendolen's "victory"—the word is too strong, and yet is right for her—but emphatically underlines the limitations of Mordecai's vision without the animation of the human (and a human that is not defined by gender), without a profoundly felt sense of "natural supernaturalism."

"Whether we were of the Israelites, or no?" Bunyan asked, as did Carlyle. George Eliot echoes both in her last novel. Alcharisi, is, literally, while Gwendolen is not. And yet this young Englishwoman is an Israelite in the most urgent way imaginable: in her suffering. Daniel Deronda must give his name to the novel because that name emphasizes its parable: Daniel—"God is my judge." In George Eliot's last "experiment in life" God may be, as Mordecai defines Israel, no more than "the core of affection which binds a race and its families in dutiful love, and the reverence for the human body which lifts the needs of our animal life into religion, and the tenderness which is merciful to the poor and weak and to the dumb creature that wears the yoke for us." But the idea of something beyond the self that enlarges our lives and gives us the power to acknowledge and then to reconcile the ideal and the demonic within ourselves must be acknowledged if the world is not to become our hell, a mirrored palace containing only Grandcourts.

The sufferings in *Daniel Deronda* recall the novel's motto—"Let thy chief terror be of thine own soul"—and recall its emblematic mirrors. Deronda, like Gwendolen, must see himself before he can finally know what he is capable of, before he can believe—not consider intellectually—Mordecai's visions. Gwendolen's case gives substance to Alcharisi's reported sufferings, and to Mirah's. And it educates Deronda to the "covenant of reconciliation": "The sons of Judah have to choose that God may again choose them . . . The divine principle of our race is action, choice, resolved memory."

And for George Eliot such a vision must be Jewish. Like Carlyle, she has no other "language" but the "nomenclature" of the Judeo-Christian religion to assert the paramount duty of fellow-feeling, and to illustrate the "pathway" towards freedom from slavery to the self and from the idolatry of a world which is alien to any better self and cares not to choose between right and wrong or anything beyond satisfying itself. In her final novel George Eliot ceases to be the historian or remembrancer we have known; memory and history have not been enough to keep vision free, unconstricted. In *Daniel Deronda* she is the sacred romancer, and baldly so. Tasso (with Handel) gives her the double plot structure to express the novel's key idea: "separateness and communication." And it gives her demons a-plenty to explore the inner life. The telling changes—indeed, reversals—she makes place the "Christians" of mid-Victorian England in the guise of Tasso's heathens, worshippers of self and of this world; and Tasso's saving Christians become in the modern retelling two Jews and one "Egyptian" whose words—"like the touch of a miraculous hand" —have something of Christ's power of love about them. The "sorceress," in both romance and novel, is converted; but beyond that we know nothing for both endings are alike. The sorceress' new life inscribes a tangent to the larger myth. Tasso's romance and Judaism show men a higher and a lower rather than a constant image of what lies about them in history's time. Romance originates in polarity, in the separation of the Hebrew from the heathen, the wheat from the chaff, the better self from the demon-empire. The Tasso and the history of the Jews together give life a vertical dimension, and man the possibility of transcendence.

The novel is called "Daniel Deronda" because finally it is the history of the development of his consciousness. Israel's history and Tasso's romance express in 1876 the path towards the natural supernaturalism possible to non-epic man. The Sterne epigraph to chapter 19, where Deronda's story is given, has told us this:

> I pity the man who can travel from Dan to Beersheba, and say, " 'Tis all barren;" and so it is: and so is all the world to him who will not cultivate the fruits it offers.

For George Eliot the only source of vision for a nineteenth century that has been travelling from Dan to Beersheba and finding all barren is in Jerusalem liberated—politically or, in the heathen case, psychologically. We are *all* Israelites.

"George Eliot's I don't rank as Novels but as second Bibles. . . . You never think or feel you are reading fiction, but biography . . . and biography of people into whose minds and hearts you can enter with the intensest sympathy." This letter, from John Brown (one of Blackwood's readers) in 1877, places precisely the effect George Eliot wanted her words to exert. She had insisted at the publication of *Silas Marner* that "the word *story*" be avoided in all announcements. In her first novels she had assertively been the remembrancer who has known Adam Bede and Mr. Tulliver. Even earlier, in "Janet's Repentance," she had insisted on her narrative position as not "the bird's eye glance of a critic" but one "on the level and in the press" with her protagonist as "he struggles his way along the stony road, through the crowd of unloving fellow-men." By the time of *Daniel Deronda* the knowing omniscient eye dominates; but it is not the eye of a Dickens narrator looking on the Dedlock world of Chesney Wold, nor that of a Carlyle sitting in judgment on the French Revolution. It is more Virgil's shade, leading us towards the vision which will allow us to say, "There is a lower and a higher!" For George Eliot only the world of romance joined to the world of mythic history can bring us into this vision (and within this text she does not hesitate to call her work a "story"). Daniel Deronda himself may never satisfy; he gazes too calmly on the demons of life, and they do not gnaw at his "bowels" as they do at the innards of Bunyan or the Old Testament Hebrews. But the reader who can not feel Gwendolen's leaving the world of despair behind has missed her strong terrible vision. Her final repetition of "it shall be better with me because I have known you" is cathartic. We must share it if we have paid attention to George Eliot's guiding voice.

We all—narrator, characters, readers—engage in constructing this book of life, "trying to make character clear before [us], and looking into the ways of destiny." For Gwendolen Harleth's inner life, as for Daniel Deronda's more outwardly connected story, we have seen that "tragic mark of kinship . . . such as has raised the pity and terror of men ever since they began to discern between will and destiny." For George Eliot, rewriting her book for the last time, only one structure was available in 1876 that she hoped would still give meaning to action and choice: that of the *Commedia, Pilgrim's Progress*, Israel in Egypt—epic, allegory, history: biblical romance. We discover our spiritual and better self only by seeing it in relation to a world larger than our own, only by breaking out of ourselves into that larger world, "above and below." As novelist—historian, seer, romancer—she offers us the parchment roll.

So she moved on, and we move on behind her.

MARTIN PRICE

The Nature of Decision

"The notion that peasants are joyous, that the typical moment to represent a man in a smock-frock is when he is cracking a joke and showing a row of sound teeth, that cottage matrons are usually buxom, and village children necessarily rosy and merry, are prejudices difficult to dislodge from the artistic mind, which looks for its subjects into literature instead of life." George Eliot evokes, as one alternative, the "slow gaze, in which no sense of beauty beams, no humour twinkles—the slow utterance, and the heavy slouching walk." She scorns sentimental idealization. "The selfish instincts are not subdued by the sight of buttercups, nor is integrity in the least established by that classic rural occupation, sheep-watching. To make men moral, something more is requisite than to turn them out to grass."

Of all English novelists, George Eliot was the most deeply concerned with moral experience, and it is from that concern that her realism emerged. To speak of moral experience is to speak of failure as much as success, of the difficulties of attaining moral freedom as much as of its exercise. When she praised Goethe, it was for his "mixed and erring" characters, "saved from corruption by the salt of some noble impulse." And she praised Goethe for a method that was "really moral" in its influence. "It is without exaggeration; he is in no haste to alarm readers into virtue by melodramatic consequences; he quietly follows the stream of fact and of life; and waits patiently for the moral processes of nature as we all do for her material processes." It is his "large tolerance" that makes for his moral superiority. "We all begin life," she added drily, "by associating our passions with our moral prepossessions, by mistaking indignation for virtue, and many go through life without awaking from this illusion." But a few learn from "their own falls and their own struggles, by their experience of sympathy . . . that the line between the virtuous and the vicious, so far from being a necessary safeguard to morality, is itself an immoral fiction." She observed elsewhere that "he who hates vices too much hates men, or is in danger of it, and may have no blame to spare for himself."

George Eliot attempted work of great subtlety, the study of how a man's virtues are implicated in and in some measure promote his errors. We can see this most sharply in the scene where Lydgate wins—or is entrapped by—Rosamond Vincy. When Lydgate seeks her out at home, she is surprised into naturalness; the usual "perfect management of self-contented grace" that she has learned at Miss Lemon's school gives way to "a certain helpless quivering." "That moment of naturalness was the crystallising feather-touch: it shook flirtation into love." When Lydgate shows concern, he elicits only tears; and her dependence brings in response an "outburst of tenderness"—because as a doctor, he is "used to being gentle with the weak and suffering." And so he leaves the house "an engaged man, whose soul was not his own, but the woman's to whom he had bound himself." The event is produced by the vulnerability and generosity of the two characters rather than by any calculation. Yet the ironic shift from the intimate rendering of mixed motives to the long-term entrapment in consequences is sharp. Even this brief scene makes clear that Eliot is concerned with the medium in which morality lives: the ways in which our choice may be limited by circumstances or even made for us—as if without our conscious consent or assertion of will—by the structure of the situation in which we find ourselves. Or we may see the converse: a decision made peremptorily by the intervention of some force we recognize as our deepest self.

Much of this vision of moral complexity arises from George Eliot's insistence upon inevitable cost. She has no patience with the teaching of her fellow-novelist Miss Jewsbury ("Constance Herbert"), that nothing we "renounce for the sake of a higher triumph, will prove to have been worth the keeping." Such "copy-book morality" is a denial of the real; "if it *were* the fact, renunciation would cease to be moral heroism, and would simply be a calculation of prudence." The notion that Duty has both a stern face and a "hand full of sugar-plums" undermines morality. It offers "something extrinsic as a motive to action, instead of the immediate impulse of love or justice, which alone makes an action truly moral." To see man as able to evade the cost and consequences of his act is to reduce him to moral insignificance. And yet there is a danger also in devoting oneself too fully to the very complexity of man's moral life, in tracing the necessary determinants of our seemingly free acts. We risk "the gradual extinction of motive—the poisoning of feeling by inference."

For responsibility carries with it the sense of our free acceptance of duties and our free recognition of obligation. The moment of decision is one in which we reveal most clearly the complexity of our nature. We can study a man's moral awareness externally and see the slow accretion of those principles and habits which gain repeated confirmation in his choices and his expectation of others. When we consider moral experience of our own internally, however, taking our point of vantage within the institutions of morality and their various offices—obligations, promises, choices—all those shaping forces drop away. We must accept as an ultimate "given," as a commanding motive, the sense of duty or obligation with which we have been inculcated. We have shifted from a study of how our moral attitudes are formed to the decision we must make in exercising them.

. . . . Jerome Schneewind [traces] the difference between Utilitarian and Intuitionist ethics in Victorian England. The Utilitarians stressed the importance of consequences, the Intuitionists of intentions. The Utilitarians were deterministic, the Intuitionists libertarian. "In a variety of ways Utilitarianism presents a morality which is . . . appropriate to the life of the large society or city and to the relations between strangers, while Intuitionism speaks more clearly for a personal morality, drawn from the life of the small group or family, from the relations between old acquaintances or close friends." The Intuitionists stressed the moral function of exemplary persons, whose character is more complex than are any of the principles it exemplifies. An exemplary person, such as Daniel Deronda is for Gwendolen Harleth (or Mordecai in turn for Deronda), is known as he knows others, through sympathy and intuition; and his personal example is more immediate and more subtle than any moral rules can be. Schneewind sees in George Eliot the "conceptual tension between an Intuitionist attitude toward morality and a determinist attitude toward the universe." *Daniel Deronda* embodies the principle that "one finds one's duty when one finds one's identity . . . and one is free insofar as one is able to love one's duty and live for its sake."

The conceptual tension of which Schneewind writes was felt by George Eliot in her reflections on the problem of moral freedom. She is aware of the claims of determinism, but she also recognizes that "to occupy the mind in contemplating human action as a chain of necessary sequences must neutralize practice."

> We are active beings because we are capable—and in proportion as we are capable—of receiving impressions and reacting in movement. But to be

considering whether impressions could have existed but for an illimitable series of antecedents, and to be regarding whatever is to be a series of necessary effects in the abstract, is to lock up the nature in a dark closet away from the impressions without which character must become a shrivelled unripe fruit.

Eliot likens this deliberation of our moral life to the "dulling, paralyzing reflection" by which a painter displaces his immediate impressions with a "dim imperfectly imagined series" of traditional images.

"Life and action are prior to theorizing, and have a prior logic in the conditions necessary to maintain them." Eliot insists upon the fact that much of our best conduct is due to "sympathetic impulses" rather than to theory. Why have people devoted themselves to caring for others? "Not because they were contemplating the greatest happiness of the greatest number of mankind—or their own achievement of utmost possible excellence [these phrases take care, in turn, of both Utilitarian and Intuitionist]—or their own happiness here or hereafter." She does not, however, see these "sympathetic impulses" merely as spontaneous feelings. They are the outcome of our lives, of our moral histories; the impulse is the stronger for the actions we have learned to perform and to accept in ourselves.

What we in turn recognize as readers is the need—if we are to read with sense at all—to feel ourselves into the moral imagination of the characters. We may shift back and forth, from inside to outside, as with Bulstrode; but we cannot begin to understand the experience the novel presents without some participation in the moral realities within which its characters live. "For there is no art which is not dependent for its characterizations either on its deep connections with life or on its want of such connections: at one extreme we have dramatic poetry, at the other pierced porcelain." The full depth of the connections with life can be seen in those sequences of perception and association out of which we create our "moral tradition." The "satisfaction or suffering" that accompany these sequences and determine our response are "deeply organic, dependent on the primary vital movements, the first seeds of dread and desire, which in some cases grow to a convulsive force, and are ready to fasten their companionship on ideas and acts which are usually regarded as impersonal and indifferent." We can see the "first seeds of dread and desire" most clearly in The Mill on the Floss, where the shaping power of childhood experience is presented with brilliant precision. There is, finally, no better account of the convulsive force of feeling in conflict with our sense of reality than the treatment of Lydgate's youthful proposal to the French actress:

He knew that this was like the sudden impulse of a madman—incongruous even with his habitual foibles. No matter! It was the one thing which he was resolved to do. He had two selves within him apparently, and they must learn to accommodate each other and bear reciprocal impediments. Strange, that some of us, with quick alternate vision, see beyond our infatuations, and even while we rave on the heights, behold the wide plain where our persistent self pauses and awaits us.

That "persistent self" is the kind of reality we are at last forced to acknowledge, a necessity we can neither circumvent nor transcend. A man is most free in Spinoza's view (as Stuart Hampshire presents it), "and also feels himself to be most free, when he cannot help drawing a certain conclusion" because of the "evidently compelling reasons" in favor of it. "Then he cannot hesitate. The issue is decided for him without any exercise of his will in decision." In contrast Hampshire describes the man who is not free, "not entirely active and self-determining but, at least in part, unknowing and passive in his motivation, since that which moved him to action was below the level of conscious thought. He was not altogether free in his decision, and he knows and feels that he was not, because he did not himself recognize its necessity." There is a peculiar fusion of logical and moral necessity in Spinoza, of the kind that George Eliot, herself a translator of Spinoza, finds in the submission to "undeviating law.". . .

MORAL DECISION

One day Mr. Farebrother, the Vicar of St. Botolph's, says to Lydgate, "The world has been too strong for me, I know. . . . But then I am not a mighty man—I shall never be a man of renown. The choice of Hercules is a pretty fable; but Prodicus makes it easy work for the hero, as if the first resolves were enough. Another story says that he came to hold the distaff, and at last wore the Nessus shirt. I suppose one good resolve might keep a man right if everybody else's resolve helped him."

The Choice of Hercules is one of the great themes of moral literature and painting. In works of Annibale Carracci, of Nicolas Poussin, of Benjamin West we see the hero standing between an austere figure of virtue who points toward a rugged upward slope and a reclining figure of Pleasure whose enticements he has just forsworn or is about to forswear. But Mr. Farebrother recalls Hercules' terrible death as well. Mortally wounded by Hercules, the dying centaur Nessus sought revenge by telling Deianira that his blood would have the power to make Hercules faithful to her. When Deianira comes to fear losing Hercules, she dips his shirt in the blood she has preserved. Its poison (perhaps the fatal poison of Hercules' own arrow) produces Hercules' terrible death: in the torture of fiery pain he tries to rip off his shirt and in his violence rips his flesh from his bones. Hercules' fate is the consequence in part of his impetuous slaying of Nessus, in part of his inducing the jealous suspicion of Deianira, in part of her yielding to the treacherous advice of Nessus. What happens is the convergence of mistaken intentions, spite, ignorance, and love: one cannot point to any single choice or act of will as the sufficient cause of Hercules' torture and death. If we blame his arrogance or impetuosity or sensuality, none of these—nor all together—demands the fate he suffers. There is something terrifyingly disproportionate in those consequences which arise out of a constellation of separate wills. The death of Hercules is the very denial of the power of choice.

"The Vicar's talk was not always inspiriting: he had escaped being a Pharisee, but he had not escaped that low estimate of possibilities which we rather hastily arrive at as an inference from our own failure. Lydgate thought that there was a pitiable infirmity of will in Farebrother." Lydgate is right to a degree he has not the means of understanding. And, even as he is right about Farebrother, whom success will make a stronger as well as happier man, he rather scornfully dismisses a condition into which he will himself descend in time.

The whole eighteenth chapter of *Middlemarch*, whose conclusion I have just cited, provides a striking instance of George Eliot's method and themes. It is a chapter about decision. Bulstrode is about to support the building of a new addition to the hospital which will give Lydgate scope for what he thinks to be proper medical practice, and Bulstrode means to have the salaried chaplaincy of the new hospital go to the evangelical Mr. Tyke instead of Farebrother, who has been performing a chaplain's duties as part of his parish duties. Lydgate is troubled because he has come to value Farebrother's fine intelligence and moral delicacy; but he is troubled as well by the mixed nature of Farebrother's character. Lydgate regards Farebrother's character somewhat as the moral north regards those "southern landscapes which seem divided between natural grandeur and social slovenliness." For Lydgate is troubled by Farebrother's way of playing cards for money and by his candid acknowledgment that the chaplaincy would be a welcome source of income. Lydgate has never suffered any lack of money, and his "ideal of life"—which we are made to see him achieve in his intransigency and boldness in medical matters—leads him to revulsion from Farebrother's "subservience of conduct to the gaining of small sums."

Without imagining the need that prompts Farebrother, Lydgate cannot help feeling contempt for such measures.

It is not that Lydgate neglects Farebrother's virtues and his lack of pretense; but Lydgate is uncomfortable with something less than moral consistency. He cannot in good conscience cast his vote for Farebrother, whom he has so much reason to favor, nor for Tyke, whose only claim is that he is Bulstrode's candidate. Even worse is the implication that to vote for Tyke would be to serve his own interest in pleasing Bulstrode. If Lydgate is uneasy in judging Farebrother, he is the more uneasy with a decision which has no simple right choice. Lydgate wants to be free to do his work, and he wants to dismiss all those small concerns that arise from the impurity of choices: he resents "the hampering threadlike pressure of small social conditions and their frustrating complexity." And he meets the problem by refusing to meet it. He does not make his choice and arm himself, as he should, with the reasons which can support it. Instead, he leaves his decision to be made when it must; and he goes to the meeting with his judgment suspended. As the lawyer Frank Hawley declares in the meeting, "Any man who wants to do justice does not wait till the last minute to hear both sides of the question." Hawley's remark is angry and illiberal; it neglects the value of disinterested discussion. But it points to the danger that Lydgate courts in waiting for something external, whatever it may be, to help him decide. When it is left for him to cast the decisive vote, Bulstrode's opponents are short of temper: "We all know how Mr. Lydgate will vote." Aware that he is expected to vote with Bulstrode, Lydgate angrily and defiantly does so; and one feels that the true reasons for the decision have been swept away in the pride with which he meets insinuations of his subservience.

Lydgate realizes later that "if he had been quite free from indirect bias he should have voted for Mr. Farebrother." He blames the "petty medium" of Middlemarch: "How could a man be satisfied with a decision between such alternatives and under such circumstances?" What Lydgate cannot allow himself to see is that he has permitted the choice to be made by circumstances rather than by the autonomy of judgment he might have reached beforehand. It is with Farebrother's continued friendliness, and even his readiness to offer others excuses for "thinking slightly of him," that the narrative turns to his self-deprecating remarks on the choice of Hercules. And Lydgate, who has failed to make a true choice, can pity Farebrother's weakness and persuade himself of his own greater moral demand upon life.

It is the difficulty of mixed or impure motives, of complex and inconsistent natures, that disturbs Lydgate, frays his temper, and disables him for responsible judgment. Such difficulties confront us at every turn, and George Eliot gives more attention than most novelists (one thinks of Richardson and of James as in some degree her counterparts) to the conditions within which our decisions are made. The conditions may be such as to deter or prevent true choice. Mr. Vincy, as he questions Lydgate's fitness as a husband for his daughter, provides a fine comic example of the avoidance of choice: "the force of circumstances was easily too much for him . . . and the circumstance called Rosamond was particularly forcible by means of that mild persistence which, as we know, enables a white soft living substance to make its way in spite of opposing rock. Papa was not a rock. . . ."

The last shift from Mr. Vincy to Papa shows us the man at his most manipulable, under the force of Rosamond's persistence, which operates with Mrs. Vincy's submissive encouragement. Mr. Vincy cannot bring himself to inquire directly into Lydgate's means, for Lydate's proud bearing daunts him. But the pride of Lydgate is only the assured courage of a man of superior status, and all the complexities of circumstance of a middle-class provincial become relevant:

> Mr. Vincy was a little in awe of him, a little vain that he wanted to marry Rosamond, a little indisposed to raise the question of money in which his own position was not advantageous, a little afraid of being worsted in dialogue with a man better educated and more highly bred than himself, and a little afraid of doing what his daughter would not like. The part Mr. Vincy preferred was that of the generous host whom nobody criticises. In the earlier half of the day there was business to hinder any formal communication of an adverse resolve; in the later there was a dinner, wine, whist, and general satisfaction. And in the meanwhile the hours were each leaving their little deposit and gradually forming the final reason for inaction, namely, that action was too late.

THE EMERGENCE OF THE SELF

In her last novel, George Eliot studied the emergence of a moral life in Gwendolen Harleth and the descent upon Daniel Deronda of an idea which can give the energy of duty to undirected moral aspiration. Eliot opens the novel with the first meeting of these two. The opening chapters of *Daniel Deronda* are intense and mysterious, mysterious because we have no knowledge of the conditions from which these events arise. "Was she beautiful or not beautiful? and what was the secret of form or expression which gave the dynamic quality of her glance? Was the good or evil genius dominant in those beams?" We see Gwendolen Harleth as Daniel Deronda first sees her; she is gambling in the casino of a German watering place, and her manner conveys "unrest," strange agitation. Her double aspect— both the physical beauty and the tortured spirit—compel Deronda's atten- tion, but compel it against his will. "Why was his wish to look again felt as coercion and not as a longing with which the whole being consents?" Much later—some eight hundred pages later—we shall look back at the "mission of Deronda to Gwendolen" which "had begun with what she had felt to be his judgment of her at the gaming-table."

This opening scene is presented externally, with the swaggering mockery of Dickens. The casino is a resort "which the enlightenment of ages has prepared . . . at a heavy cost of gilt mouldings, dark-toned colour and chubby nudities, all correspondingly heavy—forming a suitable con- denser for human breath belonging, in great part, to the highest fash- ion. . . . It was near four o'clock on a September day, so that the atmosphere was well brewed to a visible haze." This haze has the disturb- ing concreteness, and the gamblers are picked out with the contemptuous precision, that Dickens often uses:

> the white bejewelled fingers of an English countess were very near touching a bony, yellow, crab-like hand stretching a bared wrist to clutch a heap of coin—a hand easy to sort with the square, gaunt face, deep-set eyes, grizzled eyebrows, and ill-combed scanty hair which seemed a slight metamorphosis of the vulture.

Among the attitudes the gamblers reveal are the rankling "sweetness of winning much and seeing others lose" and the "fierce yet tottering impul- siveness" of the man who plays by an insane system, like a "scene of dull, gas-poisoned absorption." Later Deronda will reveal his view of gambling: "There is something revolting to me in raking a heap of money together, and internally chuckling over it, when others are feeling the loss."

Gwendolen plays willfully, restlessly, exulting as she wins, but suddenly arrested to find herself under Deronda's gaze. She has a momen- tary sense that he is "measuring her and looking down her as an inferior, . . . examining her as a species of a lower order." Her resentment prolongs her stare in turn, until she looks away as if with "inward defiance." Gwendolen has begun to imagine herself a "goddess of luck." But that fantasy is crossed by her uneasy awareness of Deronda's gaze—it seems to express a scorn that, at a deeper level, she suspects she deserves, and therefore resents all the more. Under its influence, her luck changes. She defies Deronda, still feeling his eyes upon her although she cannot turn to face him. If she cannot win, she will at least lose "strikingly."

This evening marks an epoch for Gwendolen (and to a degree for

Deronda). She has fled England rather than undertake a marriage she has seen to be degrading. Now she discovers, upon her return to her hotel, that her family has lost all its money. When she pawns a necklace with the thought that she may recover her magical luck, she is outraged and shamed that Deronda observes what she has done, redeems the necklace, and sends it back to her. She has begun to find in him a judgment of herself which she guiltily supposes to be superior and ironic. His judgment will in time become, once she recognizes its genuine concern and affection, her conscience. At last she will have internalized that judgment and made it her protection against herself. As she says to Deronda, "it shall be better with me because I have known you."

Gwendolen Harleth is the culmination of a movement in Eliot's fiction. In the story of Lydgate that is perhaps the best part of Middlemarch, there are troubling questions left by Rosamond. Eliot is brilliantly obser-vant in her rendering of Rosamond's behavior, but Rosamond's constricted mind—"there was not room enough for luxuries to look small in"—remains to a considerable degree opaque. Perhaps that is necessary in order to win sympathy for Lydgate. We hardly question the careless superiority with which he treats her until we see in her response a condescension of another kind. In her quiet assertion of will, there is no effort to explain or justify her behavior—as if to argue its rightness would only be to yield the terms of Lydgate, whose force of mind and eloquence would carry the issue. Rosamond does not choose to meet him there. She does not feel, finally, that his arguments merit respect any more than his tactless han-dling of patients and colleagues. In both there is an absence of worldly wisdom. There are small but adamantine certainties in Rosamond that allow no compromise. Yet there is also opacity; her conventional beliefs are served by a massive deficiency of imagination and an equally massive concentration of will. Her education at Miss Lemon's school and her socially ambitious parents hardly account for her formidable strength. Her selfish-ness is not the callow thoughtlessness of her brother, Fred, but quite another kind of power.

In Gwendolen Harleth, George Eliot returns to a character like Rosamond, but of a higher style and greater opportunity. Unlike Rosamond, Gwendolen is capable of growth into a moral life, and that growth is her story. In some way it is the most complex single story that George Eliot wrote, and it needs close attention.

Gwendolen Harleth fluctuates between a strong assertion of will and a terror at the possibilities that assertion raises. She has imperfect control of a manner that exhibits superiority too nakedly and reveals ironic amusement when it means to profess naivety. She does not know how to subdue herself in a role that requires her to imagine others' feelings. And there are moments when she is startled into spontaneity. When Klesmer criticizes her singing, he takes for granted standards that Gwendolen has never known. Of the music she has chosen he remarks; "It is a form of melody which expresses a puerile state of culture . . . the passion and thought of a people without any breadth of horizon . . . no cries of deep, mysterious passion—no conflict—no sense of the universal. It makes men small as they listen to it." Gwendolen's heart sinks at the space which suddenly opens around her confident drawing-room accomplishment. For, while Gwendolen has behaved "as if she had been sustained by the boldest speculations," her aspirations have been conventional enough and have made no great demands upon her. She has been living in a world not unlike Rosamond Vincy's. Her "horizon was that of the genteel romance where the heroine's soul poured out in her journal is full of vague power, originality, and general rebellion, while her life moves strictly in the sphere of fashion."

Her assertion of will is imperious in tone, but it has no high object. "My plan," she says, "is to do what pleases me." But the freedom she claims only exposes her to the terrors of the limitless. The sublime does not stir her to strength or to a sense of her own power; it fills her instead with terror. "Solitude in any wide scene impressed her with an undefined feeling of immeasurable existence aloof from her, in the midst of which she was helplessly incapable of asserting herself." At such moments she needs the presence of another person to help her recover her "indifference to the vastness in which she seemed an exile," to restore "her usual world in which her will was some avail." One may recall the imperious gestures which screen Mrs. Transome's terror of forces beyond her control.

The thought of marriage awakens no pleasure in Gwendolen: "the dramas in which she imagined herself a heroine were not wrought up to that close." She resists submission to another's closeness and independent will. She intends, instead, to, "strike others with admiration and get in that reflected way a more ardent sense of living." Yet she is startled by her own fierce revulsion at the mild Rex Gascoigne's proposal. She weeps later in her mother's embrace, exclaiming, "I can't love people. I hate them." And other kinds of limitation frighten her: "Gwendolen dreaded the unpleasant sense of compunction towards her mother, which was the nearest approach to self-condemnation and self-distrust that she had known."

S. L. Goldberg has written acutely on the problem of Gwendolen's will and on the nature of George Eliot's morality. He fears the confusion of two kinds of morality—what he calls "conduct-morality" and "life-morality." The former regulates our conscious choices; its claim is "impersonal," and it presents itself in universalized rules. In contrast, life-morality seeks to "guide the *whole* self in realizing all the finest possibilities of its human nature." It is "concerned with nothing less than the whole range of a person's active existence . . . the entire mode of its life." This includes the moral will but much more, and it considers the moral will as part of a conception of character "much wider, more complex, more holistic, and more problematical than that of conduct-morality." It would not, I think, be misleading to see these kinds of morality as Kantian and Aristotelian.

Goldberg sees in George Eliot a tendency to admire uncritically a conduct-morality that identifies the "best self" with "the practice of humility and self-abnegation." In the typical plot of conduct-morality false choices find their nemesis in "appropriate condemnation and retribution" and their issue in a "redemptory 'self knowledge' (i.e., *self*-judgment)." The plot of life-morality, in contrast, leads to "the achievement of a certain self-fulfilment, reaching a deeper and richer kind of life" or "reaching the uttermost limits of the individual's particular being as it lives itself out to the very point of death." Goldberg wants us to do justice to those qualities of Gwendolen which—somewhat like those Lionel Trilling praised in Jane Austen's Emma—have the power to charm us—they are a "force of independent life."

Beside this I would set George Eliot's words on "that idea of duty, that recognition of something to be lived for beyond the mere satisfaction of self, which is to the moral life what the addition of a great central ganglion is to animal life. No man can begin to mould himself on a faith or an idea without rising to a higher order of experience: a principle of subordination, of self-mastery, has been introduced into his nature; he is no longer a mere bundle of impressions, desires, and impulses." This conception of a moral life also stresses inclusiveness. One may see a life as shallow and incoherent for all its breadth of realization if it loses that depth of commitment (or of feeling) that gives it a new dimension and an active unity. There is no easy way of choosing between these two conceptions of morality—the emphasis upon the fullness of the self, within which morality has a limited place, and the emphasis upon moral maturity as a necessary attainment. There is a peculiar pathos in that moment when Dorothea offers Lydgate help. He smiles at her eagerness, much as men smile at Esther Lyon when she takes the stand. The smile is somewhat superior, somewhat rueful, a condescension toward and wonder at Dorothea's "childlike grave-eyed earnestness . . . blent into an adorable whole with her ready understanding of high experience. (Of lower experience such as plays a great part in the world, poor Mrs. Casaubon had a very blurred shortsighted knowledge, little helped by her imagination.)" There is reason to smile at her ignorance and to envy it; but she possesses a moral intensity that men like Lydgate, if they ever had it, have lost to the exigencies of "lower experience."

What is striking in Gwendolen is the restless assertion and its underside of fear. She attracts Grandcourt by the force of her will and the style of her self-assertion; he is, in fact, the nemesis her nature calls up by its very lack of any object beyond herself. And she has not imagination enough to allow him a will like her own, let alone one far more practiced and exacting. When Grandcourt pays court, Gwendolen holds him off, uncertain what she will do. "This subjection to a possible self, a self not to be absolutely predicted about, caused her some astonishment and terror: her favourite key of life—doing as she liked—seemed to fail her, and she could not foresee what at a given moment she might like to do." Yet Grandcourt is "adorably quiet and free from absurdities," she tells herself; she feels sure she can manage him to suit her purposes. And yet she wonders. "She began to be afraid of herself, and to find out a certain difficulty in doing as she liked." Her uncle, Mr. Gascoigne, is a clergyman with a great respect for worldly status. He encourages the acceptance of Grandcourt and even comfortably translates it into an obligation: Grandcourt's fortune, he tells her, "almost takes the question out of the range of mere personal feeling, and makes your acceptance of it a duty." Mr. Gascoigne warns against trifling with Grandcourt lest she alienate him, and he dismisses from his own mind the rumors of Grandcourt's earlier profligacy. But Gwendolen feels in response that her uncle is "pressing upon her the motives of dread which she had already felt," that he is "making her more conscious of the risks that lay within herself." When she receives a warning letter from Grandcourt's former mistress (and the mother of his children), Lydia Glasher, she finds herself thinking, "It has come in time."

But Gwendolen, once her family has lost its money, must consider means of support. When she turns to Klesmer for advice, she does it with the dread that recognizes him as part of "that unmanageable world which was independent of her wishes." There is desperation in her dream that she can become, on her own terms, a successful actress; and Klesmer reminds her of all that she has not the character to attain: "inward vocation and hard-won achievement." Gwendolen cannot begin to imagine that she must "unlearn" all she mistakenly admires in herself and undergo "unbroken discipline." But when she protests against Klesmer's judgment, he becomes crushingly explicit. After her "education in doing

things slackly for one-and-twenty years," she can expect only mortifica-
tion in her pursuit. "You would have to bear what I may call a glaring
insignificance. . . . You would have to keep your place in a crowd, and
after all it is likely you would lose it and get out of sight." There seems no
room in such a world for a gambler's luck. Gwendolen tries to rise "above
the stifling layers of egoistic disappointment and irritation" as she is forced
to accept "a vision of herself on the common level." Whatever vindictive
pleasure we might have been led as readers to take in Gwendolen's
discomfiture is checked by the author's demand for sympathy. Gwendolen
is not much different from all of us in projecting her disappointment as a
"world-nausea." "Surely a young creature is pitiable who has the labyrinth
of her life before her and no clue—to whom distrust in herself and her
good fortune has come as a sudden shock, like a rent across the path that
she was treading carelessly."

The renewal of Grandcourt's proposal—he has been stirred the
more by her flight—presents Gwendolen with a new occasion for choice.
It comes when she is in despair, and its coming brings terror as much as
triumph. The terror is once again a fear of what she may find herself
capable of doing. She consents to receive Grandcourt: "Why should she
not let him come? It bound her to nothing. . . . She could reject him.
Why was she to deny herself the freedom of doing this—which she would
like to do." When her mother observes that there is in fact some measure
of commitment in receiving him, Gwendolen swings back to the "pleasure
of refusing him." But it is only the pleasure one can take in a fantasy of
power at the moment one senses one's real powerlessness. For the constant
shifts of balance have brought Gwendolen to a "state in which no
conclusion could look fixed to her":

> She did not mean to accept Grandcourt; from the first moment of
> receiving his letter she had meant to refuse him; still, that could not but
> prompt her to look the unwelcome reasons full in the face until she had a
> little less awe of them, could not hinder imagination from filling out her
> knowledge in various ways, some of which seemed to change the aspect
> of what she knew. By dint of looking at a dubious object with a construc-
> tive imagination, one can give it twenty different shapes.

All of Gwendolen's hesitation is tied to her memory of her encounter with
Lydia Glasher. That event aroused an impulse that swept all before it—an
impulse that arose from "her dread of wrong-doing." From "the dim region
of what was called disgraceful, wrong, guilty, she shrank with mingled
pride and terror." But now she examines that fear of guilt. Might she not
help rather than injure Mrs. Glasher and her children if she were to marry

Grandcourt? But what of the "indignation and loathing" she herself has felt, or might have felt, for a man with such a past? They once more support her resolution to refuse him, and that resolution compensates for the sense of powerlessness in which Klesmer's advice has left her. The renewed sense of power is the keynote of her meeting with Grandcourt. She remains largely silent, demanding of Grandcourt that he advance without encouragement. He in turn offers to withdraw if there is not hope, and Gwendolen is suddenly aware of how much more she dreads a return to the hopelessness she has escaped by his presence. She avoids a direct reply by telling him of her family's plight.

Grandcourt has learned of the meeting between Gwendolen and Lydia Glasher, and he finds malicious pleasure in the prospect of Gwendolen's accepting him in spite of her knowledge. She, in turn, needs somehow to believe in her own power; in "this man's homage to her" lies the "rescue from helpless subjection to an oppressive lot." As he offers to remove the danger of poverty for her mother and sisters, she is stirred by this almost miraculous ascent beyond all that has threatened, into a realm of freedom and self-command. When she hesitates, even so, to accept him, Grandcourt becomes all the more fascinated by the game they are playing. "Do you command me to go?" he asks, and she at once replies, "No." "She could not let him go: that negative was a clutch. She seemed to herself to be, after all, only drifted towards the tremendous decision: —but drifting depends on something besides the current, when the sails have been set beforehand." When at last she accepts him, the word comes from her "as if she had been answering to her name in a court of justice." His tactful, undemonstrative response reinforces for the moment her sense of freedom, and she recovers her spirits. By the time Grandcourt leaves, Gwendolen has persuaded herself that he is "likely to be the least disagreeable of husbands."

And yet this decision, which she is relieved to have made, is "dogged by the shadow" of her earlier decision to reject him, "which had at first come as the undoubting movement of her whole being." She has never found a question of right or wrong awaken so much terror in her. This seems "a moment when something like a new consciousness was awakened." She is at the point of accepting the belief that it no longer matters what she does,—that she has "only to amuse herself" as best she can. But "that lawlessness, that casting away of all care for justification, suddenly frightened her." All she has chosen, all that will accomplish her "deliverance from the dull insignificance of her girlhood" seems now "like food with the taint of sacrilege upon it, which she must snatch with terror." She can repress that terror in the sense of daring she recovers on horseback, in the somewhat hectically high spirits with which she plays at "reigning."

Grandcourt is, of course, the obverse of all that Gwendolen distrusts in herself. He takes pleasure in ruling her, in bringing her to accept him in spite of aversion. "He meant to be master of a woman who would have liked to master him, and who perhaps would have been capable of mastering another man." Grandcourt disdains open brutality; his pleasure is in knowing her frustration and blocked will, in conquering her "dumb repugnance" or observing her "rage of dumbness."

George Eliot presents Gwendolen's decision with all the frightening intensity that it acquires for a young woman who has never known the check of discipline, whose will has outrun some deeper moral sense, and who has subsisted so far on the brilliant effects her beauty and her manners have won. The desolation of her marriage makes her yearn for some revival of spirit, "excitement that would carry her through life, as a hard gallop carried her through some of the morning hours." Perhaps, she thinks, "if she began to gamble again, the passion might awake." "If only she could feel a keen appetite for those pleasures—could only believe in pleasure as she used to do! . . . Her confidence in herself and her destiny had turned into remorse and dread; she trusted neither herself nor her future." She turns in imagination to Deronda: "Had he some way of looking at things which might be a new footing for her—an inward safeguard against possible vents which she dreaded as stored-up retribution?" Her desire to win Deronda's concern—she hardly seeks admiration now—is perhaps the chief vestige of regard for herself. She makes him into a "priest" and ascribes to him all the wisdom she needs to guide her. Her sense of his influence upon her acts in turn as an influence upon him. "Those who trust us educate us. And perhaps in that ideal consecration of Gwendolen's, some education was being prepared for Deronda."

It is that concatenation that gives the novel its strength, and, however one might wish to be rid of the solemnities and sentimentalities that surround the Meyricks and Mirah, the linkage cannot be broken. Gwendolen is pathetic in the blindness of her self-assertion, but Deronda's difficulty lies in his lack of trust in a self. He has discovered, as he thinks, that he is Sir Hugo Mallinger's illegitimate son, and he is somewhat terrified by the history that suggests: the disappearance of his mother, perhaps her disgrace, and the apparent insensitivity of Sir Hugo in such a matter, generous and affectionate as he has been to Daniel. Sir Hugo's failure to discuss what Deronda does not feel free to open stirs some resentment; but for the most part Deronda achieves submission in self-effacement. He has been on one occasion strongly troubled by Sir Hugo's casual suggestion (as it seems) that he train his voice for the concert stage; for this might be taken to deny his claim to be a gentleman, and he is reassured when Sir Hugo dismisses the idea. But Deronda withdraws from competition and the pursuit of any career. He devotes himself instead to helping Hans Meyrick win his scholarship; and, for motives he only partly recognizes, he spoils his own luck. He is full of uncertainty about what he can become, disabled as he feels he is by his origins, and he waits passively for the emergence of some purpose.

The image Deronda has, rowing on the Thames, of Mirah's "helpless sorrow" blends with "the strong array of reasons why he should shrink from getting into that routine of the world which makes men apologise for all its wrong-doing . . . why he should not draw strongly at any thread in the hopelessly entangled scheme of things." He lies in his boat, looking up at the brilliant sky. "He was forgetting everything else in a half-speculative, half-involuntary identification of himself with the objects he was looking at, thinking how far it might be possible habitually to shift his centre till his own personality would be no less outside him than the landscape. . . ." This moment of self-dissolution immediately precedes his rescue of Mirah and his assumption of concern, responsibility, eventually of love for her.

It is clear, once we have come to know his history, that the Deronda of the opening scene is neither so aloof nor so contemptuous as Gwendolen has imagined him. Rather, he sees her distress, her "fevered worldliness," as somehow related to the distress mingled with his own birth. Deronda, as his friend Hans Meyrick recognizes, is attracted to people by the "possibility of his defending them, rescuing them, telling upon their lives with some sort of redeeming influence." As Deronda's feelings become less diffused and more closely involved with Mirah, he finds himself more impatient for a disclosure of his origin. It might, as he knows, bring pain; but it may help him "to make his life a sequence which would take the form of duty." He wants "to escape standing as a critic outside the activities of men, stiffened into the ridiculous attitude of self-assigned superiority."

It is to this yearning of Deronda's that Mordecai's words seem so directly to apply: " 'Shall man, whose soul is set in the royalty of discernment and resolve, deny his rank and say, I am an onlooker, ask no choice or purpose of me? That is the blasphemy of this time. The divine principle of our race is action, choice, resolved memory.' " Deronda begins to recognize the weakness in his "dislike to appear exceptional or to risk an ineffective insistence on his own opinion." Once he has discovered that he is a Jew and can begin to realize that he loves Mirah, he achieves "a new state of decision," "a release of all the energy which had long been spent in self-checking and suppression." His judgment is "no longer wandering in the mazes of impartial sympathy, but choosing, with the noble partiality which is man's best strength, the close fellowship that makes sympathy practical." He has lost "the bird's eye reasonableness which soars to avoid preference"; he gains "the generous reasonableness of drawing shoulder to shoulder with men of like inheritance."

It is as a reflex of that discovery of powers in himself that he can urge Gwendolen to take on any clear duty. Other duties will arise from it, and she may then look at her life "as a debt." Nor should that be feared; what we must fear is "the want of motive." With the unfolding of duties and of new demands upon her from day to day, she will find her life "growing like a plant."

Grandcourt's death by drowning is at once Gwendolen's deliverance and her deepest source of terror: "I saw my wish outside me." Did she fail to throw the rope in time? What matters most is that the death is one she had wished for and dreamed of, and it summons up all the other forms of guilt. In her marriage, she wronged Lydia Glasher. "I wanted to make my gain out of another's loss . . . [I]t was like roulette—and the money burnt into me."

In the same city Deronda has finally met his mother—not a guilty or wronged creature, but a magnificently proud and accomplished woman. As she says, "I did not want affection. I have been stifled with it. I wanted to live out the life that was in me." She has had a great career as singer and actress. "I was living a myriad lives in one. I did not want a child." Although she has lived for something far more serious and exacting than the pleasure of doing as one likes, she shares with Gwendolen a fierce exercise of will. She is, moreover, irredeemably the actress: "experience immediately passed into drama, and she acted her own emotions." She has been humbled by a painful and fatal disease, and she can regard her father's disapproval in a new light. The defiant and vengeful daughter can now see beyond the limits of her will. In her pain, she tells Daniel, "it is as if all the life I have chosen to live, all thoughts, all will, forsook me and left me alone in spots of memory, and I can't get away: my pain seems to keep me there." She is now ready to surrender her son to his grandfather, to yield in her struggle against a father whose death has made him invulnerable.

Deronda's mother is a fine conception—stern, willful, theatrical—not another Mirah but a mature and formidable counterpart of Gwendolen. She stands out against any simple celebration of morality; she has been brought down by pain and the prospect of death, but she fights the claims of her father to the last, even in the appeasement she offers by restoring Daniel's identity. Her toughness of mind is a much greater force than Gwendolen's self-assertion, and it gives a new dignity to such assertion at the moment when Gwendolen finally surrenders hers. Henry James described the story of Gwendolen as the "universe forcing itself with a slow, inexorable pressure into a narrow, complacent, and yet after all extremely sensitive mind, and making it ache with pain of the process." Gwendolen "is punished for being narrow, and she is not allowed a chance to expand." This is too harsh. Is is true that Gwendolen seems to offer fatuous consolation to Deronda: "*You* are just the same as if you were not a Jew." And she has a "dreadful presentiment of mountainous travel for her mind before it could reach Deronda's." She is, at the last, surrounded by the large spaces and "wide-stretching purposes" in a world which reduces her "to a mere speck." She has been "dislodged from her supremacy in her own world," and, after a long period of hysteria, she wakes to feel concern for her mother, who has been sitting up with her. "I shall live. I shall be better." As we have seen in a number of such characters, for example Estella in *Great Expectations* and Marianne Dashwood in *Sense and Sensibility*, there is a loss of scale as one dwindles to a moral being; yet it is also the emergence of a self from the welter of assertion and impulse that has often provided an impressive substitute.

George Eliot makes moral experience a subject of great power, and her ultimate commitment is to the ways the world is, to the difficult, often heroically demanding recognition of both "what is unmodifiable and is the object of resignation" and what is "modifiable by hopeful activity—by new conceptions and new deeds." This moral realism is related, of course, to literary realism. Realism in the novel is often the embodiment in low or commonplace persons and events of the actions traditionally embodied in heroic, saintly, or demonic forms. It is a transposition of modes. Eliot praises Houdon's bust of the composer Gluck as a "striking specimen of the *real* in art. The sculptor has given every scar made by the smallpox; he has left the nose as pug and insignificant, and the mouth as common, as Nature made them; but then he has done what, doubtless, Nature also did—he has made one feel in those coarsely-cut features the presence of the genius *qui divinise la laideur.*" The last phrase, about sanctified ugliness, catches intimations of the sublime; and it is there—in the sublimity of moral energy, whatever its conventional goodness—that George Eliot's subject lies.

Chronology

1819	Mary Anne Evans born November 22 on the Arbury estate, Warwickshire, to Robert Evans, carpenter and estate agent, and his wife, Christiana Pearson Evans, daughter of a yeoman farmer.
1824–35	Educated first at a local dame school, then at boarding schools in Attleborough, Nuneaton and Coventry. In 1832, she witnesses the election riot caused by the first Reform Bill.
1836	Death of mother. Evans and elder sister take over management of the household.
1837	Marriage of elder sister; household management now in Evans's hands. Studies Italian, German and music under tutors.
1838	Visits London for the first time with her brother Isaac. Schooling has made Evans a zealous Evangelical. Returns to father's house.
1841	Evans and her father move to Coventry. Reads Charles Hennell's *Inquiry into the Origins of Christianity* and Bray's *The Philosophy of Necessity*. Converted from Evangelical Christianity to "a crude state of free-thinking."
1842	Refuses to attend church with her father; later returns to Coventry and to church (although not to her old beliefs).
1843–44	Stays with Dr. and Mrs. Brabant at Devizes. Works on a translation of Strauss's *Das Leben Jesu*. Leaves precipitously, probably at the insistence of Mrs. Brabant, because of her strong admiration for the elderly intellectual Dr. Brabant. Returns to Coventry, and continues work on the translation (published 1846).
1845	Rejects marriage proposal from artist friend. Teaches herself Hebrew.
1849	Death of father. Begins translation of Spinoza's *Tractatus Theologico-Politicus*. Travels to Geneva, where she remains until 1850.
1850–53	Returns to England, becomes assistant (acting) editor of *Westminster Review*. Friendship with Herbert Spencer and George Henry Lewes, critic and author.

1854	Publishes translation of Feuerbach's *The Essence of Christianity*. Takes up residence in Germany with Lewes. Meets Liszt. Begins a translation of Spinoza's *Ethics*.
1855	Returns to England, where she and Lewes take up residence in Richmond. Evans is not received by her family.
1856	Begins to write fiction.
1858	*Scenes of Clerical Life* published under the name George Eliot. Dickens writes Eliot that he is sure she is a woman; her identity is made public after the book is attributed to a dissenting clergyman of Nuneaton.
1859	Publishes *Adam Bede*. Established as leading woman novelist of the day.
1860	Publishes *The Mill on the Floss*.
1861	Publishes *Silas Marner*. Begins writing *Romola*.
1862	Publishes *Romola* serially in *The Cornhill Magazine*, of which Lewes has recently become consulting editor.
1866	Publishes *Felix Holt, the Radical*.
1868	Publishes *The Spanish Gypsy*.
1869	Meets John Cross, a wealthy businessman.
1871–72	*Middlemarch* published in parts.
1874	Publishes *The Legend of Jubal and Other Poems*.
1876	Publication of *Daniel Deronda* in parts.
1877	Eliot and Lewes received by Princess Louise and the Crown Princess of Germany, daughters of Queen Victoria.
1878	Meets Turgenev. Lewes proposes Turgenev's health as the greatest living novelist, Turgenev insists that the title belongs to Eliot. Lewes dies on November 30 of cancer.
1879	Works on preparing edition of essays, *Impressions of Theophrastus Such*, for press. John Blackwood, her publisher, dies on October 29.
1880	Eliot marries John Cross (twenty years her junior). Dies on December 22 at her home in Cheyne Walk.
1885	John Cross publishes *George Eliot's Life*.

Contributors

HAROLD BLOOM, Sterling Professor of the Humanities at Yale University, is the author of *The Anxiety of Influence, Poetry and Repression* and many other volumes of literary criticism. His forthcoming study, *Freud: Transference and Authority*, attempts a full-scale reading of all of Freud's major writings. He is the general editor of *The Chelsea House Library of Literary Criticism*.

F. R. LEAVIS was Lecturer in English at Cambridge University. Probably the most influential critic of his time, he is best remembered for his *The Great Tradition* and his studies of D. H. Lawrence.

DOROTHY VAN GHENT taught at many universities, including Vermont and Howard. Her best-known book is *The English Novel: Form and Function*.

JOHN HOLLOWAY, poet and critic, was Lecturer in English at Cambridge University. His books include *The Victorian Sage* and *The Story of the Night*, a study of Shakespeare.

BARBARA HARDY is Professor of English Literature at Birkbeck College, University of London. Her books include critical studies of George Eliot and Jane Austen.

WALTER ALLEN, critic and novelist, is the author of *The Modern Novel, The English Novel* and the novel *Rogue Elephant*.

RICHARD ELLMANN is Goldsmith's Professor of English at Oxford. His major works include biographies of Yeats and of Joyce, and a forthcoming biography of Oscar Wilde.

RAYMOND WILLIAMS is the Judith E. Wilson Professor of Drama at Cambridge University. The most influential of British Marxist critics of literature, his books include *Culture and Society, The Long Revolution* and *The Country and the City*.

J. HILLIS MILLER is Gray Professor of Rhetoric at Yale University. Among his many books are *The Poetry of Reality* and *The Disappearance of God*.

ELIZABETH WEED is Professor of French at Brown University.

ROBERT CASERIO teaches English at Oberlin College and is the author of *Plot, Story, and the Novel*.

NEIL HERTZ is Professor in the Humanities Center at Johns Hopkins University, and is the author of *The End of the Line*.

RICHARD POIRIER is Marius Bewley Professor of English at Rutgers University, editor of the *Raritan*, and one of the editors of the Library of America. His books include *The Performing Self*, *A World Elsewhere*, and studies of Frost and Mailer.

GEORGE LEVINE is Professor of English at Rutgers University, and the author of *Boundaries of Fiction* and *The Realistic Imagination*.

BARRY V. QUALLS is Professor of English at Rutgers University, and the author of *The Secular Pilgrims of Victorian Fiction*.

MARTIN PRICE is Sterling Professor of English at Yale University. His books include *Swift's Rhetorical Art*, *To the Palace of Wisdom* and *Forms of Life*.

Bibliography

Adam, Ian, ed. *This Particular Web: Essays on "Middlemarch."* Toronto: University of Toronto Press, 1975.

Allen, Walter. *George Eliot.* New York: Macmillan Co., 1964.

Alley, Henry. "New Year's at the Abbey: Point of View in the Pivotal Chapters of *Daniel Deronda.*" *Journal of Narrative Technique* 9 (1979): 147–59.

Arac, Jonathan. "Rhetoric and Realism in Nineteenth-Century Fiction: Hyperbole in *The Mill on the Floss.*" *English Literary History* 46 (1979): 673–92.

Auerbach, Nina. "The Power of Hunger: Demonism and Maggie Tulliver." *Nineteenth-Century Fiction* 30 (1975): 150–71.

————. "Artists and Mothers: A False Alliance." *Women and Literature* 1, vol. 6 (1978): 3–15.

Austen, Zelda. "Why Feminist Critics are Angry with George Eliot." *College English* 6, vol. 37 (1976): 549–61.

Auster, Henry. *Local Habitations: Regionalism in the Early Novels of George Eliot.* Cambridge, Mass.: Harvard University Press, 1970.

Beaty, Jerome. *"Middlemarch" From Notebook to Novel: A Study of George Eliot's Creative Method.* Urbana: University of Illinois Press, 1960.

Bedient, Calvin. *Architects of the Self: George Eliot, D. H. Lawrence, and E. M. Forster.* Berkeley and Los Angeles: University of California Press, 1972.

Bellringer, Alan W. "The Study of Provincial Life in *Middlemarch.*" *English* 28 (1979): 219–47.

Bennett, Joan. *George Eliot: Her Mind and Her Art.* Cambridge: Cambridge University Press, 1948.

Blake, Kathleen. "*Middlemarch* and the Woman Question." *Nineteenth-Century Fiction* 31 (1976): 285–312.

Bonaparte, Felicia. *Will and Destiny: Morality and Tragedy in George Eliot's Novels.* New York: New York University Press, 1975.

————. *The Triptych and the Cross: The Central Myths of George Eliot's Poetic Imagination.* New York: New York University Press, 1979.

Buckley, Jerome H., ed. *The Worlds of Victorian Fiction.* Cambridge, Mass.: Harvard University Press, 1975.

Carroll, David, ed. *George Eliot: The Critical Heritage.* New York: Barnes & Noble, 1971.

Chase, Cynthia. "The Decomposition of the Elephants: Double-Reading *Daniel Deronda.*" *PMLA* 93 (1978): 215–27.

Christ, Carol. "Aggression and Providential Death in George Eliot's Fiction." *Novel* 9 (1976): 130–40.

Clayton, Jay. "Visionary Power and Narrative Form: Wordsworth and *Adam Bede*." *English Literary History* 46 (1979): 645–72.

Collins, K. K. "G. H. Lewes Revised: George Eliot and the Moral Sense." *Victorian Studies* 21 (1978): 463–92.

Collins, Philip. *From Manly Tear to Stiff Upper Lip: The Victorians and Pathos.* Wellington, New Zealand: Victoria University Press, 1974.

Conway, Richard. "*Silas Marner* and *Felix Holt*: From Tale to Feminism." *Studies in the Novel* 10 (1978): 295–304.

Creeger, George R., ed. *George Eliot: A Collection of Critical Essays.* Englewood Cliffs, N.J.: Prentice-Hall, Inc., 1970.

Daiches, David. *George Eliot: "Middlemarch."* Great Neck, N.Y.: Barron's Educational Series, 1963.

Deneau, Daniel P. "Imagery in the *Scenes of Clerical Life*." *Victorian Newsletter* 28 (1965): 18–22.

Dessner, Lawrence Jay. "The Autobiographical Matrix of *Silas Marner*." *Studies in the Novel* 11 (1979): 251–82.

Doyle, Mary Ellen. *The Sympathetic Response: George Eliot's Fictional Rhetoric.* London: Associated University Presses, 1981.

Edwards, Michael. "George Eliot and Negative Form." *The Critical Quarterly* 2, vol. 17 (1975): 171–79.

Emery, Laura Comer. *George Eliot's Creative Conflict: The Other Side of Silence.* Berkeley and Los Angeles: University of California Press, 1976.

Ermarth, Elizabeth. "Maggie Tulliver's Long Suicide." *Studies in English Literature* 14 (1974): 587–601.

Fast, Robin Riley. "Getting to the Ends of *Daniel Deronda*." *Journal of Narrative Technique* 7 (1977): 200–17.

Garrett, Peter K. *The Victorian Multiplot Novel: Studies in Dialogical Form.* New Haven: Yale University Press, 1980.

Gezari, Janet K. "The Metaphorical Imagination of George Eliot." *English Literary History* 45 (1978): 93–106.

Ginsburg, Michael Peled. "Pseudonym, Epigraphs, and Narrative Voice: *Middlemarch* and the Problem of Authorship." *English Literary History* 47 (1980): 542–58.

Goodin, George, ed. *The English Novel in the Nineteenth Century.* Urbana: University of Illinois Press, 1972.

Greenberg, Robert A. "Plexuses and Ganglia: Scientific Allusion in *Middlemarch*." *Nineteenth-Century Fiction* 30 (1975): 33–52.

Greenstein, Susan M. "The Question of Vocation: From *Romola* to *Middlemarch*." *Ninetenth-Century Fiction* 35 (1981): 487–505.

Hagan, John. "A Reinterpretation of *The Mill on the Floss*." *PMLA* 87 (1972): 53–63.

Haight, Gordon S., and VanArsdel, Rosemary T., eds. *George Eliot: A Centenary Tribute.* London and Basingstoke: The Macmillan Press Ltd., 1982.

Hardy, Barbara. *The Novels of George Eliot: A Study in Form.* New York: Oxford University Press, 1967.

———, ed. *Critical Essays on George Eliot.* London: Routledge & Kegan Paul, 1970.

Harvey, W. J. *The Art of George Eliot.* New York: Oxford University Press, 1962.

Herbert, Christopher. "Preachers and the Schemes of Nature in *Adam Bede.*" *Nineteenth-Century Fiction* 29 (1975): 412–27.

Horowitz, Lenore Wisney. "George Eliot's Vision of Society in *Felix Holt, the Radical.*" *Texas Studies in Literature and Language* 17 (1975): 175–91.

Hulme, Hilda M. "*Middlemarch* as Science Fiction: Notes on Language and Imagery." *Novel* 2 (1968): 36–45.

Hurley, Edward T. "Death and Immortality: George Eliot's Solution." *Nineteenth-Century Fiction* 24 (1969): 222–27.

Ker, I. T. "George Eliot's Rhetoric of Enthusiasm." *Essays in Criticism* 26 (1976): 134–55.

King, Jeannette. *Tragedy in the Victorian Novel: Theory and Practice in the Novels of George Eliot, Thomas Hardy, and Henry James.* Cambridge: Cambridge University Press, 1978.

Knoepflmacher, U. C. *Religious Humanism and the Victorian Novel: George Eliot, Walter Pater, and Samuel Butler.* Princeton: Princeton University Press, 1965.

————. *George Eliot's Early Novels: The Limits of Realism.* Berkeley and Los Angeles: University of California Press, 1971.

Kropf, Carl R. "Time and Typology in George Eliot's Early Fiction." *Studies in the Novel* 8 (1976): 430–40.

Kucich, John. "George Eliot and Objects: Meaning as Matter in *The Mill on the Floss.*" *Dickens Studies Annual* 12 (1983): 319–37.

Levine, George. "Repression and Vocation in George Eliot: A Review Essay." *Women and Literature* 2, vol. 7 (1979): 3–13.

Liebman, Sheldon. "The Counterpoint of Characters in George Eliot's Early Novels." *Revue des Langues Vivantes* 34 (1968): 9–23.

Mann, Karen B. *The Language that Makes George Eliot's Fiction.* Baltimore and London: Johns Hopkins University Press, 1983.

Marcus, Steven. "Human Nature, Social Orders, and 19th Century Systems of Explanation: Starting In with George Eliot." *Salmagundi* 28 (1975): 20–42.

Marotta, Kenny. "*Adam Bede* as a Pastoral." *Genre* 9 (1976): 59–72.

Massey, Irving. *The Gaping Pig: Literature and Metamorphosis.* Berkeley and Los Angeles: University of California Press, 1976.

McGowan, John P. "The Turn of George Eliot's Realism." *Nineteenth-Century Fiction* 35 (1980): 171–92.

Meckier, Jerome. " 'That Arduous Invention': *Middlemarch* Versus the Modern Satirical Novel." *Ariel* 4, vol. 9 (1978): 31–63.

Miller, J. Hillis. *The Form of Victorian Fiction: Thackeray, Dickens, Trollope, George Eliot, Meredith and Hardy.* Notre Dame, Ind.: University of Notre Dame Press, 1968.

Mintz, Alan. *George Eliot and the Novel of Vocation.* Cambridge, Mass.: Harvard University Press, 1978.

Newton, K. M. *George Eliot: Romantic Humanist.* Totowa, N.J.: Barnes & Noble, 1981.

Noble, Thomas A. *George Eliot's "Scenes of Clerical Life."* New Haven: Yale University Press, 1965.

Paris, Bernard J. *Experiments in Life: George Eliot's Quest for Values*. Detroit: Wayne State University Press, 1965.

Pinion, F. B. *A George Eliot Companion: Literary Achievement and Modern Significance*. Totawa, N.J.: Barnes & Noble, 1981.

Roberts, Lynne Tidaback. "Perfect Pyramids: *The Mill on the Floss*." *Texas Studies in Literature and Language* 13 (1971): 111–24.

Roberts, Neil. *George Eliot: Her Beliefs and Her Art*. Pittsburgh: University of Pittsburgh Press, 1975.

Shaw, Patricia. "Humour in the Novels of George Eliot." *Filologia Moderna* 13 (1973): 305–35.

Smith, Anne, ed. *George Eliot; Centenary Essays and an Unpublished Fragment*. Totawa, N.J.: Barnes & Noble, 1980.

Spacks, Patricia Meyer. "Us or Them." *Hudson Review* 31 (1978): 34–52.

Stang, Richard, ed. *Discussions of George Eliot*. Boston: D.C. Heath & Co., 1960.

Stump, Reva. *Movement and Vision in George Eliot's Novels*. Seattle: University of Washington Press, 1959.

Sullivan, William J. "Piero di Cosimo and the Higher Primitivism in *Romola*." *Nineteenth-Century Fiction* 26 (1972): 390–405.

Swann, Brian. "*Silas Marner* and the New Mythus." *Criticism* 18 (1976): 101–21.

Thale, Jerome. *The Novels of George Eliot*. New York: Columbia University Press, 1959.

Wiesenfarth, Joseph. *George Eliot's Mythmaking*. Heidelberg: Carl Winter, Universitätsverlag, 1977.

Wilt, Judith. "George Eliot: The Garment of Fear." In *Ghosts and Gothic: Austen, Eliot and Lawrence*. Princeton: Princeton University Press, 1980.

Wolfe, Thomas P. "The Inward Vocation: An Essay on George Eliot's *Daniel Deronda*." In *Literary Monographs* 8. Edited by Eric Rothstein and Joseph Anthony Wittreich, Jr. Madison: University of Wisconsin Press, 1976.

Zimmerman, Bonnie. "*Felix Holt* and the True Power of Womanhood." *English Literary History* 46 (1979): 432–51.

Acknowledgments

"The Early Phase" by F. R. Leavis from *The Great Tradition* by F. R. Leavis, copyright © 1948 by George W. Stewart, Publisher, Inc. Reprinted by permission.

"*Adam Bede*" by Dorothy Van Ghent from *The English Novel: Form and Function* by Dorothy Van Ghent, copyright © 1953 by Dorothy Van Ghent. Reprinted by permission.

"*Silas Marner* and the System of Nature" by John Holloway from *The Victorian Sage: Studies in Argument* by John Holloway, copyright © 1953 by Macmillan & Co. Reprinted by permission.

"The Moment of Disenchantment" by Barbara Hardy from *The Review of English Studies*, New Series, 19, vol. 5 (July 1954), copyright © 1954 by The Clarendon Press. Reprinted by permission.

"*The Mill on the Floss*" by Walter Allen from *George Eliot* by Walter Allen, copyright © 1964 by Walter Allen. Reprinted by permission.

"Dorothea's Husbands" by Richard Ellmann from *Golden Codgers: Biographical Speculations* by Richard Ellmann, copyright © 1973 by Richard Ellmann. Reprinted by permission.

"Knowable Communities" by Raymond Williams from *The Country and the City* by Raymond Williams, copyright © 1973 by Raymond Williams. Reprinted by permission.

"Optic and Semiotic in *Middlemarch*" by J. Hillis Miller from *The Worlds of Victorian Fiction* edited by Jerome H. Buckley, copyright © 1975 by the President and Fellows of Harvard College. Reprinted by permission.

"The Liquidation of Maggie Tulliver" by Elizabeth Weed from *Genre* 11 (Fall 1978), copyright © 1978 by The University of Oklahoma. Reprinted by permission.

"*Felix Holt* and *Bleak House*" by Robert Caserio from *Plot, Story, and the Novel: From Dickens and Poe to the Modern Period* by Robert Caserio, copyright © 1979 by Princeton University Press. Reprinted by permission.

"Recognizing Casaubon" by Neil Hertz from *Glyph*, vol. 6 (1979), copyright ©
1979 by Johns Hopkins University Press. Reprinted by permission.

"*Middlemarch*, Chapter 85: Three Commentaries" by Barbara Hardy, J. Hillis
Miller and Richard Poirier from *Nineteenth-Century Fiction* 3, vol. 35 (December
1980), copyright © 1980 by The Regents of the University of California.
Reprinted by permission.

"The Scientific Texture of *Middlemarch*" by George Levine from *The Realistic
Imagination: English Fiction from Frankenstein to Lady Chatterley* by George
Levine, copyright © 1981 by The University of Chicago. Reprinted by permission.
"Speaking through Parable: *Daniel Deronda*" by Barry V. Qualls from *The Secular
Pilgrims of Victorian Fiction: The Novel as Book of Life* by Barry V. Qualls,
copyright © 1982 by Cambridge University Press. Reprinted by permission.

"The Nature of Decision" by Martin Price from *Forms of Life: Character and Moral
Imagination in the Novel* by Martin Price, copyright © 1983 by Yale University.
Reprinted by permission.

Index